Theory, Culture & Society

Theory, Culture & Society caters for the resurgence of interest in culture within contemporary social science and the humanities. Building on the heritage of classical social theory, the book series examines ways in which this tradition has been reshaped by a new generation of theorists. It also publishes theoretically informed analyses of everyday life, popular culture, and new intellectual movements.

EDITOR: Mike Featherstone, *Nottingham Trent University*

SERIES EDITORIAL BOARD
Roy Boyne, *University of Durham*
Mike Hepworth, *University of Aberdeen*
Scott Lash, *Goldsmiths College, University of London*
Roland Robertson, *University of Pittsburgh*
Bryan S. Turner, *University of Cambridge*

THE TCS CENTRE
The Theory, Culture & Society book series, the journals *Theory, Culture & Society* and *Body & Society*, and related conference, seminar and postgraduate programmes operate from the TCS Centre at Nottingham Trent University. For further details of the TCS Centre's activities please contact:

Centre Administrator
The TCS Centre, Room 175
Faculty of Humanities
Nottingham Trent University
Clifton Lane, Nottingham, NG11 8NS, UK
e-mail: tcs@ntu.ac.uk
web: http://tcs@ntu.ac.uk

Recent volumes include:

Feminist Imagination
Gelealogies in Feminist Theory
Vikki Bell

Michel de Certeau
Cultural Theorist
Ian Buchanan

The Cultural Economy of Cities
Allen J. Scott

Body Modification
edited by Mike Featherstone

Paul Virilio
From Modernism to Hypermodernism
edited by John Armitage

Subject, Society and Culture
Roy Boyne

Norbert Elias and Modern Social Theory
Dennis Smith

Development Theory
Deconstructions/Reconstructions
Jan Nederveen Pieterse

Occidentalism
Modernity and Subjectivity
Couze Venn

Simulation and Social Theory
Sean Cubitt

THE CONTRADICTIONS OF CULTURE

Cities: Culture: Women

Elizabeth Wilson

SAGE Publications

London • Thousand Oaks • New Delhi

First published 2001

Published in association with *Theory, Culture & Society*
Nottingham Trent University

SAGE Publications Ltd
6 Bonhill Street
London EC2A 4PU

SAGE Publications Inc
2455 Teller Road
Thousand Oaks, California 91320

SAGE Publications India Pvt Ltd
32, M-Block Market
Greater Kailash – I
New Delhi 110 048

British Library Cataloguing in Publication data

A catalogue record for this book is available
from the British Library

ISBN 0-7619-6974-8
ISBN 0-7619-6975-6 (pbk)

Library of Congress catalog record available

Typeset by Mayhew Typesetting, Rhayader, Powys
Printed in Great Britain by Biddles Ltd, Guildford, Surrey

CONTENTS

ACKNOWLEDGEMENTS

'The Invisible *Flâneur*' is a revised version of the article that originally appeared in *New Left Review*, no. 191, January/February 1992.

'The Unbearable Lightness of Diana' originally appeared in *New Left Review*, no. 226, November/December 1997.

'Looking Backward: Urban Nostalgia' is a revised version of an article which was published in *Imagining Cities*, ed. Sally Westwood and John Williams, Routledge, 1997.

'Living Dolls' originally appeared in Elizabeth Wilson, *Hallucinations*, Radius, Random House, 1988.

A different version of 'Dogs in Space' appeared in *Harvard Design Magazine*, Fall 1997.

A different version of 'Feminist Fundamentalism: The Shifting Politics of Sex and Censorship' appeared in *Sex Exposed*, ed., L. Segal and M. Mcintosh, Rutgers University Press, 1993.

A very different version of 'These New Components of the Spectacle: Fashion and Postmodernism' appeared in *Postmodernism and Society*, ed., R. Boyne and A. Rattansi, Macmillan, 1990.

1
INTRODUCTION

The essays in this collection were written under the shadow of postmodernism/postmodernity. They are linked by an interest in the position of women, although few address feminism directly. Exploring fields of study whose profile has been raised over the past fifteen to twenty years (fashion, the consumption of urban space) or in which there have been major revisions of past assumptions (feminism), they offered a commentary on aspects of life across the postmodern landscape, but do not address postmodern theory as such. A lack of training in philosophy and an ambivalence about the postmodern has prevented the staking out of a position, with the result that I may seem to be trying to have it both ways, combining what might best be described as a flirtatious approach to postmodernism with an implication that my heart is still in the right (i.e. leftwing) place, while approaching the theoretical issues only obliquely.

Ambivalence has been a common reaction to postmodernism; Alex Callinicos (1990a, 1990b) and Zygmunt Bauman (1988), for example, both note the tendency among intellectuals to respond ambivalently to the whole postmodern phenomenon, whether because its positive and negative attributes are so finely balanced or because it is, in postmodern language, 'undecidable'. Callinicos (1990a) suggests the ambivalence arose because while radical intellectuals recognised postmodernism as intimately related to the 'retreat of the Western labour movement and the "overconsumptionist" dynamic of capitalism in the Reagan–Thatcher era', it could act as 'a floating signifier by means of which this intelligentsia . . . sought to articulate its political disillusionment [but simultaneously] . . . its aspiration to a consumption-oriented lifestyle' (Callinicos, 1990a: 115). At least some academics and intellectuals, he suggests, were torn between condemnation of the social and political developments they deplored and the considerable rewards they enjoyed in terms of the lifestyle that came (for them) as part of the package.

As has been widely recognised, it was by developing the theories and discourses hauled in under the umbrella term of postmodernism that western intellectuals attempted to come to terms with the demise of the USSR and of 'actually existing socialism' in Eastern Europe, with the 'death' of more utopian aspirations towards socialism within the West itself, with the globalising economy, with the impact of communications technologies in creating a new, image-dominated world, and with the consequences of these changes for our notions of self and identity. Not that there was ever an undisputed definition of the postmodern. Terry Eagleton

(1996: vii) distinguishes between postmodernism as 'a form of contemporary culture' and postmodernity as 'a specific historical period', but then, while conceding that the distinction is 'useful', states that he will dispense with it, using the term 'postmodernism' to refer to all aspects of what he discusses. The two terms cover such a wide range of subjects and objects of study that his decision, paradoxically, seems reasonable, and implies a recognition of the promiscuity of the term, which has led to an endless debate as to what it means, and a persistent doubt as to its value, combined with a refusal to leave it alone. Such has been the volume of commentary that it would be easily possible for any writer attempting a comprehensive survey of the subject to realise Walter Benjamin's ambition of constructing a text consisting entirely of quotations from other authors.

Much of this vast commentary has been uneasy. Already in 1988 Mike Featherstone's introduction to the special issue of *Theory, Culture & Society* on postmodernism struck an apologetic note: 'Any reference to the term "postmodernism" immediately exposes one to the risk of being accused of jumping on a bandwagon, of perpetuating a rather shallow and meaningless intellectual fad,' he wrote (Featherstone, 1988: 195). He also pointed out that as early as 1975 postmodernism had already been pronounced dead. It may have been dead, but it wouldn't lie down; in the succeeding decade not only did the works on postmodernism multiply, but the concept was taken up in broadsheet journalism and even advertising, so that – like the late nineteenth-century idea of the *fin de siècle* to which it has often been compared – it has become a fashionable term for the zeitgeist, mood or style of the time.

Jean-François Lyotard, who wrote one of the most influential contributions to the subject (Lyotard, 1984), welcomed the end of the 'grand narratives' of Western Enlightenment mastery which, he claimed, postmodernism signalled. The attack on grand narratives has particularly meant an attack on Marxism. There has, for example, been no corresponding attack on psychoanalytic theory as a 'grand narrative' (which it certainly is), although that may be partly because its Lacanian variant has been highly amenable to poststructuralist interpretations, so that it has been possible to construct an arguably postmodern Freud in a manner not possible in the case of Marx (although see Carver, 1998). Yet it is now so familiar as to be almost a truism that Lyotard's theory of the disintegration of grand narratives is itself a grand narrative in its own right, that 'the narrative of the death of metanarrative is itself grander than most of the narratives it would consign to oblivion' (Osborne, 1995: 157), and that 'for all its talk of difference, plurality, heterogeneity, postmodern theory often operates with quite rigid binary oppositions' (Eagleton, 1996: 25). Moreover, while it may be true that some weary ex-leftist western intellectuals have abandoned 'grand narratives', Lyotard appears not to have taken into consideration the worldwide expansion of re-invigorated religious fundamentalisms and extreme forms of nationalism, the two sometimes united in narratives quite awesome in their terrifying and all-encompassing grandness.

Nevertheless, although the development of postmodern theory was associated with the retreat from Marxism, from socialism and even from political engagement of any kind, and although theorists associated with it, such as Richard Rorty, have avowedly championed versions of the existing social order, so protean is postmodernism that it has taken a well-developed Marxist as well as an anti-Marxist form. Fredric Jameson, for example, characterised postmodernism as the cultural moment of Ernest Mandel's late capitalism, a cultural explosion of which the underside was 'blood, torture, death and horror' (Jameson, 1984: 57). Alex Callinicos (1990a, 1990b) and Mike Davis (1985: 106–114) have acknowledged the importance of Jameson's analysis of postmodernism, while criticising it on empirical grounds, and Perry Anderson argues that Jameson's work has been more significant than that of any other theorist in redefining the field. From his 'founding text', a lecture at the Whitney Museum in 1982, onwards, he 'redrew the whole map of the postmodern at one stroke – a prodigious inaugural gesture that has commanded the field ever since' (Anderson, 1998: 54). This was because Jameson not only theorised the postmodern as the analogue of multinational capital and the globalising information economy, but argued that postmodern culture became 'virtually coextensive with the economy itself' (Anderson, 1998: 55), and that it involved the eclipse of nature and a 'schizophrenic' 'waning of affect' – a change in the nature of subjective experience characterised by depthlessness and a strange mingling of euphoria and horror, which Jameson referred to as the 'hysterical sublime'. Furthermore, argues Anderson, 'Jameson's work has been . . . a majestic expansion of the postmodern across virtually the whole spectrum of the arts, and much of the discourse flanking them' (Anderson, 1998: 58). Jameson's analyses of postmodernism combined a relentless denunciation of the world order that brought forth its grotesque mani-festations with a rhetoric that itself suggested the 'hysterical sublime' and a kind of euphoric reaction to the schlock of modern mass culture and the degradation of the urban landscape.

Jameson's work was influential in fixing the note of lamentation and denunciation combined with fascination that has been so characteristic of writings on postmodernity. Norman Denzin (1991), for example, writing about postmodern film, defined postmodernism in terms of a sense of loss and a bleak impotence in the face of the dominant system, which was yet transformed into an aesthetic melancholy. For, as Callinicos suggested (1990b), postmodernism articulated a critical and cultural pessimism, expressive of the feelings of radical, or once radical, academics during the period of Thatcherism, Reaganism and renewed cold war.

Yet optimists were by no means absent from the debate. Positive interpretations were particularly likely to associate the postmodern turn with advances in liberation struggles around gender, sexuality and ethnicity. The poststructuralist attack on essentialism and binary oppositions was perceived as an advance for pluralistic and transgressive identities, and for a new kind of feminism or postfeminism that was more concerned with subjectivities than with what was seen as an assimilationist and liberal-humanist project of equal rights. It was the sliding signifiers of difference rather than false universalisms that now interested the forces of erstwhile radicalism.

In the mid-1980s Angela McRobbie, Craig Owens and Andreas Huyssen welcomed the way in which postmodernism made it possible for the 'new movements' to come forward. Owens in particular argued that post-modernism challenged the overemphasis of orthodox Marxism on class. He acknowledged the danger of polarising feminism and Marxism, but proceeded to do exactly that:

> Marxism [with its] fundamentally patriarchal bias . . . privileges the characteristic masculine activity of production as the *definitively human* activity. . . . What is at issue, however, is not simply the oppressiveness of Marxist discourse, but its totalising ambitions, its claim to account for every form of social experience. But this claim is characteristic of all theoretical discourse, which is one reason women frequently condemn it as phallocratic. (Owens, 1983: 63)

No doubt well intentioned, this position reproduced an unfortunate binary opposition between masculinity (or indeed men) = intellect/theory/domina-tion, and femininity (or women) = feeling/particularity/ oppression.

Angela McRobbie cheerily welcomed postmodernism as 'a breath of fresh air':

> The reason why postmodernism appeals to a wider number of young people, and to what might be called the new generation of intellectuals (often black, female, or working class) is that they themselves are experiencing the enforced frag-mentation of impermanent work, and low career opportunities. Far from being overwhelmed by media saturation, there is evidence to suggest that these social groups and minorities are putting it to work for them. This alone should prompt the respect and the attention of an older generation who seem at present too eager to embrace a sense of political hopelessness. (McRobbie, 1989a: 178)

Andreas Huyssen, who understood postmodernism as a fundamental shift, not just in the arts but in the whole cultural realm, felt that

> it was especially the art, writing, film-making and criticism of women and minority artists with their recuperation of buried and mutilated traditions, their emphasis on exploring forms of gender- and race-based subjectivity in aesthetic productions and experiences, and their refusal to be limited to standard canonisations, which added a whole new dimension to the critique of high modernism and to the emergence of alternative forms of culture. (Huyssen, 1986: 198)

Chapter 2 will question whether postmodernism has been as significant for women as the foregoing arguments maintain.

Huyssen believed that women artists had made an especially important contribution to the attack on the 'great divide' between high art and mass culture:

> One of the few widely agreed upon features of postmodernism is its attempt to negotiate forms of high art with certain forms and genres of mass culture and the culture of everyday life. I suspect it is probably no coincidence that such merger

attempts occurred more or less simultaneously with the emergence of feminism and women as major forces in the arts, and with the concomitant reevaluation of formerly devalued forms and genres of cultural expression (e.g. the decorative arts, autobiographic texts, letters, etc.). (Huyssen, 1986: 59)

Jameson likewise regards the collapse of the high art/low culture divide as central to postmodernism, an overturning of the traditional hierarchies in the arts, resulting in 'the emergence of new kinds of texts infused with the forms, categories and contents of the very culture industry so passionately denounced by all the ideologues of the modern', expressive of

> intellectual fascination with a whole degraded landscape of schlock and kitsch, of TV series and *Reader's Digest* culture, of advertising and motels, of the late show and the grade-B Hollywood film, so-called paraliterature, with its airport paperback categories of the gothic and the romance, the popular biography, the murder mystery and the science fiction or fantasy novel. (Jameson, 1991: 2–3)

Whether or not this is accurate, the academic study of popular and mass forms represented by cultural and media studies has certainly flourished in the past two decades. It predated the identification of postmodernism, even if it emerged in the 1960s, the period many have perceived as inaugurating postmodernity. An emphasis on consumption, for example of fashion and of urban space, may be seen as a result, although I shall argue against such a view, particularly in the case of fashion.

Fashion can certainly be seen as part of popular culture; likewise it has its subversive and transgressive aspects (Wilson, 1985). This makes it compatible with the general trajectory of cultural studies, which, particularly as it developed in Britain, saw itself as above all a radical project, celebrating the empowerment of popular audiences and finding a history of rebellion in the enjoyment of mass forms. In this, cultural studies, whether consciously or inadvertently, adopted and endorsed an association of culture with radicalism and even revolution which goes back at least to the French cultural dissidents of the 1830s, the first bohemians. From those early romantics until the high noon of the avant-garde in the early twentieth century, 'the shock of the new' was wielded as a weapon against the bourgeois, the philistine, the reactionary. The revolutionary art of the avant-garde, especially from the 1870s to 1918, conceived of art as part of a general social and political revolution; revolutionary art and revolutionary politics marched together, the cultural vanguard carrying the banner of a political transformation that was to include every aspect of daily life and every aspect of the aesthetic realm (Wilson, 2000). During that time the avant-garde looked to the popular arts for inspiration, but the enemy was not 'high art', it was rather conformism, academicism, salon art and 'midcult'. It is therefore rather inaccurate to equate the breaching of the cultural divide with postmodernism, since this had been a major plank in the avant-garde project.

The pre-First World War avant-garde looked to folk and popular culture for inspiration, but their art equally assumed the importance of experiment. For example, Seurat, who seems to have been associated with the anarchist movement – some of his friends, at least, were anarchists (Clark, 1999:

109–10) – developed his experimental pointillist technique in paintings of popular leisure scenes, parks, the circus and the music hall. When Schoenberg incorporated into his work a melody from the popular song 'Du liebe Augustin', the effect was shock and outrage. At this period, when culture was 'the modernist or romantic resistance to capitalism' (McGuigan, 1999: 66), quotations from or reappropriations of mass and/ or popular culture reinforced or drew attention to the high culture/mass culture divide, but they did also question it.

In the 1950s, modern movements in art and architecture became, in the United States especially, cultural weapons in the cold war, wheeled into action against communism (Guibaut, 1983; Saunders, 1999), but in the 1960s, American avant-garde art took provocation to new extremes with happenings, performance art and other experiments, such as the Living Theatre Company fronted by Julian Beck and Judith Malina (Tytell, 1997). Most famously of all, Andy Warhol developed an art based on the imagery of mass consumption America. His Factory was a crucible of extreme art and behaviour (Cagle,1995) and his films took experiment to the limit – movies lasting for eight hours which simply showed the Empire State Building or a man asleep in real time. Yet at the same time, his productions were postmodern in their depthlessness. In a well-known passage, Fredric Jameson contrasted Warhol's *Diamond Dust Shoes* with Van Gogh's *A Pair of Boots*. Whereas the Van Gogh painting constitutes 'a celebration of labour', 'confers artistry on mundane objects' and thus 'articulates a utopian vision, the autonomous and transformative capacity of art' (McGuigan, 1999: 71), Warhol's image is all about commodification. The flat, depthless image refuses interpretation, being rather an ambiguous anti-commentary on the consumer culture it may or may not celebrate or critique (Jameson, 1984: 58–60). Warhol was nevertheless *received* as avant-garde and as the genius who in some sense shaped the counter-culture of the 1960s; art and dissidence were still twinned.

In Britain the 'Underground' and the counter-culture were equally radical, but were fertilised by a more explicitly leftwing tradition. In the 1950s the after-effects of an earlier period lingered on: the wartime Utility programme and the postwar Festival of Britain (in 1951) had been based on the belief that good design could be mass-produced for the many; and that this good design was modern design. In the 1960s the garment and music industries were able to produce just that, although not in quite the way earlier planners had envisioned, for the entertainment and embellishment of the 'affluent' adolescent, and innovators who are still household names today – Mary Quant, the Beatles – forged a new way to look, new music, new film, new mass media and new images with which to identify. That a number of the new stars came from working-class backgrounds was widely celebrated.

The desire for a more forward-looking culture had begun in the 1950s, when it had been more literary than visual. The so-called 'Angry Young Men' had shoved aside the 'effete' playwrights left over from the 1930s, and put an older generation of novelists in the shade; and Richard Hoggart, first director of the Centre for Contemporary Cultural Studies at Birmingham, had written *The Uses of Literacy*, first published in 1957.

This influential text, and some of the novels from the period, nostalgically celebrated a traditional working-class way of life, the industrial world of the back street, the factory, Friday nights at the pub and baths in a tub in front of the living-room fire. It is said, indeed, that the long-running soap opera *Coronation Street* was inspired by Hoggart's book, which celebrated this world of corner shops and local pubs, of gossiping women and horny-handed men.

Nostalgia notwithstanding, the caricature of the reactionary fifties and the radical sixties is an inaccurate one. At least from the mid-1950s, 'fundamental economic difficulties and social dissatisfactions became apparent [and] a vivid phase of cultural and political challenge began' (Sinfield, 1989: 4). Integral to this was the theoretical work of intellectuals, some of whom, like Hoggart, and, notably Raymond Williams, themselves came from the working class. The first New Left arose at this time, organised around dissident ex-communists such as E.P. Thompson and independent Marxists such as Stuart Hall. Reacting to the shock waves of the 20th Congress of the Soviet Communist Party, the invasion of Hungary by Stalin in 1956 and the British adventure at Suez (almost the last gasp of an expiring imperialism), non-aligned leftists forged a culture of dissent encompassing CND, jazz and folk music, a theatre of protest, radical poetry, coffee bars and D.H. Lawrence (Sinfield, 1989: Chap. 12). The radicalism of the 1960s took more from the American student movement, but meanwhile the writings of Hoggart and Williams had become part of an intellectual and theoretical project most notably carried through at the Centre for Contemporary Cultural Studies. This project continued to link radical protest with cultural and aesthetic forms of expression. Alternative dress and popular music continued to be the most visible and widely understood forms of cultural protest, and they were always linked – in CND, where marchers in duffle-coats and (for women) black stockings strode along to the sounds of jazz and folksong (although this was largely a middle-class subculture), and in the sixties, when Mary Quant and the Beatles epitomised 'swinging' Britain. However, it was only when Malcolm McLaren and Vivienne Westwood appeared on the scene in the seventies that Punk explicitly fused the dress and music scenes economically and in business terms (Mulvagh, 1999).

The Mayday Manifesto in 1966 and the Dialectics of Liberation Conference at the Round House in North London a year later brought together Marxist and non-Marxist socialists, radical psychiatrists and hippies, anarchists, peaceniks and LSD. Written by E.P. Thompson, Raymond Williams and Stuart Hall the Manifesto was representative of a leftwing and explicitly Marxist tradition of interest in the cultural and the political and the links between the two that were so formative of British cultural studies. It was therefore not surprising that a major focus of the

Centre for Contemporary Cultural Studies under the leadership of Richard Hoggart and Stuart Hall was the analysis of working-class youth subcultures.

Today media studies tends to be cited by British journalists and politicians as both an example and proof of the 'dumbing down' of higher education, but this is a misunderstanding of its project. The study of popular and mass culture was initially the study of social forms and ideologies. Its purpose was to understand the sources of popularity of mass culture and how it functioned – whether it was, as Theodor Adorno and Max Horkheimer believed, a new opium of the people, or whether it had radical potential. The CCCS project had a long pre-history, and was essentially of a piece with the work of Matthew Arnold and F.R. Leavis, both of whom had argued passionately for the importance of high culture in creating a civilised society. The difference now was that cultural theorists took mass culture seriously instead of merely denouncing it (although Hoggart's celebration of the working-class culture of the North of England set against it the negative influence of American mass culture).

Mass culture deserves serious analysis: the researcher learns as much from an investigation of a comic book, a film or the back of a cereal packet as from perusal of modern classics or atonal music, possibly more; in other words, these are 'texts' rich in ideology and tell us much about our own culture. Such an analysis rejects the Frankfurt School belief in the false consciousness of the duped masses – a mass audience does not simply, sheeplike, allow itself to be manipulated by every latest trend in pop and television, but displays discrimination in what it chooses to watch or hear, and only those texts which have some relevance to the audience at some level will in fact become popular. This is an illuminating idea, and even if it does occasionally seem as if we are seeing the transformation of a sow's ear into a silk purse as we read accounts of this or that audience heroically transgressing, resisting, poaching and transforming some humble cultural object or activity, the study of popular culture has been challenging and fascinating.

Yet by the 1990s there were those who were questioning what appeared to have become the populism of cultural theorists, some of whom did little more, or so it was alleged, than celebrate the market in all its forms: the consumer is triumphant and never gets it wrong (McGuigan, 1992). This created a new set of exclusions; now those who enjoyed 'high art' were in danger of being dismissed as elitist as postmodernist perspectivism rendered absolute aesthetic judgements inadmissible; instead the once mass audience was fragmented into a series of 'tribes', each with its own tastes, uniforms and (perhaps) ideological take on the world (Maffesoli, 1996), and relativism forbade the passing of any moral or aesthetic judgements or the construction of hierarchies of discrimination. By means of liberal tolerance and the celebration of any and every 'difference' as a form of 'resistance' or act of 'transgression', cultural studies adjusted to the loss of the left's political project. Marooned in the vistaless landscape of decaying social democracy, this intellectual generation apparently failed to notice that mass culture had meanwhile adopted the insignia of revolt while divesting them of content (Wilson, 2000).

It is not simply that feminism, once so marginal yet so challenging, has been incorporated into political correctness and at the same time shorn of its 'revolutionary' credentials, dwindling into the analysis of subjectivities rather than a programme for empowerment. Nor is it simply that cultural studies, which developed as a validation of the tastes and desires of 'ordinary people', is now accused of acting as ideologue of market forces and of an obsession with the trivial and vulgar. It is rather that the fundamental link between mass culture and radicalism needs to be revised now that the revolutionary tide has receded and left a residue of intellectual assumptions scattered along the sand.

The study of youth cultures was congruent with a belief in the subversiveness of the avant-garde because such youth cultures were dissident and oppositional, and because of their use of what could be seen, above all in the case of Punk, as avant-garde forms of dress, music and behaviour – Johnny Rotten of the Sex Pistols was compared to Rimbaud, the antics of the band to Dada protest. Yet since the 1970s the belief that the culture of the dissonant, the dissident, the shocking and the submerged are somehow inherently and eternally radical has had the last drop of transgression squeezed out of it. This has been achieved by the marketing of every form of culture shock, from music to fashion and from the fine arts to film. Fashion, MTV, popular music and literature have incorporated aspects of the avant-garde. The avant-garde also believed in the revolutionary potential of the sexual act, but as this has become the staple of mainstream film and television it has surely lost its radical force.

The incorporation of the avant-garde into the popular does seem to confirm the idea that postmodernism has confounded the division between the two. That does not in itself invalidate the cultural studies project, but it does throw into question its exclusive concern with mass culture and the continuing assumption that there is anything necessarily radical about this. Even Jim McGuigan, for example, in an admirable survey of postmodern culture that questions many of its radical claims, supports the study of mass culture on political grounds:

> From my point of view, mass-popular culture is the primary terrain of cultural struggle and, I believe, there is more space there for a cultural politics than, perhaps, Jameson would allow. To illustrate the argument, I would suggest that a mass-popular genre such as television situation comedy is at least as likely to articulate progressive possibility and disturb a prevailing sense of 'reality' as that which often seems to function as research and development for future advertising discourse in video art. (McGuigan, 1999: 68)

In other words, while he recognises the way in which the avant-garde has been incorporated into commercial culture, he wants to hang on to the belief that the popular, paradoxically, still embodies 'progressive possibility'. But not only can there be no guarantee that it does, there is also no reason why it should; and even if it does, this justification of the study of mass culture reproduces one of the major problems of 'orthodox' social-isms, which, from Proudhon onwards, justified art in terms of politics. That art was good which forwarded the revolutionary project – a point of view that leads ultimately to socialist realism.

Art, however, cannot be judged in terms of political correctness. As Ien Ang points out in connection with Janice Radway's account of *Reading the Romance* (Radway, 1991), such an analysis takes insufficient account of 'pleasure *as pleasure*', and amounts to a 'functionalist explanation . . . one that is preoccupied with its effects rather than its mechanisms. Conse-quently, pleasure as such cannot possibly be taken seriously in this theor-etical framework, because the whole explanatory movement is directed towards the *ideological function* of pleasure' (Ang, 1996: 104–5). Of course the idea that pleasure is a good in itself, no matter what elicits it, is not a view likely to meet with universal approval were the subject under dis-cussion food, pornography or killing people. Equally, Ang's insistence on 'pleasure as pleasure' could be dismissed as an 'art for art's sake' account of culture. Yet even if we regard the 'political' as in some sense omnipresent in all works of art and all productions of mass culture (which I do), this has to be balanced by the recognition of beauty and the importance and validity of aesthetic judgements. Aesthetic judgements are the very ones, however, that have been banished within cultural studies. Indeed, in audience research, the nature of work or text in question becomes largely irrelevant, its meaning inherent only in its symbolic function, its social signficance and the uses made of it.

This is not the way in which audiences themselves respond to or evaluate what they read, watch and listen to; on the contrary, audiences continually make aesthetic judgements – a point also made by Terry Eagleton (1996: 94) – and therefore such an analysis becomes supremely elitist, although elitism is the cardinal sin from which cultural studies has always fled in horror, even when couching its abhorrence in language so abstruse as to be virtually incomprehensible.

As Eagleton further argues, 'that one should study *Dallas* rather than *Little Dorrit* is not a levelling of values, but a reordering of them. To claim that one should study them both is not a collapsing of values but a different kind of valuation' (Eagleton, 1996: 95). Note that this does not mean that we should reject the 'self-evident truth that some issues and artefacts are more precious than others'; that would be a category mistake. Those radicals who reject opera, for example, on the grounds that the tickets cost a lot of money and only 'toffs' go to the opera anyway, confuse the social circumstances that have grown up round opera in some countries with the value of the art form itself, and also, of course, in this particular case, ironically neglect its radical history in France, Belgium and Italy.

Ironically also, those cultural theorists who attack the alleged elitism of the study of classical art forms are themselves in danger of perpetuating the educational elitism, at least of Britain, where attendance at public (i.e.

private) schools and prestige universities still presupposes familiarity with a range of liberal culture, and exclusion from which still, to some extent, carries negative social consequences. As an Afro-Caribbean student of mine said, referring to the whole sweep of modern art, 'We were not taught about this at school. Why have we been excluded?' To assume that steel bands are what inner-city comprehensive schools need and that classical music and the Victoria and Albert Museum are 'irrelevant' to their students is to perpetuate the very racism and elitism that such well-meaning gestures aim to eliminate. The exclusive insistence on mass culture as the only form relevant to the masses implies, furthermore, that the mass audience is incapable of understanding high art, and – in a reductionist reading of Bourdieu (1980) – asserts that a taste for opera, Proust and all high art is *nothing other than* the search for distinction, in other words cultural snobbery. The logical conclusion of such a position is, then, that those audiences who believe they do enjoy high art are, at best, suffering from the very false consciousness which was denounced in the discussion of the popular. The concept of false consciousness was criticised because it suggested that those who allegedly suffered from it were in need of enlightenment by more politically advanced cadres; this was rejected as elitist and authoritarian in itself. Yet the cultural theorists who denigrate the audiences for high culture are themselves guilty of just that kind of authoritarian judgement.

The essays that follow are collected around topics, in Part One primarily fashion and the discourse of the body and in Part Two urban space, that have themselves become fashionable under the sign of postmodernism, but that should not be read as an endorsement of the 'anti-elitism', or, rather, inverted snobbery, I have discussed above. I have taken as my motto in linking these topics a passing comment by the literary critic Franco Moretti: 'Fashion links beauty, success and the city' (Moretti, 1983: 113). This may suggest a purely celebratory approach to the phenomena I discuss, and indeed I have been criticised for just that; but what I am attempting is more complicated and perhaps more contradictory. In exploring the surface phenomena of style, dress, urban street life, pleasure – in other words, forms of consumption – my intention is not simply to demonstrate the importance of aspects of daily life that, having once been dismissed as trivial, and, indeed, 'feminine', have allegedly been rescued by the postmodern project; I wish to challenge the belief that there is anything inherently 'postmodern' about such subjects. To take the most obvious example of fashion: although postmodern studies may have legitimated its study within the academy, fashion has no particular connection with postmodernism, nor is it simply to be equated with consumption and pleasure. Nor does writing about it support the ideological position that postmodernism alone permits the discussion of topics previously considered trivial.

It is even more mistaken to link postmodernism with the coming forward of minority movements, given that the emancipation of women and subordinate ethnic groups began as projects of the Enlightenment. Terry

Eagleton argues that we should not assume the politics of postmodernism to be nothing but a retreat into reactionary melancholy or alternatively complacency, since they represent

> the appearance on the theoretical centre stage of millions who have been dumped and discarded, as often by traditional leftists as by the system itself . . . not merely a fresh set of political demands, [they amount to] an imaginative transfiguration of the very concept of the political . . . a veritable revolution in our conception of the relations between power, desire, identity, political practice. . . . Any socialism which fails to transform itself in the light of this fecund, articulate culture will surely be bankrupt from the outset. . . . The complicities between classical left-wing thought, and some of the dominative categories it opposes, have been embarrassingly laid bare. At its most militant, postmodernism has lent a voice to the humiliated and reviled. (Eagleton, 1996: 22–3)

But this greatly overstates the claim of postmodernism to have *for the first time* insisted on articulating the claims of those 'others' outside the dominant socialist category of class. Postmodernism simply does not deserve that much credit.

On the other hand, there is no reason why the study of dress, the body or any aspect of mass culture need imply a rejection of the study of political economy and production, as has been sometimes suggested; these (very binary) oppositions merely reproduce vulgar separations between consumption and production and between 'hard' and 'soft' objects of investigation that Marxism actually questioned, but which with the waning of Marxism have returned in pseudo-radical forms.

By the mid-1990s, in any case, the mood and the terms of the postmodern debates had changed. The melancholic euphoria and the horrified fascination had been displaced by more nuanced texts; the celebratory tone was equally muted. Perhaps intellectuals had grown accustomed to postmodernisation so that it no longer so effectively made strange our cultural world. It may also be that the continuation by social democratic, 'left of centre' governments in many western countries of free market 'Thatcherite' economic and social policies shed a different light on postmodernity. In the 1980s the novelty of postmodernism had made it appear to some intellectuals as a viable alternative to the arid and abstract debates that had too often characterised orthodox Marxism, but today few theorists believe that this is 'post capitalism'. Perhaps because the fevered debates within the left of yesteryear have become at most a distant folk memory, the postmodern alternative has also lost some of its power. New contributions to the debate, for example by Terry Eagleton and Jim McGuigan, had little truck with the grander claims of the postmodernists. Eagleton's uncompromising and indeed devastating attack on the postmodern turn, and above all on its politics of retreat and even (he suggests) incipient fascism, exposed its political and philosophical incoherence, and demonstrated that the plurality, fragmentation, desire and other features celebrated by many postmodernist critics might be little more than an ideology well suited to the shopping mall and commercialised media entertainment (Eagleton, 1996:

132). McGuigan meanwhile located postmodernity firmly within the modernity of a new phase of global capitalism and revanchist politics, and questioned its grand claims for the liberation of identities and subjectivities.

For my part I have returned to my original intuition of postmodernism as, after all, more like the idea of the *fin de siècle* than anything truly rigorous: a seductive name for a mood, a style, a sensibility, a zeitgeist, and a suggestive set of ideas for the analysis of both mass and experimental aesthetic forms; but while cognisant of the significance of the globalisation of economies, relatively lacking in explanatory power and certainly in moral or political values. Its very widespread usage and the definitional discourse that it has generated may also have obscured trends and events that could not be successfully linked to it, so that it has occluded as much as it has illuminated. Perhaps the best that can be said is that, again like the *fin de siècle*, it is a transitional and decadent mode, expressive of a moment in which we western intellectuals of goodwill are caught between past utopian dreams and an uncertain future.

In 1998 I viewed an art-work constructed from the bits of plastic and metal flotsam the artist had collected from the beach near where she lived. These bits of detritus had been worn into strange and beautiful abstract shapes by the friction of water and sand. Many former radicals feel themselves to be beached along with the flotsam of discarded ideas. Yet many of those ideas may also be recycled and transformed into something new and beautiful. In any case, the apparent exhaustion of what was once our project does not excuse us from holding to the importance of constructing a better system of ethical, political and aesthetic values, and of asserting that some things are better than others. To borrow, finally, another of Eagleton's cutting phrases, we do not have to pretend that there is 'nothing to choose between Goethe and Goebbels', or indeed between Madonna and Marx.

PART ONE

2

INCOHERENT FEMINISM

On 1 May 1997, the Labour Party victory in the general election was heralded not simply as a new era for Britain, but as a new dawn for women. With the rout of the Tory Party, women, mostly Labour, made up 25 per cent of the new intake of MPs. Some of these had benefited from the brief period when the Labour Party had instigated all-women short-lists in the selection of parliamentary candidates;[1] but while some represented safe seats, many, perhaps significantly, had triumphed in marginal seats or even 'safe' Tory seats they had never been expected to win. Immediately after the election the new Prime Minister, Tony Blair, was photographed at the centre of this bouquet of women, all of them dressed in neat, middle-management suits; and soon jubilant predictions were being made that their arrival would inaugurate not only a more family-centred timetable within Parliament, but also a woman-oriented government.

A bare six months later, however, when Natasha Walter interviewed several women from the new intake disillusionment had already set in. She felt that the new young women MPs had identified so totally with the new government that they 'run the risk of losing the connection with the people who put them in power'. Some of them already seemed a little weary and a lot more cautious. Walter concluded that 'they seem to believe they will achieve more as a quiet obedient herd than if they pull in different directions . . . and seem oddly slow at expressing discomfort even with things they can't help but feel unhappy about' (Walter, 1997: 7). These – nicknamed 'Blair's Babes' – were among the most docile and even apolitical in the House of Commons. Despite the huge Labour Party majority, few of them joined rebels who voted against measures to pressurise single mothers into work, nor indeed were they vocal on any other controversial issue. It was also widely noted that there was no Minister for Women in the Cabinet, and that although to begin with a woman (Harriet Harman) was in charge of social security, since her departure there has been no woman minister in charge of a big-spending department. And in the year 2000 one woman Labour MP, who has had twins, has announced that she will not seek re-election, on the grounds that the arcane ritual practices of Parliament and the unnecessarily long hours make family life impossible.

The particularities of this situation relate to Britain, but they are emblematic of what appears to be the general situation of western women at the millennium. Women are the butt and object of a confusion that existed a hundred years ago, but which has seemed only to increase as they have gained more rights and opportunities.

The confusion reaches into every corner of women's – and men's – lives. The changing roles of men and women are endlessly discussed, as is the alleged decadence (although that word is seldom used) of contemporary consumer society, the fate of children and the family, and the transformed nature of work. On the one hand, we are told that girls now outperform boys at all levels of the educational system – yet any satisfaction that may be felt that girls are doing so well is outweighed when their success is recast as the *problem* of the underperformance of boys. Boys, by contrast, are, it appears, at risk of becoming deviant, criminal, unemployed and suicidal; for 'de-industrialisation' has destroyed the work structure for men while creating new jobs for women in the tertiary sector. At one moment the macho male culture suited to the old industries of mining and iron and steel production is diagnosed as the problem, yet at another the advancement of women is blamed as so threatening for men that it has decimated their sperm count and created a need for Viagra. No-one quite dares openly to suggest that women should be returned to the home (apart from anything else, they are too useful in the workforce). Instead, writers such as the 'communitarian' Amitai Etzioni (1995) set out a vision of a society which includes a return to traditional family and marriage patterns, but refuse to draw the obvious conclusions of this for women: that the allegedly traditional 'breadwinner/ homemaker' model of the nuclear family (which lasted only for a short period in history) was predicated on a domestic role for the wife and her subordination to her husband. Meanwhile the rise of evolutionary psychology offers a 'theory' of why men must always be dominant and why gender behaviour can never change. Our genes 'demand' that men spread their seed about as widely as possible in order to increase their chances of immortalising their genes; but women look for one stable provider in the interests of preserving theirs – an amazingly brazen justification for male promiscuity and female fidelity, which seems to amount to little more than the rhyme: 'hogamous, higamous, man is polygamous; higamous, hogamous, woman is monogamous'.

Yet at the same time we are told that women have more opportunities than ever before, that feminism is no longer needed since women are doing so well, that single mothers must be encouraged into the workforce, that women – younger women at least – are becoming as drunken, promiscuous, 'laddish' and obscene as their male peers, and that even if the glass ceiling hasn't yet been shattered, this too is only a matter of time. Different stereotypes and partial truths conceal a reality in which women are still – as they have been for the last fifty years – 'juggling' their lives. Research into domestic labour suggests that they still shoulder almost the whole burden of domestic work, even when working full-time; and one survey revealed that most men would, if other things were equal, still prefer to have a wife who stayed at home. There is a yawning gulf between the over-sexualised images of women and heterosexual relations splashed all over the media and the often drab and insecure reality of daily life; older women, and especially the very old, are often lonely and very poor.

The implication of the anguish and uncertainty expressed in the debate is that men's position is under threat; anxieties about women are anxieties, too, about men. This may seem to be an obvious point, and has been recognised for some years in academic circles, where 'gender studies' has displaced 'women's studies' and the study of masculinity has become as influential as the study of women. Yet it is a point still worth making insofar as policy pronouncements and attempts to implement, say, equal opportunities policies tend not to confront the fear that equal opportunities for women mean *fewer* opportunities for men. Is this a zero-sum game, or do all members of society, women, men and children alike, benefit from the feminist revolution? This was what optimistic socialist feminists used to argue in the 1970s, but it didn't necessarily convince.

The confusion surrounding women's place has not revitalised feminism. On the contrary, confusion is as characteristic of feminism as of any other discourse on women. This may be because, as Terry Eagleton (1996) suggests *à propos* postmodernism, we are in a transitional period. Things have got both better and worse for women during the past twenty-five years. Indeed, things have got both better and worse for some of the *same* women (now you have a career but your husband's gone off with the nanny); but also there are growing differences between the life chances of different women. The gulf that has widened between rich and poor in Britain and the United States means, as a number of women have pointed out, that it is even harder than it was in the 1970s to conceptualise western women as a single homogeneous group, while worldwide, the gulf between the rich and poor countries creates a further set of differences and differing life chances for women.

So far as the West is concerned, it may be that the career prospects of professional and managerial women are liable to be to some extent thwarted by the men in their environment, by prejudice, sexism and the glass ceiling, but they have made rapid progress, and it appears that *childless* younger women, working slightly longer hours, also earn slightly more than comparable male colleagues (Segal, 1999: 204, quoting Franks, 1999). These are also the women most likely to be in the privileged position of making the choice *not* to work, at least for a period, when they have children. Maureen Freely (1999) suggests that there is a new generation of high-powered women (admittedly they have to have rich husbands if they can afford to retire from paid employment) who have willingly left their harried lives as hotshot barristers, managing directors or media stars in favour of the 'richness' of meeting the kids from school, making friends with other mothers at the school gate and going on impromptu picnics. But the mothers who have no choice but to stay at home or work part-time might have a wry smile for this grand rediscovery of the joys of domesticity by a privileged minority.

At the other end of the scale, unemployed women are often attached to unemployed men. Surveys suggest that unemployed men do not necessarily help more than those in work with domestic duties and child care; and the experience of women trapped in the 'dependency culture' of welfare leads to depression and low self-esteem. In any case there is a huge gulf between rich and poor women, and between women from different ethnic and minority groupings – but wealth and poverty divide women within those groups as well. And, while in the 1970s it was politics that seemed further to divide women, today competing religious – and anti-religious – beliefs seem just as, if not more, important.

Women are certainly no longer invisible. One of the main achievements of the feminism of the 1970s was to rescue women from that invisibility so that they were no longer 'hidden from history'. Yet the media attention that has recognised the existence of the 'woman problem' is selective and more often adds to the confusion than bringing clarity to the debate. A caco-phony of competing views merely reflects rather than providing an analysis of the huge social ambivalence from which women suffer. And women feel ambivalent about themselves too. As Rosalind Coward (1993) has pointed out, women are pulled in different directions by their desires: for inde-pendence, for heterosexual passion, for motherhood, for freedom, for the love of a good man; and some, she has asserted, are frightened of success, or not prepared to make the sacrifices it demands. Winifred Holtby observed similar tensions and temptations in the 1930s, but would have no truck with them:

> If it is true that many women better equipped to be engineers, lawyers or agri-cultural workers, waste their time on domestic activities which husbands, sons or professional employees might more effectively perform, it is even more true that other women who . . . enjoy domestic work, use it as an excuse to do nothing and know nothing else. . . . 'Oh, I'm only a housekeeper. I'm a private person' . . . they say complacently, finding it easier to be a good housewife than a good citizen. So long as their own children are healthy and happy, why worry because others are ill and frightened? It is agreeable to . . . squeeze oranges and mix nourishing salads; it is not agreeable to sit on quarrelling committees, listen to tedious speeches, organise demonstrations and alter systems, in order that others – for whom such . . . pleasures are at present impossible – may enjoy them. (Holtby, 1978: 148–9)

The mass media have not seriously addressed the ambivalence felt by men *and* women towards women and women's issues, and perhaps could not do so, but equally their contributions to the debate need not have been quite so unhelpful as they often have been. The media-created Superwoman, the 'woman who has it all', was one kind of mystification; Camille Paglia provided another with her strident assertions, allegedly *from a feminist viewpoint*, that creativity and 'genius' are the phallic property of the mas-culine. Taken up by the media because she provided good copy, she became

Paglia

a celebrity famous for her 'controversial' ideas, her status as a lesbian who adored men, and as a feminist who attacked other feminists, as the defender of Madonna and Diana as feminist icons, as an Ayn Rand for the 1990s. Her wit and sometimes common sense did not compensate for the under-lying incoherence of her ideas, but there is a sense in which she has been as much a victim of the media's continual demand for novelty and shock value as the 'icons' she celebrates.

She was a gift to the media because she represented in her person the popular wish to have it both ways – misogyny and feminism combined in one person. For to add to the confusion, women, including feminists, no longer face today the open contempt for women against which both first- and second-wave feminisms had to struggle: 'gross and unapologetic pre-judice against women is no longer an unremarked-upon given of everyday life', by contrast with the 1950s and 1960s, when 'the prevailing assumption of the inferiority of women was the starting point from which one planned one's moves and shaped one's life' (DuPlessis and Snitow, 1998: 4). As a single example of this state of affairs, it is salutary to remember that at that time in Britain selective entry to grammar schools through the 'eleven plus' examination was skewed: because girls did better than boys, the standard for them was raised in order to ensure that equal numbers of both sexes made it into the academic institutions. This was not public knowledge, but hidden, secret prejudice.

There have been real and dramatic changes since the 1970s, and from the point of view of consciousness and access to opportunity no-one would deny that the lives of many women have changed for the better. Govern-ments on both sides of the Atlantic have endorsed – and indeed enforced – women's 'right' to paid employment (especially if they are single mothers), and the 'woman problem' has been declared defunct as a crazy assortment of feminine role models are simultaneously celebrated and demonised. From the millionaire British businesswoman Nicola Horlick, top banker and mother of five, to Madonna, from the British Prime Minister's barrister wife, Cherie Booth, to Cabinet minister Mo Mowlam, active and successful women are (up to a point) applauded, although we have only to mention the ambivalence and hostility with which both Hillary Rodham Clinton and Monica Lewinsky have been treated by the American public to realise that gender issues remain essentially unresolved in modern western society. Like postmodernism itself, western society's attitude towards the position of women is utterly incoherent, with discourses from Darwinist geneticists competing with deconstruction, and calls for a return to traditional values competing with paeans of praise for women's superior ability to survive in the world of globalised markets and touchy-feely management. Worldwide, the turn to fundamentalisms functions – like neo-Darwinism – as a denial of that ambivalence, an attempt to pretend that the conflicts between family life and the global market, emancipation and patriarchal authority do not exist, or, rather, may be resolved only by a reassertion of gender difference. As globalisation threatens patriarchal, masculine authority in many different ways, restrictions on women's lives have become the symbolic (but for women themselves very real, of course) negation of change.

Recent responses by feminists to the prevailing ambivalence towards what used to be called 'the woman question' have been of several kinds. There have been popular 'new' feminist analyses; and there have been attempts by feminists from the 1970s to defend and extend their rather more complex critique; and while Maureen Freely criticised those original second-wave feminists for forgetting about mothers, Susan Faludi and Rosalind Coward turned their attention to men. Many of the activists from the women's movements of the 1970s have migrated to the universities or have become psychotherapists; while a younger generation have more typically come from the media. Some, like Camille Paglia or Rosalind Coward, have bestridden the two. A single chapter cannot possibly do justice to all, or indeed any, of these contributions, but it may be possible to identify some themes, and to assess the degree to which they have lessened or added to the ambivalence and confusion which, I have suggested, are the chief characteristics of the discourse on women today.

In 1997 the British 'left of centre think tank' Demos published *Tomorrow's Women* by Helen Wilkinson and Melanie Howard. This report was critical of provision for women in the UK by contrast with a number of European countries. Women's equality at work is hindered in Britain because employers are reluctant to make adequate provision for maternity leave and generally to recognise women's family responsibilities. Scandinavia has coped much better, and in countries such as France and Belgium women are more likely to be employed full-time and enjoy better childcare and nursery school provision. In Britain, by contrast, 'work has not been adequately adapted to the needs of the family and parenting'.

Feminists have been pointing to these inequalities and campaigning for change for over 100 years, and the feminists of the 1970s certainly placed them at the centre of their campaigns. Where the Demos report differs from the writings of the seventies generation, however, is in emphasising the differences between different groups of women. Not that there was anything original in this either: the women's movement of the 1970s and 1980s was riven with fissures and splits; black women, for example, pointed to the racism of white feminists who promoted an unthinking universal sisterhood, which was seen as a denial of or refusal to recognise the different oppressions of non-white women both within western society and in the developing world, and as an imperialist claim that white, western middle-class women could speak for all women. But not only do Helen Wilkinson and Melanie Howard present as a new discovery the way in which class, ethnicity, earning power and varying value systems act to fragment women, they also argue that this makes the revitalisation of a single, unified women's movement unlikely; there will be feminisms, not feminism, because women's life experiences are so diverse today that the idea of a single, unifying women's movement no longer makes sense:

Only fifteen per cent of women now define themselves primarily by gender, fewer than define themselves by their intelligence. Although women are becoming more assertive, they are unlikely to coalesce into a single movement, and politicans, advertisers and businesses will find it increasingly hard to appeal to a 'typical' woman. (Wilkinson and Howard, 1997: 9)

The unity of all women was always, of course, a fiction. Nonetheless it is mistaken *automatically* to conclude that because women's lives and aspirations vary so greatly, a feminist movement is an inappropriate goal. Political movements and parties are always coalitions that actively construct the constituencies they aim to represent (as demonstrated by both the fragmented Tory and Labour Parties).

An additional problem with the Demos report is that it assumes too glibly that its data, based on market research, can be unproblematically translated into politics. In fact, as we know, the goal of marketing is to create and amplify consumer differences – the opposite of the goal of a political movement.

Third, the report tries to have it both ways. It makes much of the advance of so-called 'feminine values' – environmentalism, the therapeutic agenda and 'spirituality' – falling for the stereotype that biological women largely share such values, yet at the same time it emphasises the increasingly 'masculine' behaviour of some women. Women's lives are of course contradictory, and the report tries to illustrate this by describing the five types of nineties woman: Networking Naomi, New Age Angela, Mannish Mel, Back to Basics Barbara and Frustrated Fran (there's no sign of Dinosaur Daphne, the socialist feminist).[2]

Across the lives of these five types the old problems are clearly visible. The report, for all its desire to stress the positive in terms of 'women's lives', and the negative in terms of the future for feminism as a movement, cannot conceal that for many women the problems identified not only by women's liberation in the seventies, but by the suffrage movement 100 years ago, remain with us, unresolved.

Helen Wilkinson and Melanie Howard acknowledge the widening gulf between rich and poor women – there are more successful professional and businesswomen in the 'enterprise culture'; but there are also more women sinking into the 'benefit culture' of welfare dependency – the two groups euphemistically renamed the 'time-rich' (i.e. unemployed) and the 'time-poor' (i.e. well-paid women with professional partners who don't share the burden of housework and childcare fairly). The report's solution for this divergence of opportunity is to suggest that there is 'a common interest in encouraging working women to buy more services from currently unemployed women': in other words, the return of the domestic servant – hardly the optimum solution for the decline in unionised, adequately paid manufacturing or white-collar work.

In the 1970s, feminists would have been shocked by the very idea of employing other women to do their domestic work for them. Times have changed, and a servant class has re-emerged anyway; domestic work is probably the best available option for some women, and it is certainly better paid than some other forms of service work. Nevertheless, most domestic workers are ununionised, unprotected and lack benefits such as social insurance and holiday pay, at best dependent on the goodwill of individual employers. Nor does the existence of nannies and cleaners resolve all the problems of professional women forced to put in excessive hours at work yet wishing they could spend more time with their children. For some it means the decision to postpone motherhood, and in turn some of them leave it so long that the 'biological clock' has moved too far forward.

Tomorrow's Women is essentially a reflection rather than an analysis of contemporary attitudes, which are well caught (better, possibly, than the authors realise) in the report. Demos is close to the 'New Labour' agenda of Tony Blair's government, and seems to share with it a concern with the media, presentation and the mindset of the new managerial class. There is much Blairite rhetoric about the future, and about being 'modern', and a wish to be in the mainstream of contemporary mass culture with references to the Spice Girls, the soap opera *EastEnders* and the women's road movie *Thelma and Louise*, but the end result is rather the same as the new Labour government – a wish to make all the right noises and support the right 'radical' causes such as environmentalism, but an equally strong wish not to offend the powerful, and not to appear to be 'rabidly' feminist. Above all, like New Labour, it has no alternative economic strategy that might mitigate the effects of monetarist 'flexibility' on both women and men in the work-place. As things stand, there seems no reason to feel optimistic that employers will listen to Helen Wilkinson, Melanie Howard and Demos, and 'reduce working time, providing support to make sure that childbearing and work are genuinely . . . compatible' (Wilkinson and Howard, 1997: 161).

Published a year later, *The New Feminism*, by the journalist Natasha Walter, strikes a similar bright note of optimism tempered by reality. Her arguments are backed up by the meticulous deployment of facts and informed by interviews with many women in all sorts of situations. Moreover, like Rachel Blau DuPlessis and Anne Snitow she rightly insists on the dramatic changes in (some) women's lives that have occurred since the 1970s, let alone since 1900.

Towards the end of the book she puts herself in the picture, describing how she sits in a bar and drinks a glass of beer, watching the women in the street outside wearing comfortable minimalist clothes, yet in a whole variety of styles. She quotes Rebecca West, who wrote of the women's fashions of 1900 that they were 'a handicap and a humiliation, heavy, crippling, loaded with rows of buttons and hooks and eyes . . . and boned in all sorts of places', whereas Walter's own wardrobe contains 'pretty silk dresses and spindly sandals as well as stout clothes in dull colours . . . for gardening or walking or working' (Walter, 1998: 255). She can drink alone in a bar and live with a man to whom she is not married, whereas Lydia Bennet in *Pride and Prejudice* was 'lost forever. . . . Loss of virtue in a female is irretrievable

. . . one false step involves her in endless ruin . . . [her] death would have been a blessing in comparison of this' (Walter, 1998: 255).

Yet Walter recognises the contradiction that all this freedom goes hand in hand with continuing inequality. She cites lucidly and in detail all the forms of discrimination against women in the workplace, the welfare system and the courts; nor does she shirk an account of women's victim-isation by men, whether rapists or pimps. Yet ultimately, like Helen Wilkinson and Melanie Howard, she lays out but cannot solve the contradictions between the idea that 'the future is female' and the con-tinuing obstacles faced by women. Indeed, she largely blames the women's movement of the 1970s for the persistence of inequalities in the public sphere. This, she believes, was because Women's Liberation shut men out and became too inturned. In retrospect I think she is right to argue that (some) feminists from that period were responsible for the widely held view that feminists are man-haters, although of course this has since the nineteenth century been the first slur cast at women the moment they dare to complain. Certainly slogans such as 'all men are rapists' were open to misunderstanding, to say the least. Yet there was a reason why, and Walter does not sufficiently acknowledge that the demand for women's-only meetings and women's-only groups was a direct response to the open denigration of women referred to earlier. Indeed, it was rather shocking to read that her late father, the well-known anarchist and libertarian Nicholas Walter, wrote letters 'to *Spare Rib* and the *Guardian* women's page under an assumed [presumably female] name, because he wanted to enter a debate that would otherwise have been closed to him' (Walter, 1998: 145). His daughter may have a point in her criticisms of the ways and extent to which feminists excluded men, but her father's arrogance in refusing to respect women's wishes and the underhand fashion in which he circum-vented them provide a good example of the reasons for that exclusion.

Yet Natasha Walter makes a powerful point when she argues that the essential link between the private and public, the personal and political, emphasised by seventies feminists who 'showed how personal life was constructed in the image of wider inequalities of power, and . . . how political life could never be divorced from private values', became increas-ingly an *overemphasis* on the personal at the expense of the political – epitomised, incidentally, by the importance of psychoanalysis both as a theory and as a therapy to this generation of feminists. This resulted, Walter argues, in a concentration on sexuality in particular at the expense of more outward-looking campaigns; she relates this obsession with the personal to an identity politics that fragmented the women's movement by insisting on the differences that divided women rather than what could bring them together.

Although I was one of those who in the 1970s accepted and argued for the view that sexuality formed the core, in some way, of women's oppression, it is possible to see today how it is, at best, only one aspect of women's difficulties. There have undoubtedly been changes for the better in the sexual arena. Sex is more freely discussed – although many young women, even if they know about contraception, are still too scared to go on the pill or insist on the use of condoms because then they will be labelled as 'slags'. Different sexualities are more acceptable, and the importance of women's pleasure is more widely acknowledged. All this is good in itself and may well have increased the general sum of human happiness. What it has not done is caused a *general* improvement in the position of women. Sexual behaviour has been revealed as one arena of struggle for women, but not as central in the way many feminists used to believe.

The 'modern' voices of contemporary (semi-)feminism, then, found in *The New Feminism* and *Tomorrow's Women*, provide few solutions for the problems they cogently describe. Yet the voices of the feminists who were already writing in the 1970s do not seem quite right for the millennium either. In 1997 Ann Oakley and Juliet Mitchell, two of the most influential British feminists of an earlier time, published an edited collection of articles, *Who's Afraid of Feminism: Seeing Through the Backlash*, which followed their previous collections, *What is Feminism?*, published in 1987 and *The Rights and Wrongs of Women* a decade before that. The articles in their most recent volume are scholarly and serious and quite devoid of the studiedly bright tone of Walter and Wilkinson. Most address specific issues of relevance to women that have arisen in recent years; nevertheless, to organise a whole book round the assertation that there has been a 'backlash' against feminism, which these editors do, seriously oversimplifies the ways in which women's lives have changed during the last three decades, and does scant justice to the extraordinarily contradictory experience it has been, or to the ambivalence I have identified as crucial to our understanding of women's contemporary situation. Had there been a backlash pure and simple, women might have been pushed back into the home, or deprived of gains they have made; but ambivalence has produced a kind of stalemate, with numerous problems identified (often quite sympathetically, for example, by government bodies) yet solutions in short supply so that women are both held back and pushed forward by competing interests – and above all by the competing demands of the globalising economy.

Margaret Walters in *Who's Afraid of Feminism?* looks back with nostalgia at the hopes of the early seventies, and especially to its sexual optimism and to the importance accorded to the sexual revolution:

> It's hard in this climate to recall the optimism and the robustness of the women's movement of the late 1960s and early 1970s. A concern with how we lived our lives sexually was central. . . . It was no idyll: we pontificated about 'sexual liberation' as if it were there for the taking; we were naïve about political power, about our relationships with men and with each other, and about our own darker selves. We were muddled and inconsistent . . . but what happened to the vitality of that attempt to examine and explode the clichés we had grown up with – that men are active, women are passive, and that nice girls don't? (Walters, 1997: 59)

Walters' article cogently demolishes the overblown rhetoric of the anti-pornography campaigners Andrea Dworkin and Catharine MacKinnon and the bombast of Camille Paglia's wilder claims, but her article ends on a note of despair that seems exaggerated, as though all other feminisms had left the field. In fact Dworkin's stentorian tones have not won the day – on the contrary, her attempts to legislate against pornography were defeated.

Lynne Segal's magisterial survey of feminist discourse since the 1970s *Why Feminism?* is equally scholarly and provides a compendium of arguments to combat the more simplistic arguments against feminism as well as a path through the thickets of theoretical debate. Yet her book too contains a note of nostalgia, for while she recognises that 'what will engage the attention and further the interests of one group of women will not be most relevant to the needs of another' (Segal, 1999: 232), she looks to the socialist feminist vision as the way of harmonising this diversity of interests.

This is not inconsistent with the postmodern perspective that has, as Lynne Segal herself suggests, created 'spaces for more women to flaunt the diverse pleasures, entitlements and self-questioning to which recent feminist thinking has encouraged them to aspire (often, disconcertingly, in line with late capitalist consumerism' (Segal, 1999: 232). As she also argues, however, the postmodern celebration of diversity, fragmentation and pleasure can easily become a 'feminism without politics', a narcissistic (albeit rather shaky) hedonism of which the fictional Bridget Jones has become the popular representative.

So where, then, are women – and feminists – at the millennium? Just as the gloomy claims of a direct backlash against female emancipation assign too great a clarity and certainty to the forces of patriarchal reaction, so the optimism of postmodernists seems facile. The fragmentation which, it is alleged, has permitted alternative movements, the 'others' of orthodox leftist movements, to come forward has led to a celebration of any and every woman as a feminist, thus emptying feminism of any meaning whatsoever. Angela McRobbie emphasises the camp parody of postmodern culture, and the 'witty' way in which it subverts old meanings. In this spirit *Bridget Jones's Diary* can be cast as a parody of the anxieties that beset young women. Yet while it is healthy to be able to laugh at one's own absurdities, Bridget Jones – and Ally McBeal – merely *express* the contemporary incoherence which, I argue, is the current state of things. Sure, they claim to do no more than provide light entertainment with a woman-friendly touch, and it is of interest that they ventriloquise so successfully the confused world we live in. Yet parody, irony and wit have a way of undercutting the very ground from beneath one's feet, while jokiness is a way of warding off anxiety; in the end these young representatives of the contemporary middle-class woman make any serious attempt to investigate the problems they touch on seem, well, just too serious and heavy. Moreover, as Llewellyn Negrin (1999) points out, this playful hedonism is very much in tune with contemporary consumer capitalism.

At a more analytical level, the main achievement of postmodern feminism, or postfeminism, as it has sometimes been termed, has been at a theoretical level to query the very category 'woman' and at the level of representation to

embrace a wholesale relativism, so that however a woman presents herself –
as lesbian, homemaker, romantic, career woman, wild child or nun – it is all
equal in the public arena of performance and spectacle. It was for these
reasons that in her death Princess Diana could appear not only to condense
in her single person all the contradictions of contemporary women's lives,
but to become a saint for this new 'feminism'. The death of Diana is
discussed in my next chapter; what is demonstrated by the ambivalent
collective attitude from which she suffered and which she shared, albeit on a
grander scale, with the iconic women I have mentioned above is the unease
with which western culture views the spectacle of women in public.

Notes

1. This was later challenged by a male would-be candidate and declared illegal on equal
opportunities grounds.
2. For those who were feminists in the 1970s, these caricatures were also unpleasantly
reminiscent of a notorious article by a psychiatrist, Jasper Gayford, attached to the then
Chiswick Women's Refuge, in which he argued that battered women actively sought violent
men or else brought violence upon themselves by their own (mis)behaviour. He gave his
stereotypes names such as 'Flirtatious Fanny' and 'Violent Violet'.

3

THE UNBEARABLE LIGHTNESS OF DIANA

Myth

In the week after Princess Diana's death I was baffled and deeply alienated by the public response to the horrifying accident and its amplification by the mass media. I could neither understand nor share the apparent outpouring of grief, nor the explanations thought up by media commentators for the flowers, the poems, the queues and the candles. Of course, it was terribly sad – the death of a young woman and mother when on the threshold, as seemed at least possible, of a happier period in her life – but I did not feel I had lost a friend or a member of my family. On the contrary, since a neighbour of mine had just died, I was painfully aware of the difference between the death of someone who actually *was* a friend and the more ethereal loss of someone known only as a media figure.

Nor did I believe that the tragic event had in any real or permanent sense 'united the nation', as we were being told. I did not believe that this marked the beginning of a transformation of the British personality as we shed our stiff upper lips, and openly expressed our emotions; I did not believe this meant that the nation had become 'feminised', nor that henceforth we would become a different, more 'caring' society.

In the first week after the accident the only public expression of dissent from these prevailing views appeared in the *Guardian*. Its columnist, Mark Lawson, reported that the BBC had been inundated with demands from television viewers for *less* coverage of Diana's death and its aftermath, and the readers' letters column in the *Guardian* newspaper expressed anger and scepticism in varying degrees. 'Broadcasters . . . seemed determined to create rather than reflect the mood of "a nation in mourning",' wrote C.J.R. Abbott on 2 September. 'Don't they realise that the strange mixture of hedonism, self-pity, media manipulation and noblesse oblige displayed by the former Princess of Wales in recent years mattered very little in most people's lives?' Mike Pokorny, meanwhile, admitted that 'I never realised that Diana had single-handedly led the campaigns for the eradication of Aids, leprosy, landmines and youth homelessness. And to think I had always assumed that this selfless and saintly woman only ever used the media to manipulate her own image.' But the very next day the heretics were slapped down in no uncertain manner by Andrew Heath as: 'curmudgeonly; clever-clever; slightly nasty minded; and above all wholly contemptuous of what ordinary people think and care about. Your letters page yesterday was a useful and pretty representative sample of the attitudes of the British intellectual left.' The following week Linda Grant devoted the whole of her column to a similar attack on the 'sneering, Puritanical distaste' of 'the Left' (whatever that is – we weren't told). 'The Left', she pontificated, can't cope with beauty, is terrified of feelings, and guilty of 'sneering, elitist condescension'.

Between the death of Princess Diana and Dodi Al Fayed and the funeral of the Princess, I felt desperate to write something, to try to mount a serious challenge to the apparent general consensus. Then, gradually, several journalists wrote thoughtful articles that went against the general grain. In particular, Nikki Gerrard in the *Observer* wrote 'let's hear it for stoicism', and questioned whether the unfettered outpouring of vicarious grief was as wholly virtuous as everyone seemed to have assumed. She and Mark Lawson in the *Guardian* voiced my doubts and my resentment, and expressed my disquiet in the whole way in which the aftermath of the Princess's death had played. So perhaps there was nothing further to be said after all.

In the following weeks, however, the ongoing media discourse on Diana continued to evolve. Despite all the protestations of guilt, despite the regrets of those who admitted they had bought the tabloids which had – perhaps – contributed to the Princess's death, the revised version of Andrew Morton's *Diana: Her True Story* headed the bestseller lists the moment it appeared. There was intense debate on the Internet as to the cause of her death, and there and in newspapers in Egypt and other Arab states a conspiracy theory developed that she had been murdered by MI5 in order to prevent her marriage to a Muslim. At the same time the continuing investigation into the causes of the crash shifted the focus of blame from the paparazzi of the media to the chauffeur and drunken driving.

Yet despite the flood of daily coverage and comment, certain silences were maintained. This was a classic case of the way in which Roland Barthes argued that a 'myth' is created. In *Mythologies* Barthes (1957) developed the idea that a myth is a representation which, in articulating one set of meanings, silences possible alternatives. His best-known example was of the photograph of a black soldier in French army uniform saluting the Tricolour; in the 1950s, in the context of the Algerian troubles, Barthes interpreted this as a statement that there are (good) black men who are loyal to France. Thus, the image he deconstructed silently buried the arguments in favour of decolonisation, substituting a subliminal message reassuring to conservative opinion and white racism. This message was not openly uttered; it was more subtly implied. The very silences of the 'myth' covered up what could not be said, 'suturing' over the cracks.

In investigating the 'myth' 'Diana', which is, of course, much more complex than any single photograph, it is just as necessary to look for what is not said. The exploration of this myth of our times is a search for the cracks in credibility that fissure our society.

Opera: Romantic Tragedy

Surprisingly little was made of the operatic nature of the love story between Princess Diana and Dodi Al Fayed. Yet this had every ingredient of what the French romantic novelist Théophile Gautier called 'modern love'. 'The fallen woman and the fatal man' were, for Gautier (1874) the essential components of 'modern love', and 'modern love' was the staple of the narratives upon which many of the great nineteenth-century operas were based.

Although western societies have consciously rejected the very idea of the 'fallen woman', Diana fitted to perfection a contemporary version. Today we have confused women, women finding themselves, women breaking free from restricting relationships; yet underneath it all the image of the fallen woman remains, the woman, that is, who, from love or desperation, breaks her marriage vows and accordingly finds herself in a no-(wo)man's land of social ambiguity. Of course, since this was 1997, Princess Diana was not cast out of polite society and condemned to a *demi-monde* of kept women, as was the lady of the Camelias, Violetta. Yet her fate was not so dissimilar, since once she left the Royal Family there was no clear social group or caste to which she belonged, no clear social role for her. Tina Brown, of *Vanity Fair*, described a luncheon she had with the Princess and the editor of American *Vogue*, at which Diana told them she thought it unlikely she would marry again: 'Who would take me on? I have so much baggage,' she reportedly said. Her social situation was unique. She was as much in uncharted waters as the *demi-mondaines* of Edith Wharton's *The House of Mirth*. In that novel the heroine, Lily, fatally descending the social scale eventually to destitution, found herself at the mid-point of her downward spiral in a strange half-world of unanchored women living in unexplained ease in luxury hotels:

> Through this atmosphere of torrid splendour moved wan beings as richly upholstered as the furniture, beings without definite pursuits or permanent relations, who drifted on a languid tide. . . . High stepping horses or elaborately equipped motors waited to carry these ladies into vague metropolitan distances, when they returned . . . to be sucked back into the stifling inertia of the hotel routine. . . . [They] seemed to float together outside the bounds of time and space [and] . . . through this jumble of futile activities came and went a strange throng of hangers-on – manicurists, beauty-doctors, hair-dressers, teachers of bridge, of French, of 'physical development'. (Wharton, 1952: 298–302)

The life of the Princess was not pointless nor exclusively dedicated to self-indulgent luxury in this way – the difference a hundred years has made is that even princesses have more opportunities for independence and self-development, and Diana was making use of such opportunities, although she was hampered by her attachment to the world of international royalty, where, it seems, women are still defined overwhelmingly in terms of marriage and their relationship to men. That made her 'independence' highly ambiguous. Diana's predicament after her divorce, however, also illustrated the ambiguity of *all* women's lives, was a paradigm of contemporary confusions. There is really no consensus whether women should concentrate on being mothers or go out to work, whether they are still oppressed by men, or have overtaken them and now threaten masculine identity.

So while Diana's situation was not defined in the moralistic terms of nineteenth-century social rules, she did to some degree play the fascinating role of 'fallen woman'. The media permitted and even encouraged acts of excess and a lifestyle that, like Violetta's, seemed both glamorous and slightly out of control, the waltz always threatening to become a *danse macabre*, while Edith Wharton's cloud of 'strange hangers-on' were certainly reincarnated in some of the psychics, trainers and gurus to whom Diana turned for help.

And then the fatal man appeared in the form of Dodi Al Fayed. Whether he was really suited to this role we shall never know, and we can tantalisingly forever play out different alternative scenarios of what Diana's life with him might have been. As she was rumoured to have said she intended, she might have retired from public life to live in idyllic, albeit jet-setting, happiness and become simply a wife and mother once more (a pronouncement that raises questions as to the strength of her commitment to the causes she had made her own). On the other hand it might have all gone horribly wrong, so that, ten years down the line, we might have known that she had embarked on a series of less and less 'suitable' relationships, seeking, like ageing film stars before her, a series of ever more bizarre consorts, gigolos and toy boys. Dodi Al Fayed, who was older than she, was not exactly a toy boy. Neither did he seem quite to match the Byronic ideal of doomed romantic hero, although his lifestyle did, as it turned out, transform him, however unintentionally, all too literally into the 'fatal man'.

Yet precisely because the love of Princess Diana and Dodi Al Fayed was extinguished seemingly at the very moment of its consummation, it becomes forever operatic. It fits with a long western tradition of doomed love, of romantic passion as inextricably linked to death; it is a reworking of Romeo and Juliet, of Tristan and Isolde, of *Wuthering Heights, Anna Karenina* and *Rebecca*. For this reason it touched a deep, unconscious chord. Like the real-life drama of the suicides of *Mayerling*, the tragedy will surely be the raw material for films, for theatre, for whatever art forms there are in a hundred years time. Unfortunately, it is musically more likely to be Andrew Lloyd Webber than Verdi.

This aspect of the Diana myth effectively occludes any concerns or doubts that could be labelled 'feminist'. Glamorised, tragic, operatic love is so potent that, caught up in it, we no longer worry about whether Diana really was, after all, a feminist icon, a woman reaching for independence, and refusing the humiliating traditional role of virtuous but betrayed wife (a role still seemingly much in fashion in the Conservative Party, and, indeed, not unknown in American presidential circles).

Soap Opera

So we had 'Candle in the Wind' rather than *La Traviata* (the title of which, translated, means 'The Misled'). This was opera, but it was also soap opera. If opera is very often melodrama dignified and made sublime by music, then soap opera is melodrama domesticated. We have long grown used to the idea that the whole of the Royal Family has become a soap opera. There can be little more to say about this, other than that Diana played the familiar role of the heroine who becomes the evil woman, only to then undergo further transformations into the strong woman, the survivor, a heroine of a different kind.

Soap opera characters must invite the identification of an audience if they are to be truly successful; and Diana was perfect for this, since she embodied in her person a number of contradictory, even incompatible, roles. To begin with she was simply the *ingénue*, the fairy princess, but she rapidly became mother, crazy neurotic, wife betrayed, self-obsessed narcissist, glamour star, bulimic, woman-struggling-for-independence, survivor and, latterly, saint, strong woman, and even political interventionist. This excess, this surfeit, amplified by the media, meant that she became a living simulacrum, that is to say, a copy without an original, a multiple personality with no 'real' Diana to which her public could return. But that did not matter; on the contrary, it made her more than ever an object of fascination and multiple identifications. It is hardly surprising that so many women expressed grief at her passing, queued to sign books of condolence and left flowers, prayers, candles and poems, for she was anything and everything. Or at least her image was. And yet what does it say about our ideas of beauty if so many women of all creeds and colours identify with a woman who was white, blonde and thin, the most traditional style of beauty.

This image was a massive wish fulfilment. For it had two completely contradictory messages for the public. To the unhappy divorcée, to the bulimic wracked with guilt, to the betrayed lover, to the woman of a certain age, it seemed to say, on the one hand: to be rich and beautiful does not make you happy; on the other: if you suffer, maybe you can be like her. There was consolation of a conservative kind in her at times obvious misery; yet her looks and wealth cast a veil of glamour over even the dreariest chapters of her life – which is also the role of soap opera. It is about 'ordinary people', but the very fact that they are actually television stars or personalities removes their 'ordinary' – life-and-death – problems from the very realms of ordinariness they were supposed to represent. Thus the Diana myth, while *appearing* to address the contradictory nature of women's lives today, undermined its own potential radicalism by burying it in glamour and melodrama.

Her position was unique and exceptional, yet her difficulties were similar to those of many women: an unhappy marriage, an insensitive and unfaithful husband, hateful in-laws, a snatch at happiness with another, on the face of it rather unpromising, lover. Her looks and clothes glamorised her predicament, yet her bulimia reminded her audience that the search for feminine beauty is a poisoned chalice. Finally her efforts to find a new role for herself must also have resonated with many women. She was in fact a confused, contradictory individual, iconic of the incoherence of our society's attitude towards its women. As Linda Holt points out, however, 'Diana's solutions remained personal, individual and traditional' (Holt, 1998: 195), and today the glee with which some feminist writers adopted her as a feminist icon seems bizarre. Even stranger was the way in which a populist feminism saw her as the representative of 'ordinary people'. For after all, Diana was not like 'us', but was caught in an imperial time warp, and instead of noting the similarities between her position and that of so many women, it might be more constructive to measure the distance and the difference between her and us. The way in which writers such as Beatrix Campbell, Linda Grant, Elaine Showalter and Suzanne Moore elevated Princess Diana to the status of a feminist saint after her death is illustrative less of feminist truths than of the weak thought of postmodernism and postfeminism. Unable to understand the difference between 'feminine' and 'feminist', these writers, as Linda Holt pointed out, turned the two inside out so that the stereotype of woman as emotion and woman as victim became something to be gloried in rather than analysed or questioned.

Beatrix Campbell went so far as to see in the outpouring of emotion the wholesale 'feminisation' of British culture. This reaffirmed a reactionary stereotype of women as the only sex with feelings, the only ones with tear ducts, the only ones who 'care'. We could only become a more 'caring' society, went the argument, if we were a 'feminised' society. Yet the idea that men are incapable *ever* of feeling, of caring or of nurturing is a pseudo-feminist cliché. To suggest this is to parrot the unhelpful stereotype that to be a woman is to feel, to be a man to think. It is an argument predicated on the belief that nature counts for more than nurture; that both men and women are programmed hormonally and genetically from the start to such an extent that an essential maleness and femaleness can never be altered. This is not feminism, but a cry of despair. If men can't change, what hope is there for women, or children? All civilisation is based on the belief that human individuals can and do change.

Don't Cry for Me, Cry for *Gran Britannia*

One aspect of the event 'Diana's death' was the way in which a cloud of 'pundits' of various kinds tried to make sense of the apparent 'outpouring' of grief. In a particularly unenlightening round-table discussion for the London *Observer*, for example, Stuart Hall said it meant something complicated, while Simon Jenkins said it didn't mean anything much at all. It certainly seems to have been the case that many individuals felt able to revisit and work through tragedies and losses of their own in the context of this shocking public event. Perhaps, as some cynics suggested at the time, it also revealed an emptiness in the lives of those who had felt so bound up with Diana's life without having ever met her. (For those who *had* met and been charmed by her, the situation was clearly different.)

The Church of England seemed to take heart from the unexpected and at least partly spontaneous creation of a kind of secular religion, or religiosity, but surely it revealed rather the extent to which official Christianity in Britain has become almost entirely bankrupt, unable to connect with the lives of most people in any meaningful way. For me, one of the most profoundly depressing aspects of the events was just this empty religiosity. It may seem unfair, or, in Linda Grant's terms, 'elitist', to dismiss as empty the way in which millions of individuals sought to express genuine grief. Yet it was rather indulgent, for if it was 'compassion', it had no 'hard edge'. I always thought that religion – or any decent secular philosophy, for that matter – involved rules, precepts and beliefs that were necessarily sometimes hard to follow, hard to live up to. Mourning for Diana, by contrast, was soft-centred in the extreme. It seemed simply to be, if we are to believe the media, an outpouring of 'caring', an expression of 'emotion' (what emotion?), without an accompanying clear morality or set of spiritual beliefs. What was really so great about all this vague and formless emotion? Far from rejoicing at the way in which this ectoplasm enveloped the land, I am appalled by the idea that the expression of emotion – any emotion – is necessarily always good.

One of the hidden agendas may have been – as some suggested – a generalised regret for eighteen years of Thatcherism. I suspect that many people in Britain do now regard those eighteen years as being years of missed opportunity and a decline in public values; but, as opinion polls show, the British seem to want the goodness and 'caring' without hard choices: the NHS, but low – or preferably *no* – taxes; better working conditions, but no trade unions; fair shares and better times for all, but no redistribution of wealth; a society stripped of deference, but wall-to-wall *Hello!* magazine. Grief for Diana expressed that perfectly. You could emote all you wanted without having to think hard about anything.

The media, as Mark Lawson pointed out, put a brilliant spin on things. At first, the media were the villain: paparazzi had hounded the Princess to her death, and they had done so because the tabloids, like the insatiable plant in *Little Shop of Horrors*, demanded ever more food in the shape of human lives to satisfy their hunger. For a moment it even seemed as if the grieving public was itself to blame for having read the tabloids in the first place. Soon, however, the spotlight was turned on the hateful, out-of-date Royals.

This was the expression of 'feeling' at its worst. There was something very unpleasant about the way in which the Royal Family was bullied and hounded for not displaying emotion in the way in which the tabloids approved (and I write as a convinced republican). It made some people feel better and gave them someone other than themselves to blame; but how did it make Diana's sons feel? It was shoddy and cheap to condemn the Queen for refusing to express a depth of grief she surely could not have felt, and I felt embarrassed by her little bob as the Princess's coffin passed.

The big blame story became the Royals' inability to move with the times, and one of the more permanent 'lessons' to be drawn from Diana's death was that the House of Windsor must be reformed. This was possibly the most depressing aspect of the whole affair: that an opportunity for finally getting rid of the whole fake pageantry and undemocratic claptrap of the monarchy was seemingly missed; instead Diana may actually have saved the antiquated institution. Indeed it has since become clear that this was always Tony Blair's intention, and the curtailment of royal budgets coupled with Blair's eulogy to the Queen on the occasion of her golden wedding skilfully worked to this end. Thus the myth performed the further task of *appearing* to address outworn privilege, while actually strengthening it.

The Politics of Diana's Death

The Prime Minister, Tony Blair, played an important role in encouraging the expression of emotion by his own reaction to the death of the 'People's Princess'. He even managed to create the impression that there was a link between the nation's mourning of Diana and the victory of the Labour Party in the election on 1 May. The rejoicing on election night seemed to be an outpouring of relief that the country had finally got rid of those embarrassing, seedy, unpleasant, clapped-out Tories, and the election night 'myth' obscured the fact that – wonderful to relate – we had done it without ditching any of their policies! A brilliant squaring of the circle had been magically achieved, but what this really meant in terms of unchanged monetarist policies is only now beginning to sink in – or rather the 'sutures' cobbling up the cracks are beginning to unravel.

The Labour Party seems to assume that it won the election *because* it ditched anything resembling a 'leftwing' policy. No-one, however, has thoroughly investigated the real reasons for the Labour victory. It may have been that 'middle England' no longer felt scared of the unions or feared another winter of discontent. It may have been determination to get rid of a hated government. It may have been – indeed it is likely – that some voters hoped that the Labour Party would prove more radical in government than in opposition. Such hopes have so far been largely disappointed. Under Tony Blair the government has pursued what are for the most part right-of-centre policies, particularly in relation to the economy and law and order issues, but has presented them in a new way.

The link to Princess Diana is in the domination of emotion over content, and in the individualisation of collective issues. Tony Blair appealed, and continues to appeal, to formless, vague yearnings for an undefined good. The Labour Party is identified as the person of Blair himself: in his *On the Record* television 'apology' (BBC1, 16 November 1997) for the events surrounding Formula One motor racing and tobacco advertising,[1] he said 'trust me', never 'trust the Labour Party': '*I* am a pretty straight guy' – '*I* didn't get it all wrong' – 'In the end the country has got to look at *me* and decide whether the *person* they believed in is the same person they have got now' (emphasis mine). His evangelical style has been noted, and the Evita/Diana/Blair axis mobilises the emotions of the crowd in the service of what Stuart Hall named as 'authoritarian populism'. By this Hall (1980b, 1983) meant the way in which a populist leader (he was writing of Margaret Thatcher) could ventriloquise popular feelings (that is, appear to say what 'the people' were feeling), for example fear of crime, and could use this popular emotion as a springboard for undemocratic moves and authoritarian policies. Whereas Mrs Thatcher tended towards the confrontational, Tony Blair appears more consensual, and has attempted, with some success at first, to clothe the continuation of Thatcherist policies in more 'caring' language. The link between Diana's death and Blair's government may be quite tenuous. The feelings aroused by the Princess's death, however, were mobilised to create the impression that the 'caring', 'unified' nation in grief was the same nation that voted Tony Blair into power, and that in showing its feelings, the nation somehow endorsed Blair's 'vision' – whatever that really is.

For me, therefore, the hidden, oblique politics of Diana's death were profoundly conservative. They masqueraded as progressive, but they were populist. They claimed to be modern, reforming, a call for change, but they were undemocratic and intolerant.

The last, and most serious, aspect was the way in which her own best acts and interests were mobilised in the interests of charity. The eighteen years of Tory rule saw a concerted and continuous onslaught on the very notion of the public sphere. All collective, state provision was rubbished; the idea that progressive taxes constituted a fair and rational method of redistributing wealth was denounced; the thought that anyone had a responsibility to do anything for anyone other than their 'family' was sidelined. The way in which, for example, Tony Blair defended the decision of the then Cabinet minister, Harriet Harman, to send her son to a selective school was to say that of course she would do her best for 'her children'. The idea that doing 'your best' for your own children might involve damaging the prospects of *other people's* children was right outside the frame. The reality – that universal free comprehensive education only works if everyone signs up to it – was never mentioned. For Tony Blair as for Mrs Thatcher, it seems as if there is no such thing as society – we have a duty only to our own families; a narrow creed if ever there was one.

This is a good example of the way in which debate has narrowed as the public sphere has declined, and, sadly, the good Princess Diana did has acted to reinforce these assumptions. No-one would wish to belittle the importance of her gesture in shaking hands with a patient with HIV. That did enormous good. No-one would deny that her patronage of Centrepoint, the charity for the young homeless, that her campaign for the abolition of landmines and that the other causes to which she devoted herself were beneficial and often brave.

Yet it would seem that her work has also acted to reinforce the idea that charity can substitute for the public sphere. The shortfall in public spending in all the important areas of life that affect us so much is to continue. The only way – and the only *correct* way, it seems – in which the gaping void can be filled is by charity, because in charitable giving the individual chooses how to spend her or his money. It is not taken away by the state; the giver makes the choice.

Unfortunately the giver too often does not make the choice, and charitable giving has declined, even if the Princess Diana Memorial fund is awash with lucre and the Lottery mounts up. Of course, the obscene manner in which the arts are to be funded by what has often been termed a voluntary tax on the poor shows how much, or rather how little, this government, like the last, really cares about the arts. But in the context of Princess Diana, the message of the myth is that charity is good, the state bad. We are good, and we feel good if we give to charity; but the state is greedy and authoritarian if it takes these matters out of our hands. Yet surely, it would be more rational, honest and adult if, in voting (we hope) for a better NHS and education system, we also recognised that we have thereby signed up to a financial contribution to these public goods.

The emphasis on charity ignores one of the hardest-learned lessons of the nineteenth century: that charity simply does not work. Throughout the whole of the Victorian epoch successive governments, reformers and moralists clung desperately to the idea that state intervention was an evil and that philanthropy was and must be the only route for the amelioration of poverty and misery. The utter failure of charity to do this job pushed Parliament slowly and painfully towards the state intervention that now, one hundred years later, is being inexorably destroyed. Read Dickens if you want an accurate picture of the charitable society.

One of the media gurus who had a field day in the wake of Diana's death was the psychologist Oliver James. On an edition of the *Moral Maze* (BBC Radio 4) he was moved to yelp rather desperately that Tony Blair had got it all wrong: it wasn't that we needed to get back to traditional morality, in fact we couldn't because this was what late capitalism did – it created atomised societies, it split up families and destroyed communities in its search for profit. The only solution he suggested, in an article in the *Guardian* (James, 1997: 3), was a more caring form of neo-capitalism, which to some of us may seem like a contradiction in terms.

Lastly, there is the riddle of why feminist columnists such as Linda Grant believed that anyone who didn't sign up to the grief-for-Diana syndrome was an elitist member of a 'Left' that couldn't cope with feeling. It seemed particularly strange that this grossly reactionary stereotype should be mobilised at a time when 'the Left' is in such utter disarray.

This was possible because the rump of the Left – and it is hard even to define who or what this is – has been marginalised so completely that today it plays the hopeless role of Cassandra, the prophetess who was doomed never to be believed. So thoroughly has the very idea of anything resembling socialism been delegitimated that those who attempt to speak in and/or renew its discourse cannot be heard; it is the babblings of madness. The disintegration of the Soviet Union and its evident corruption has been the excuse for the rise of a doctrine that nothing other than what is can ever be: the end of history. There is no alternative to monetarism even if as a doctrine it is far emptier than socialism and spawns regimes every bit as corrupt as the USSR.

In the case of Diana's death 'the Left' could be attacked also because socialism was a product of the Enlightenment that it is now fashionable to demonise as a terorristic project: there was never 'reason', there was only a different form of domination masquerading as rational. Thus grief for Diana privileges the values of feeling over reason and is therefore a good, whereas ideas associated with socialism, such as justice and equality, make a fatal claim to rationality and are therefore bad. The attack by post-modern philosophers on the 'white, male, western' reason (or pseudo-reason) of the Enlightenment has a point; there was a complacency and a one-sidedness in the eighteenth-century belief in the superiority of reason and the unimportance or inferiority of the emotions and the body. Yet in the twentieth century we went to the opposite extreme, and over-valued feelings at the expense of reason. This may be due in part to the legacy of psychoanalysis. Freud himself, however, believed that if the irrational forces of the unconscious were brought to consciousness (insofar as that is ever possible), they would be open to rational control. He envisaged, in other words, the cooperation of reason and feeling. That was not the atmosphere at the close of the twentieth century.

In his novel *The Unbearable Lightness of Being*, Milan Kundera explored the idea of how bearable, how 'light', seem the sorrows and tragedies of the affluent society at one level. Likewise, in her analysis of soap opera, Ien Ang (1983) saw the genre as expressive above all of the sorrow that has no name, of the vague griefs and discontents of the welfare societies of the West. In the week after the car crash that killed Princess Diana and Dodi Al Fayed, it was surely just this unbearable lightness of being that poured out, our grief that the consumer society, which claims to offer us everything we could ever want, actually gives us so little. Princess Diana embodied that unbearable lightness, the suppressed consciousness of an emptiness at the heart of our coarse and philistine society.

Into this massive political vacuum of thought stepped the twin figures of Tony Blair and Princess Diana. And, just as 'Candle in the Wind' reduces the whole complex story of Diana to one single, easy sob, so the myth of the 'People's Princess' condenses the whole complex political challenge of our times into one poignant moment of regret without real change.

As we wept for Diana we forgot how we kicked the homeless and loathed the poor. We forgot that the other side of the coin of Diana-worship is the bullying of the Royal Family, just as emotional support for Louise Woodward went hand in hand with intolerance and even violence towards individuals who failed to express 'adequate' support for her, and coincided with the renewed demonisation of the two disturbed ten-year olds who killed the toddler Jamie Bulger.[2]

Instead we were wafted to the heavens, and Diana smiled upon us, as in one of those Catholic oleographs in which rays of light surround the saint like bolts of lightning. Diana's halo was our halo. Indeed, Diana *was* our halo, and we wore her with pride.

Notes

1. Following a donation of £1 million to the Labour Party from Bernie Ecclestone, the Formula One motor racing magnate, the government exempted Formula One motor racing from its ban on tocacco advertising. It was later forced to return the donation.

2. English girl Louise Woodward was a nanny to an American couple, and was found guilty of having killed their infant son. The case was controversial on both sides of the Atlantic. Although the two boys who killed Jamie Bulger appear to have been disturbed and neglected, tabloid newspapers orchestrated demands for their prolonged incarceration and one prosecution lawyer even referred to them as 'evil monsters', thus reflecting an apparent widespread lack of understanding of mental disturbance and a refusal to confront its complexity.

4

FEMINIST FUNDAMENTALISM

The Shifting Politics of Sex and Censorship

Debates within Feminism

Almost from its beginnings the feminism of the 1970s was divided between those who saw men as the 'main enemy' and those who linked women's subordination to a number of different structures in society, including the state and capitalist production. The first group were labelled – or chose to be called – 'radical', 'revolutionary' or 'cultural' feminists; the second usually, in Britain at least, were 'socialist' feminists. In the United States a third category, of liberal or mainstream feminists, existed, identified with the organisation NOW (National Organisation of Women).

These labels were not always helpful, and could perpetuate or reinforce stereotypes. For example, it was sometimes alleged that socialist feminists were interested only in employment and welfare issues, or believed that women's oppression was solely due to industrial capitalism, when in fact most socialist feminists argued that men as a group were responsible for the oppression of women, and many were happy to use the term 'patriarchy'. However, they recognised that neither men nor women constituted a monolithic group, nor did women's oppression emanate from a single source, but was the outcome of the complex interaction of a number of causes: state, social formation, industrial capitalism and powerful men combined. Radical feminists, by contrast, were seen as being interested only in issues relating to sexuality and violence, yet they were often equally critical of capitalism and of the state as well as of men as a group.[1]

However, in the context of the politics of sexuality the differences between radical and socialist feminists were very real and the gulf widened towards the end of the 1970s and in the early 1980s. Radical feminists were more likely to be critical of heterosexuality itself as an instrument of male domination. They also placed greater emphasis on male violence towards women, and were latterly largely responsible for raising the issue of the sexual abuse of children. Socialist feminists were more interested in 'coalition politics' and regarded some men, or groups of men, as potential allies, sympathetic to demands for equality and capable of being won over to an anti-sexist stance.

This rift might seem like ancient history, and an irrelevance at the millennium, but if that is so, it is partly because it came to a head in the pornography debate and was partly or even largely responsible for the collapse of feminism as a movement. The decline of activist feminism has also coincided with the 'culturalisation' of society – the expansion of media technologies and the growing importance of the cultural sphere – in mass entertainment, electronic communications and the Internet. One feature of this expansion is the increase in the amount of printed and visual material. The production of pornography has expanded as part of this more general expansion.

Despite their differences, feminists of all kinds fought active campaigns in the 1970s and early 1980s – for better or specific provision for women in the fields of employment, health and education, for legislation against violence and rape, for changed attitudes within the juridical system and the police force, for the provision of universal childcare, and in the early eighties, for peace. In the Reagan/Thatcher years, however, as the battles for concrete material change became harder, declining feminist activism meant in practice an increasing shift from struggles to change the world to struggles to change representations, a shift that culminated in the campaigns against pornography.

There was a second shift here too. From the beginning Women's Liberation had developed a critique of representations of women. Some American feminists have suggested that the 'bra burning' demonstration was a myth, but women certainly demonstrated and campaigned against the Miss World contest, against striptease, against the irrelevant use of women's bodies in advertising, and against the cultural stereotypes that equated feminine beauty with youthful, slender, blonde whiteness. They objected to the division of women into madonnas and whores, sex objects and mothers, sluts and virgins, slags and uptight bitches.

Feminist campaigns were radical in refusing also to accept the line drawn by conventional society between the 'decent' and the 'indecent', between 'family viewing' and the 'obscene', between 'clean' and 'smutty' images. They also challenged the norms whereby written and visual material is judged in terms of what should or should not be censored or restricted. For the purposes of censorship, the dividing line is often between what is merely suggestive and what is sexually explicit. Thus, in practice, *Penthouse* images of nude or semi-nude women in alluring poses may be purchased in newsagents, but any image that included an erect male penis would be judged sexually explicit and therefore restricted. Feminists rejected this convention, refusing to accept that an image that shows sexual activity is in and of itself automatically 'obscene'. What feminists criticised were images of women that reinforced stereotypes or pandered to masculine prejudice. The 1980s film *Nine and a ½ Weeks*, for example, might offend some feminists, not because it contained sexual scenes, but because the film suggested that women enjoy bondage and masochistic sex. (Other feminists, of course, would argue that some women *do* enjoy bondage and masochistic sex.) In the 1970s, however, the feminist response to an objectionable film or to objectionable images would not have been that they should be banned; the idea was rather to generate debate and criticism of sexist images, or to produce alternative 'positive' images of women's sexual enjoyment and of their own bodies. Such demands would have been linked with related demands for women to be depicted in a wider range of non-sexual roles: as fire-fighters and engineers, for example. There would have been demands for images of older women, of women with disabilities, of non-white women. Everything about the way in which western society depicted women was up for grabs, and sexual imagery was only one target of a much wider critique.

At the same time, while it was objectionable if women were depicted *only* as sexual objects, feminists argued that it was important for women to be able to explore their varying responses to sexually explicit material – and, again, to produce their own non-sexist erotica if they wished. It was possible, for example, to acknowledge that some women *might* have fantasies of being raped, without concluding that this therefore meant that women really wanted to be raped in real life. Rape and other masochistic fantasies might or might not be common, and they were problematic, but it was important to confront and explore such responses – to understand their sources and their power – if anything about sexual behaviour was to change. But the pornography campaigns contributed to a shift from the attempt to understand how women respond sexually – to understand the diversity and variability of that response, to understand how and why women internalise oppressive notions of femininity and female sexual response – to a simpler position which laid the blame squarely on pornography for creating a climate of sexual violence and terrorising women.

Andrea Dworkin's influential *Pornography: Men Possessing Women* (1980) can retrospectively be identified as the opening shot in what became the pornography wars among feminists. This powerful polemic argued that pornography was a completely transhistorical phenomenon, which, since ancient times, had caused the enslavement of women. Because the word 'pornography' came from the ancient Greek terms for 'writing' and for 'prostitutes' it followed that it had existed in ancient times, Dworkin argued, seemingly unaware that the word was a Victorian back formation – and indeed that the concept was itself a very Victorian one. In ancient Greece and Rome sexually explicit images were *not* separated off into a discrete, pornographic sphere, but were commonly found on walls, on domestic vessels in daily use as well as in a religious context (e.g. Etruscan tombs). Evelyn Hunt (1993) has much more convincingly argued that pornography *is* historically specific, and that it arose with merchant capitalism. Only in the nineteenth century did the British state become interested in legislation against sexually explicit material (see Feminists Against Censorship, 1991: Chap. 2).

Many feminists, however, were not interested in the historical inaccuracies of Dworkin's account, swept up by its emotional power and its black-and-white message: on the one hand of the horror of pornography itself, and on the other hand of a simple solution. If women *saw* pornography, they would understand the depth of the misogyny it betrayed, yet by that act of seeing they would somehow destroy its power.

With the lawyer Catharine MacKinnon, Andrea Dworkin campaigned to introduce legislation, not to ban pornography, but to make it possible for any woman who felt she had been harmed by pornography and/or pornographers to bring an action against it/them. Ultimately the strategy failed, defeated because it was found to contravene free speech, but not before the fundamentalist Christian Right had taken up the issue in the United States.

In Britain, which lacked both a constitution and a powerful fundamentalist constituency, feminists were nevertheless inspired to campaign in a number of different ways against pornography and pornographic images. One early protest was the attempt at the Communist University of London[2] in 1981 to halt a screening of Michael Powell's film *Peeping Tom*. Although controversial when first made, in 1960, it was later reinterpreted as a ground-breaking exploration of voyeurism. To the feminists who objected to its being shown, however, it was an outrage simply because it depicted a murderer who kills women as he photographs them by means of a blade attached to his camera; in other words, even to show such a man was to condone, or even perpetrate, the murderous act. In the early eighties a similar, more protracted campaign was mounted against the Brian De Palma Film *Dressed to Kill*. Women's groups in a number of cities also demonstrated outside porn shops, and organised marches through red-light districts, including London's Soho.

The British Labour Party

Because of the different constitutional situation in Britain, it was never likely that legislation of the kind framed by Dworkin and MacKinnon would be placed on the statute books. In true British style, however, the issue attracted the attention of a number of individual members of Parliament, and for a time it seemed possible that a 'private member's' or even a government bill to restrict pornography nationally might pass into law. The most sustained attempt to produce such a law was that introduced by the Labour MP Dawn Primarolo. She tried to introduce a bill that would have removed soft porn magazines such as *Playboy*, *Penthouse*, *Mayfair* and *Hustler* from ordinary newsagents (where they are usually displayed on the top shelf) to special sex shops. Ironically it was at just this time that women's groups in Ms Primarolo's constituency in Bristol were trying to close sex shops down altogether.

This was in the mid- to late 1980s when the Labour Party had been in frustrated opposition for some years. It has come to be the received explanation for the Labour Party's eighteen years in the wilderness that it moved too far to the left and became 'unelectable'. Whether or not this is a wholly adequate analysis, the embattled Left within the Labour Party was desperate for campaigns that would be both popular and radical, and from this point of view the campaign against porn was a godsend. It was noted that this was a campaign that originated within feminism, yet which had widespread populist appeal, and it was taken up particularly by women Labour MPs, including some of the most radical, for example the late Jo Richardson, who had a superb record of defending and extending women's rights. Yet it was hardly surprising that these leftwing women attracted support from some of the most rightwing parliamentarians, including the Conservative Jill Knight, anti-abortionist, scourge of homosexuals, and an ardent supporter of capital punishment. A number of evangelical MPs also supported moves to restrict the sale of pornography as part of a traditionalist, 'pro-family' stance.

No doubt the Labour Party women were acting from conviction, at a time of great difficulty and despondency for the Left as a whole, brought to its knees by the breakaway of the SDP (the short-lived Social Democratic Party), the defeat of the controversial miners' strike of 1984–5, and the continual attacks by the Thatcher governments on trade unions, employment rights and regulation of all kinds. In a way it was the inverse of the 1960s when the Labour Party was in power. Then, it had come to power in adverse economic circumstances and was unable to fulfil its pre-election promises to modernise British industry and revitalise the economy. In winning the elections of 1964 and 1966, the Labour Party had to gain support beyond its core constituency, which was then still the organised working class. Accordingly it rode the bandwagon of the rising demand for the liberalisation of a number of laws relating to personal conduct, and in particular to sexual behaviour, but also to other humanitarian causes. This wave of reform had been building since the late 1950s, with the publication of the Wolfenden Report on homosexuality and prostitution in 1957 and the introduction of the defence of literary merit into obscenity trials in 1959.[3]

Thus in the 1960s – the era of so-called 'permissive legislation' – suicide ceased to be a crime, the death penalty was abolished, the laws relating to abortion and homosexuality were relaxed, and divorce law was reformed. Most of these changes were brought about by means of parliamentary action through the mechanism of private members' bills, thanks to the support of the Labour government, which thus satisfied its liberal constituency by means of these cost-free measures at a time when libertarianism was in the ascendancy. Without impugning the motives of liberals such as Roy Jenkins (Home Secretary for part of this period), it is fair to say that it was comparatively easy for the then Labour government to support permissive legislation since the tide was already running that way, and it had the added advantage that it thereby gained the support of the young and of progressive sections of society. That is not to say that this permissive legislation was as liberal as it may now appear. Stuart Hall (1980a) has rightly argued that in some respects it increased the state regulation of behaviour and rested on a strong distinction between behaviour in public and in private. Second-wave feminists always challenged the distinction between public and private, since it historically meant that men could behave as they wished in the privacy of their homes and that women had almost no protection from their violence in the domestic sphere. Nevertheless, despite these qualifications, the legislation of the 1960s marked a step forwards and improved the lives of many men and women.

In the 1980s and 1990s the climate was becoming in some ways less liberal as, initially influenced by 'Thatcherism', the whole political climate shifted away from tolerance. That is not to say that the views of the majority of the population have actually moved away from liberal positions. By the 1990s little stigma attached to divorce or illegitimacy, nor has popular support developed for further restricting access to abortion (although a recent survey suggests that the young of both sexes are more hostile to the idea of abortion than the generation above them [Travis, 1999: 3]).[4] Even homosexuality has lost much of its stigma, at least in metropolitan circles.

In this changing political climate the feminist campaigns against pornography seemed to offer an embattled Labour Party a wonderful opportunity for appearing to support feminist demands without incurring political debts they would be unable to repay – for as with the permissive legislation of the 1960s, anti-porn legislation was cost-free. The anti-porn position was, however, also consistent with the new respectable image they were seeking to develop, and they hoped it would attract women's votes across a wide spectrum.

During this time Clare Short, another Labour MP, mounted a related campaign to get topless 'Page 3' pinup girls banned from the tabloid newspaper the *Sun*. This attracted widespread support from women – 5,000 wrote letters to her in support of her efforts – but, again, there was little consideration of how effective such a ban would be in changing attitudes.

However, the attack on pornography and *Sun* pinups was consistent with the pro-law-and-order image the Labour Party sought; it was also consistent with a long tradition of Fabian authoritarianism. The Labour Party has traditionally been a 'broad church'. It gave a home to many of liberal and libertarian views, but its Fabian strand was never libertarian. Fabianism saw progressive change coming about in society through a process of the implementation of policy plans designed by a confident professional and administrative class on behalf of the less fortunate. Some of the ideas of two of the leading Fabians of the early twentieth century, Sidney and Beatrice Webb, were prescriptive, some were directive, and some draconian. They were in favour of compelling the unemployed to attend labour camps; and there was even a Fabian pamphlet which advocated the sterilisation of the 'unfit'. This was hardly mainstream (although eugenics, from which this idea came, *was* widely influential right across the political spectrum until the Nazis took the 'science of race improvement' to its logical conclusion). A further dimension of the Labour Party inheritance was from the Methodist movement and a Christian philanthropic tradition, and the anti-porn campaigns in a curious way reworked the patronising and protective attitude of some reformers – including feminists and socialists – in the late nineteenth century (see Walkowitz, 1982). Typical of this was the refusal of the anti-porn campaigners to believe that any woman could possibly or reasonably disagree with them. It was no accident that they commonly cited children, and women in the developing world 'sex slaves', as the primordial victims of pornography. For them, less fortunate women were invariably positioned as victims, while they, the campaigners, were rescuers. This was the classic nineteenth-century reforming scenario. Feminists who – astoundingly – disagreed with them were labelled 'liber-tarians'. That the term 'libertarian' should have become a term of abuse was itself rather astounding given that in the 1970s the term referred to anti-Stalinist Marxists, socialists, anarchists and community activists, and implied an anti-authoritarian critique both of East European and Soviet socialism and of the capitalist state. Then, libertarianism was on the side of autonomy and democracy, choice and self-determination. For the anti-porn feminists, however, the label was no longer positive; to be in favour of liberty appeared, so far as they were concerned, to be dangerous and even sinister – an alarming indication of the authoritarianism at the core of their thinking. But in any case, even 'libertarian' feminists were denied auto-nomy, since the anti-porn campaigners liked to accuse them of being in the pay of the porn industry or even of being pornographers themselves.

The Meanings of Pornography

The anti-porn analysis of pornography was incorrect and mistaken for a number of different reasons. Empirical arguments were chiefly concerned with the *effects* of pornography on the viewer, and addressed the question whether contact with porn made men more likely to assault women (see Segal and McIntosh, 1993).

A second debate was concerned with drawing a line between art, on the one hand, and porn, on the other. Leading art historian Kenneth Clark, for example, in his evidence to Lord Longford's Committee on Pornography (a privately established group which met in the early 1970s), defined the difference between art and porn as follows:

> To my mind art exists in the realm of contemplation, and is bound by some sort of imaginative transposition. The moment art becomes an incentive to action it loses its true character. This is my objection to painting with a Communist programme, and it would also apply to pornography. (quoted in Nead, 1993: 280)

This is a statement of the view that while art is a reflection of the highest ideals and social values of society, pornography is the underside: 'if art stands for lasting, universal values, then pornography represents dispos-ability, trash' (Nead, 1993: 282). In a reworking of this opposition, which concentrates more directly on sexual issues, pornography is contrasted with erotica: erotica is the life-loving, positive expression of affirmative sexual values and erotic love; pornography then becomes the expression of negative sexual impulses, desires and acts.

The attempt to define pornography was always an attempt to draw a clear line between 'good' and 'bad' sexual imagery, and by implication between that which should be 'permitted' to circulate and that which should be regulated, banned or hidden. The very meaning of the word 'pornography' was changed by the feminists who campaigned against pornography in the 1980s. Before that, it had referred to sexually explicit images whose purpose was to arouse; but now it was redefined as sexually explicit material which 'must depict women as enjoying or deserving some form of physical abuse' and 'must objectify women, that is, define women in terms of their relationship to men's lust and desire'.[5]

To try to define pornography is understandable, but the fact that it has always resisted clear definitions reveals an underlying problem. It perpetuates the illusion that pornography is a single definable entity, that it is 'a discrete realm of representation, cut off and clearly distinct from other forms of cultural production', and that 'the pornographic resides *in* the image, that it is a question of content rather than form, of production rather than consumption' (Nead, 1993: 280). Just as there is no such thing as a transhistorical 'pornography' stretching from the Etruscan tombs to *Linda Lovelace*, so there is no genre 'pornography' that can be neatly defined in terms of both content and effects. Two completely different aspects of visual culture have become locked together in the term: the representation of – usually – women's bodies; and the response of the individual who looks at the image.

It is therefore necessary to unpack the whole concept of 'pornography'. Indeed, it would make more sense to abandon the term altogether, and to discuss rather forms of cultural production of which some are sexually explicit. This would not prevent the moral and aesthetic evaluation of any work, but only if we view the sexually explicit in the context of the whole range of visual and written texts will we challenge the dominant sexual ideology of our society, which is that 'the sexual' should be cordoned off and separated from the rest of life. This is a variation of the general division between the public and the private which is so marked in western society. It actually contributes to the idea that *all* sex is somehow something tainted that should be hidden from view and to a more general ambivalence about the body.

Rather than continually attempting to define pornography, we should instead be raising questions about this cordoning off of the sexually explicit. What is needed is to examine what has been labelled as pornography 'in relation to other forms of cultural production' (Nead, 1993: 280). Then, for example, we can see how some fashion photography uses protocols drawn from porn, and how the erotic may be as present in classical painting as in *Playboy*. It does not follow from this that *all* visual culture is therefore pornographic, although some feminists did follow a reductionist line of argument whereby paintings by Titian, Courbet or whomever were redefined as 'just tits and bums for rich men'.

If we look at what is labelled as pornographic at any period in relation to other works from that period, we see that it has more in common with them than with 'porn' from a different era. John Cleland's novel *Fanny Hill*, for example, was written as a parody of one of the earliest English novels, Samuel Richardson's *Pamela*, and is an implicit critique of the Richardson novel, which would fall outside any definition of pornography, yet which is prurient and titillating. *Fanny Hill* is also much more like other novels of its time, such as Daniel Defoe's *Roxana*, than it is like a contemporary video or magazine.

Feminist anti-porn campaigners were not concerned with works such as *Fanny Hill*; but nor, more surprisingly, were they concerned with videos and other visual material, which had, and have, much in common with contemporary porn, but which are not sexually explicit. Any video shop will have, alongside its 'adult' films, a section devoted to violence pure and simple – war movies, revenge movies, vigilante movies, horror movies, slasher movies. If violence is male and men are violent, as the 'radical' feminists argued, it surely followed that such material confirmed and activated men's violent impulses, which were likely to be directed at women.

If, on the other hand, as research suggested, some convicted sex offenders were turned on by images of women knitting, were *any* images of women safe? Peter Sutcliffe, the 'Yorkshire Ripper', who murdered thirteen women, became obsessed with a waxworks museum which contained models of women in various stages of pregnancy and of people suffering the effects of venereal disease. It might therefore follow that medical textbooks and exhibitions should be banned. For it is the imagination and not the image that is pornographic.

The anti-porn campaigns ultimately foundered on the absence of a consensus as to what pornography actually was. In Canada, attempts to enact anti-sexist forms of legislation against pornography on the grounds of its offence to women resulted only in actions against a lesbian and gay bookshop. The effects on lesbian and gay imagery of any restrictive legislation is always a touchstone of what is really going on, since there are, still today, many persons in positions of power who believe that homosexuality is an illegitimate, unacceptable and deviant activity in itself, and that any representation of homosexuality must therefore automatically be essentially 'pornographic' or obscene. After all, Radclyffe Hall's famous lesbian novel *The Well of Loneliness* was banned for many years, although the nearest the lovers in it get to an explicit act is the deathless sentence 'and that night they were not divided'.

The anti-porn campaigners argued that sexual imagery is necessarily different from all other imagery, thereby reproducing the assumptions of the dominant culture. To challenge this view is not to take the opposing view of the 1960s 'sexual liberationists', who tended to argue as if simply to *show* more sex was itself progressive and liberating. Sexually explicit representations, images and text are neither reactionary nor liberating in and of themselves. On the one hand, to hide them away simply reinforces and confirms their power. On the other hand, simply to legalise everything does not solve the problem of misogyny and sexist representations of women. The meaning of pornographic images, like their effects, is not always clear or predictable, and may be the focus of a struggle for meaning.

It is not that we should not be disgusted by sadistic images of women being tortured or children being raped. Such imagery is, however, not restricted to what is termed pornography, and while what really concerned most feminists was the sexism and misogyny of so much imagery in our culture, the focus on porn actually detracted from the wider issue. Whatever its intentions, it also gave the impression of wanting to 'save' women from 'male lust', and this, ironically, actually objectified, women, who were positioned as passive objects of men's desire – precisely the aspect of porn to which the campaigners themselves objected. The campaigners took the fantasy world of porn at face value – a world in which men were always ready to perform, erections were always repeatable and ejaculation never premature. Thus they reinforced the misinformation about sexuality which they accused porn of purveying.

The anti-porn campaigns constituted a form of secular fundamentalism. By fundamentalism I mean a world-view, a philosophy and way of life which insists that the individual lives by narrowly prescribed rules and rituals, and which insists that only *this* world view is the correct one. Those who do not follow the truth and the light are rejected and demonised – and this certainly happened to feminists who disagreed with the anti-porn campaign. Fundamentalist faiths offer certainty. Change and uncertainty, by contrast, can lead to anxiety, even collapse; yet the price paid for certainty is rigidity and intolerance, and the belief that those who do not follow the 'true way' must be either destroyed or saved. Fundamentalisms have usually been associated with restrictive attitudes towards women and the maintenance of rigidly patriarchal authority.

Undoubtedly feminists against pornography believed they were attacking patriarchy, yet, especially in the United States, the style of the campaign was taken directly from evangelical Christianity, with preacher-style harangues, 'testimony' from women who had 'seen the light', conversion rituals and shock-horror denunciations (Smart, 1993).

A feminist, egalitarian agenda on sex, sexuality and representation would emphasise the need for sex education for children; it would attack sexism as a manifestation of male power, rather than attacking sexual material as a representation of men's sexuality; it would challenge the quasi-monopolistic ownership of the mass media, it would challenge political as well as sexual censorship. It would attack the sexual abuse of children and the exploitation of women (and men where necessary). But these latter issues are linked as much to ideologies of the family and opportunities for employment as to pornography – indeed, more so. To have made pornography both the main cause of women's oppression and its main form of expression was to wipe out almost the whole of the feminist agenda; and, indeed, its main achieve-ment was the fragmentation and demise of the women's movement itself.

A decade later, however, the issue is dead and buried. A younger generation of women has either rejected the idea that representations are important at all (Walter, 1998) or has seemingly come to the conclusion that postmodern irony takes the sting out of *any* image of women, no matter how 'sexist' it might once have been deemed. Triumphant 'New Labour' has still sought cost-free measures to please its leftwing, but has preferred gay and animal rights over the rights of women, however conceived (or misconceived).

The most that may be learnt from this episode is perhaps that there is no simple remedy for the incoherence of our culture. We have, at least, rejected the view, taken to an extreme by Catharine MacKinnon (1994), that a representation is *just as bad as* an action – that we are as much violated by the depiction of a rape as by an actual rape. Yet it is surely equally misguided to argue that representations matter not at all. In an increasingly global media- and image-saturated culture, the opposition to this culture – with its endless incitements to participate in a consumerism from which the majority of the globe's inhabitants are excluded – comes from religious funda-mentalisms which have no inhibitions about criticising representations. Rather than incoherently swimming – or sinking – in the cultural sea of contradictory imagery, a postmodern abdication of discrimination, we need to find a way of reasserting cultural values without resorting to dogma.

The group Feminists Against Censorship, which campaigned against the anti-porn groups in the early 1990s, sought a 'third way' between censor-ship, on the one hand, and 'anything goes' libertarianism, on the other. Third ways invariably seem elusive, or even illusory, yet surely we cannot be satisfied with the choice between the shopping mall and the cathedral/ mosque; between anything goes and therefore nothing matters, and every-thing matters and must therefore be policed; between a rigid external authority and an abandonment of all discrimination. The pornography debates, therefore, which even at the time seemed narrow and today appear quite arcane, gestured towards larger issues of global culture, and the problems they threw up remain just as relevant today.

Notes

1. That this brief summary makes no mention of race reflects the absence of an awareness of racism in the early days of Women's Liberation.

2. Throughout most of the 1970s this annual event organised by the Communist Party of Great Britain was a highly successful week-long educational conference, attracting attendances in the thousands to lectures and seminars by well-known academics and in some cases political figures.

3. However, we should note that the reforms around prostitution tightened regulation and were not liberalising. See Weeks (1981).

4. This is likely to be at least partly due to the fact that with the ending of attempts in Parliament to restrict abortion rights, the arguments in favour of liberal abortion laws are no

longer being made, so that young people are likely to be aware chiefly of highly emotionally charged arguments against abortion.

5. This was the definition used in a resolution put to the annual general meeting of the National Council for Civil Liberties (Liberty) in April 1990, when feminists were attempting to push Liberty into an anti-porn stance.

5

THESE NEW COMPONENTS OF THE SPECTACLE

Fashion and Postmodernism

Traditionally, fashion came at the bottom of the hierarchy of academic study, dismissed – and not only by intellectuals – as trivial and unworthy of serious discussion. It was associated with the body and therefore assessed as low and degraded; it was associated with women and therefore dismissed as frivolous; it was associated with capitalism and therefore denounced as exploitative; it was associated, especially in utopian socialist thought, with inequality, ugliness and unhealthiness and therefore rejected on all three grounds. For over a century feminists in particular disavowed an interest in dress because it seemed incompatible with their political project.

My interest in fashion is not simply a postmodern inversion of these priorities. Dress is one of the most fundamental fields of social expression and aesthetic taste, a universal form of expressive communication and a subtle and protean indicator of identity. Nevertheless, when, in the late 1980s, I contributed an article on fashion to a collection of essays on postmodernism, I argued that fashion was in particular a neglected aspect of the postmodern, when it should have been central. Fashion was especially congruent with postmodernity for a number of reasons: it was, rightly or wrongly, primarily associated with woman and the feminine, one of the most important of the Others for whom postmodernism claimed to have found a voice; it was connected to aesthetic movements and practices, although as the degraded or unacceptable face of art; in the postmodern world, moreover, designer mass fashion seemed more important than ever – 'style' was the buzz word of the moment and fashion's blatant consumerism shocked the culture whose heart it yet spoke so well. Furthermore, fashion, seen as a popular form, a manifestation of pluralism, pleasure and the demotic, offered an opportunity to re-evaluate popular, kitsch and 'low' aesthetic and cultural forms, and to break down the distinction between high art and popular culture. Finally, the intense ambivalence fashion produced was congruent with a more general postmodern ambivalence.

By 'fashion' is meant a changing cycle of styles in which novelty and difference are highly valued. It was until recently accepted that the style cycle applied exclusively to western dress. Jennifer Craik (1994) has challenged this idea. She argues that it is ethnocentric to (mis)perceive 'fashion' as essentially western; on the contrary dress in all cultures and throughout the world is always culturally meaningful. Craik equates 'fashion' with 'dress' as a general term. To treat fashion as unique to the culture of capitalism is, she believes, to assume that fashion is 'a marker of civilisation' and that this is the reason for its exclusion 'from the repertoires of non-western cultures. Other codes of clothing behaviour are relegated to the realm of costume, which, as "pre-civilised" behaviour, is characterised in opposition to fashion, as traditional, unchanging, fixed by social status, and group-oriented.' This analysis, she suggests, 'fails to account for the circulation of changing clothes codes and stylistic registers in non-European societies. The relation of bodies to clothes is far deeper than the equation of fashion with the superficial products of "consumer culture" permits' (Craik, 1994: 4).

It seems that two separate, or at least separable, concerns are confused here. It is surely the case that in all societies dress and adornment have played an essential role as part of culture. Nonetheless it is still useful to reserve the term 'fashion' for a more restrictive use: to refer to the *distinct* form taken by western dress. It is true that in no societies have clothing styles remained absolutely static. Yet there is something specific about the increasingly rapid and production-generated changes characteristic of western fashion; these differentiate it from the more slowly paced evolution seen elsewhere – and indeed Craik (1994) accepts that 'fashion under capitalism exhibits peculiar features such as planned obsolescence'.

Western fashion as we understand it arose in Europe in the thirteenth century, with early cloth trading and the very earliest manifestations of a consumption oriented society (Mukerji, 1983). To begin with it was the preserve of a courtly aristocracy, yet there is evidence that the rising bourgeoisie of the sixteenth and seventeenth centuries equally aspired to be fashionable. Sumptuary laws passed in many European countries, for example, could never be enforced and were abruptly dropped in the early seventeenth century (Baldwin, 1926).

Quentin Bell (1947) put his finger on a central paradox of fashionable dress when he described how it is individualistic and conformist *simultaneously*. We dress to be part of the crowd, yet to stand out from the crowd. We may dress to rebel, yet somehow that rebellion usually ends up being just another style. In the pre-industrial period, or so the argument goes, fashionable dress was primarily important in expressing status and wealth. The rich alone could afford to be fashionable, and the splendour of their dress with its elaborate embroidery, use of jewels, lace and gold thread and the luxury of the fabrics used – silk, satin, velvet – was a straightforward statement of rank and power.

With industrialisation and the beginnings of mass manufacture dress underwent profound modifications as the production of cloth and clothing was revolutionised by technology. Mass production began with clothes intended for the lowest sections of society. In the US clothing for slaves was mass produced, as were military uniforms on both sides of the Atlantic, along with some forms of workwear. Uniforms and working clothes were sold in the 'slop shops' of ports and slums. Fashionable dress, however, continued to be made by tailors and dressmakers at all levels of society. This was partly because, as Ellen Leopold has pointed out, the fashion industry remained in many senses technically backward, and has continued to be based on a 'made to measure' model that has aped *haute couture*. She believes that:

> the seemingly anarchic and rapidly changing proliferation of style in women's clothes, a feature that has distinguished it not just from other industries but also from other branches of the clothing industry, has served as a substitute for technical innovation, arising not in response to a rise in incomes or to changes in consumer preferences or to the exhaustion of possibilities arising from early mass production, but rather from the industry's failure ever fully to embrace mass production techniques. (Leopold, 1992: 102)

One result of the technical backwardness of clothing manufacture was that the majority of working class and even lower middle class men and women relied largely on second-hand clothing, a flourishing trade in Victorian London and elsewhere. (And well into the twentieth century the lady's maids of rich women expected to have their employer's clothes passed on to them, as one of the 'perks' of the job.)

Mass production might have ended up in the 'nightmare' of *Brave New World* and *1984* – uniforms for everyone. Yet although mass production began with uniforms, and despite the continuing emphasis on made to measure and on the 'whole garment' method (whereby the tailor or dressmaker is an artisan who deals with every aspect of the production of the garment), mass production eventually led to the dissemination of greater and greater varieties of fashionable styles, until by the mid-twentieth century all classes were included in fashion's embrace. Even as late as the 1920s class difference is signalled, for example in cartoons in the British magazine *Punch*, by differences in dress (a young wife dressed in the latest short shift issues orders to a servant who still wears a long skirt and almost Edwardian style blouse); but after the Second World War mass production made versions of the latest fashion accessible to almost everyone.

So far as masculine dress is concerned, many have argued that in fact male dress *did* develop as a uniform from the beginning of the nineteenth century onwards. The psychoanalyst and dress reformer, J.C. Flugel, argued that with the 'great masculine renunciation', as he termed it, of the early nineteenth century, fashion became a wholly feminine preserve and has remained so ever since, and until recently this view was widely accepted. Indeed he continues to be cited reverentially, partly perhaps due to the continuing popularity of psychoanalysis as a form of cultural theory; and also because he recognised the importance of gender. Kaja Silverman, for example, referred to his *The Psychology of Clothes* (Flugel, 1930) as 'the classic psychoanalytic text on the subject' (Silverman, 1986: 140). Peter Wollen (1993) equally appears to accept the idea of the 'great masculine renunciation', a view earlier popularised by the costume historian James

Laver (1969), who argued that the men's suit, dominant since the nineteenth century, was an unchanging, sober, un-self-displaying form of uniform.

Gender is, certainly, of central importance in dress. It is arguable that dress became increasingly gendered during the eighteenth century, and that rather than being a form of 'renunciation', the changes in men's dress which resulted in the rise of the suit constituted an accentuation of masculinity. In the Regency period in Britain the dandies, especially Beau Brummell, adapted the country dress of the landowning class (navy woollen coat, tight buff breeches, long leather boots and snowy linen and cravat) for day wear, and were among the first to abandon the wig in favour of short, unpowdered hair. Yet in certain, crucial respects, dandyism represented an even more marked form of display than the silks and satins of eighteenth-century men's court dress. Woollen cloth could be shaped more closely to the body than silk; breeches became extremely tight and revealing. Even the abandonment of cosmetics by men was less the renunciation of beauty and exhibitionism than the inauguration of a new and different style of male beauty, one that was more gendered, more 'masculine'. Charles Baudelaire (1971) argued that the dandy's preoccupation with appearance was an attempt to create the self as a work of art; the dandy's appearance was a performance on the urban stage.

In any case, men's fashions did continue to change throughout the nineteenth and twentieth centuries, albeit more slowly than women's, and Christopher Breward (1999) has unearthed a whole history of the nineteenth-century male shopper as a consumer as much as his female counterpart. The industrial period also saw the proliferation of masculine uniforms and ritualised forms of dress for men in public, satirised by Virginia Woolf in *Three Guineas*, where she wrote of the astonishing elaboration of uniforms, military, religious and judicial: 'After the comparative simplicity of your dress at home, the splendour of your public attire is dazzling. But far stranger . . . every button, rosette and strip seems to have symbolical meaning' (Woolf, 1938: 23).

Such rule-bound rigidity might seem the very opposite of fashion, but Woolf drew attention to the display and exhibitionism it involved. Self-display was never renounced, even when displaced onto ceremonial attire. The 'great masculine renunciation' was rather, as Craik succinctly puts it, a form of 'disavowal' by men, a refusal to admit their psychological involvement in their appearance – the 'great masculine renunciation' was a myth of masculinity that took the form of 'a set of denials' such as that

> there is no men's fashion; that men dress for fit and comfort rather than for style; that women dress men and buy clothes for men; that men who dress up are peculiar (one way or another); that men do not notice clothes; and that most men have not been duped into the endless pursuit of seasonal fads. (Craik, 1994: 176)

Masculinity, in other words, was naturalised; whereas the fashionable woman represented artifice. Anne Hollander (1994) goes further, emphasising the modernity and above all the highly sexual allure of the suit; she argues that by a kind of cultural lag women continued to be dressed as objects of display throughout the nineteenth century and that only in the twentieth did they 'catch up' with men, adapting the men's suit for themselves to create a form of dress adequate to modernity, a point also made by James Laver, who associated the revolution in women's dress primarily with Chanel.

The coming of mass fashion (for both sexes) meant more than just the availability of low-cost fashions; it meant the proliferation of fashion as a central component of the spectacle of modern life. Western societies and increasingly the whole globe have become saturated with fashion and images of fashion, a process associated as much with urbanisation as with industrialisation. Fashion served to underline the elaborate rituals of bourgeois life – there was an appropriate costume for every activity and every hour of the day or evening – but fashion also served to signal to the other strangers in the crowded streets and public places the class and status of the individual, thus countering to some extent the apparent social disorientation threatened by urban life (see Sennett, 1974).

As mass fashion increasingly took over in the twentieth century, it could be used to designate not merely class, status and gender, but an expanding repertoire of elaborate self-definitions and group affiliations – individual and collective identities. The new fashions renounced obvious luxury and could therefore seem classless. Chanel's 'little nothing' clothes – a uniform for the street, an 'anti-fashion' according to Cecil Beaton (1954), clothes adapted to the life of the typist, the office girl and the shop assistant – were beautifully made for her rich clientele in costly materials and with minute attention to detail; yet they could be relatively easily and cheaply copied, thus producing a representation of democracy and of 'the modern'. These new fashions for women really were more functional than the old. Between the two world wars dress was one means whereby women, even women from the slums, were better able to escape the worst aspects of their environment than their menfolk. Women's fashions 'embodied postwar newness . . . a consciously radical transformation . . . clothes were clearly indicative of a dramatic redefinition of femininity at this time'. This was at a time when 'the factory was becoming a structural element in a new "feminine" culture', and working girls were beginning to be perceived as fashionably dressed. Even a queue of young ex-munitions workers queueing for their dole money were described in one local newspaper in the 1920s as 'a well dressed queue; the musquash and seal coat, eloquent of the former munition worker, was not absent' (White, 1986: 191–2).

After the Second World War, mass-produced fashion received a further impetus as *haute couturiers* developed diffusion lines. Although the 1950s has been caricatured as a period of conservatism and the rolling back of women's emancipation, it was in 1954 that Chanel made a successful return to fashion. She rejected the backward-looking 'New Look' fashions popularised by Dior, with their long, full skirts and tightly corseted waists, as inappropriate for the modern woman; she now aimed explicitly to cater for the woman in the street: 'I am no longer interested in dressing a few hundred women, private clients; I shall dress thousands of women. But a widely repeated fashion, seen everywhere, cheaply produced, must start from luxury' (quoted in Wilson, 1985: 89). But by luxury she meant simplicity of style and perfection of cut, the very opposite of 'conspicuous consumption'.

Until the 1980s, theories (as opposed to historical accounts) of western fashion were undeveloped and dominated by writers who commented on fashion from outside. So long as costume history was embedded within a conservative art history that focused on empirical details of dating and provenance, this was bound to be the case; but the new art history and with it the new dress studies has made possible an escape from the functionalist sociology of Thorstein Veblen and (at least in regard to fashion) Georg Simmel, and others who regarded fashion as a kind of aberration that needed to be explained *away*. In the influential *Theory of the Leisure Class*, Veblen (1957) argued that dress was merely an aspect of conspicuous consumption, functional for capitalism and for the status of the bourgeoisie, and that it represented the enslavement of women, symbolising their continued existence as symbolic chattels. He was influenced by dress reform ideology, which wished to abolish fashion (in the sense of a changing cycle of styles) altogether; and he entirely failed to understand either its relationship to art and aesthetic practices, or its expressive potential for the individual and the group. Flugel was similar in this respect. Far from being a 'classic text', the eugenicist preoccupations of *The Psychology of Clothes* (Flugel, 1930) tie it closely into its epoch. Flugel was a member of the Men's Dress Reform Society, whose aim, between the wars, was to assimilate male attire to the more 'rational' dress of women at that period. The Society argued that men should wear shorts and lighter materials, to free them from the fusty three-piece suits, stiff collars, spats and other items which still imprisoned them. Male dress, the Society's members felt, was now lagging behind the healthy minimalism of women's fashions. Flugel also, like other writers of the period, held an evolutionist view of human progress, and expected that the human race would eventually be able to renounce not only masculine fashion but the whole 'neurosis' of clothing altogether. Fashion was irrational, a neurotic symptom, a compromise formed to reconcile the conflicting demands of exhibitionism and modesty; but although this 'explanation' has some salience, it completely misses the social and symbolic significance of dress – and, taken to its logical conclusion, his view, like that of Veblen, implies a rejection of all cultural forms. Adorno (1967), in fact, criticised Veblen on precisely these grounds. Flugel's views were not too far removed from those of J.D. Bernal, the leftwing scientist, and of H.G. Wells, both of whom imagined utopias of the future in which not only clothing but even the body itself would have atrophied with the increasing development and dominance of the mind and the machine.

The functionalism characteristic of much theoretical writing on fashion until the mid-twentieth century and beyond was inadequate to the challenge of mass fashion, since it tended to be based on a rejection of the elitism of *haute couture*. By the 1960s, and partly under the influence of the rise of the mass media, it was becoming obvious that 'fashion' was being displaced by 'fashions', which made possible an expanding repertoire of new and increasingly self-conscious, knowing performances. For Andy Warhol the fashions of the sixties contributed an essential element to the New York avant-garde scene – but this scene was both avant-garde and pop, indeed Pop Art dissolved the distinction between high and low, stylistically at least, and created an iconoclastic atmosphere which brought high fashion, the popular and counter-cultural fashions together. The relationship of John Lennon with Yoko Ono embodied the marriage of pop and the avant-garde. Mary Quant and the pop bands of the period drew on similar sources of inspiration – although as noted in the Introduction (see p. 8), it was not until Malcolm McLaren and Vivienne Westwood developed their versions of Punk in the mid-1970s that the fashion and music industries were formally and economically united (Mulvagh, 1999).

Punk was avant-garde in the way in which it collapsed the boundaries between life and art – at least in Peter Bürger's (1984) definition of the avant-garde. Quite apart from Punk, the fashions of the 1970s were in general greeted with bewilderment by fashion journalists; it became a popular cliché to say that there was no longer fashion, only fashions, or no longer fashion, but only styles. For decades, Simmel's 'trickle-down' theory of fashion had been accepted as a reasonable explanation of the style cycle. This was the idea that fashions originated with high-status groups, were copied by inferior classes, were therefore rejected by the innovators who had to find a new style by which to distinguish themselves, and so on, endlessly. A more careful examination of the origin of styles demonstrates that throughout the nineteenth century new fashions were at least as likely to come from more marginal groups, such as dandies, performers and *demi-mondaines* (of whom Chanel herself was originally one). The trickle-down theory was also unsatisfactory in constructing a one-dimensional picture of fashion, which failed to take into consideration the many different fashions of different groups within society.

By the 1970s this was clearly recognised. The use of ethnic, historical and retro styles signalled the change. Sometimes fashion journalists, puzzled by the 'confusion' of a plurality of styles, attributed them to feminism. An oscillation between romantic nostalgia and masculine and Punk modes signified uncertainty as to women's roles, they argued. Alternatively it was possible to argue that with a dominant fashion in abeyance, women could now dress as they liked – an overstatement of liberal permissiveness.

Then, in the early 1980s, postmodernism began to be widely discussed. Although, as I have argued, fashion seemed likely to play an enhanced role in postmodernity, one of postmodernism's most highly regarded theorists, Jean Baudrillard (1981), denounced fashion with almost as much ferocity as a fifteenth-century divine. Like Veblen, he defined fashion as inherently ugly, and perceived it as an artificial irritant to encourage ever higher levels of consumption, while ideologically it functioned to mask the unchanging nature of domination under capitalism. Fashion was especially pernicious in its masking of social inequalities by means of its claim that fashion is accessible to all. His rejection of consumer society had developed out of a Situationist repulsion for the boredom, alienation and conformity of the modern bourgeois order. But this drew him into a crude functionalism: for him fashion arose from the 'needs' of capitalism, which required continually changing styles of dress, interior decoration and indeed all aspects of consumption. The compulsion towards change was part of the irrationality of fashion. At this stage, Baudrillard implied that change and variety in style were somehow intrinsically wrong, indeed this was taken as read. No defence was offered for such a view, Baudrillard merely bringing forward an undefined ideal of 'beauty' to set against the 'ugliness' of fashion and fashionable ephemera. Beauty, he assumed, resides in function (an argument that reproduced the views of modernists such as Adolf Loos whose famous article 'Ornament is Crime' was published in 1908). Baudrillard, like earlier functionalists, posed 'consumption' against 'use' and emphasised its wastefulness.

There were many unexamined assumptions here. It is not clear how we should define the 'useless' or why useless objects should necessarily be ugly. It does not necessarily follow that change must be wasteful. Baudrillard was here modernist rather than postmodernist in advocating some universal and timeless set of styles, the imposition of which might be seen as tyrannical, and, indeed, puritanical. His argument was also reductionist. For him, *everything* in the capitalist order expresses capitalist values, and there is therefore no room for contradiction or escape, no vantage point from which critique or rebellion may be mounted. Nor, certainly, is there any room for the idea that the most civilised form of life resides in the cultivation of beauty for its own sake. Yet as Freud put it, 'as though seeking to repudiate these utilitarian achievements [the achievements, that is, of an over-rationalistic Enlightenment order], we welcome it as a sign of civilisation . . . if we see people directing their care to what has no practical value whatever, to what is useless . . . to reverence [of] beauty' (Freud, 1949: 54).

Roland Barthes (1957) was equally dismissive of the fashion system. He argued that its function was to 'naturalise the arbitrary', and, as did Baudrillard, felt it acted to mask the unchanging nature of capitalism.

Yet as Llewellyn Negrin has pointed out, Baudrillard's point of view shifted radically in his later writings, and especially in *Seduction* (Baudrillard, 1990). Now, writes Negrin, 'he celebrates . . . fashion, which, for him epitomises the society of the spectacle where the cult of appearances is all important. Fashion revels in the creation of images, making no pretence about their fabricated nature.' The society of the spectacle, moreover, is 'superior to the earlier phases of capitalism which were dominated by the logic of production . . . [and] represents a liberation from the tyranny of technocratic reason which subjected the free play of the sense to the iron rule of practical necessity' (Negrin, 1999: 114).

Fashion has indeed taken on certain traits that might be described as 'postmodern'. There has been a blurring between mainstream and counter-cultural fashions; fashion has become 'stagey' about its own status as a discourse, about its irrationality, about its message. Jean-Paul Gaultier, for example, drew inspiration from Punk, recycled Punk anti-fashion for *haute couture*, and this was then popularly disseminated by Madonna, who wore his corsets as outerwear in her performances in the 1980s. Old-fashioned 'granny' corsets were adapted by the original punks as a statement of hatred and rebellion (see Savage, 1991), but when the 'subversive' ques-tionings of Punk appear on the Paris catwalk, it is difficult to say what is real and what is parody. Gaultier's own pronouncements on his work added to this uncertainty, since he appeared to mount an attack on the very notion of fashion: 'People who make mistakes or dress badly are the real stylists. My "you feel as though you've eaten too much" collection [clothes deliberately designed to look "too tight"] is taken from exactly those moments when you are mistaken or embarrassed,' he announced to *Vogue* in the mid-1980s (Wilson, 1985: 10). Carl Lagerfeld, meanwhile, at Chanel was producing outfits that parodied the original Chanel styles, and 'pudding' hats which mimicked the Surrealist fashions of the 1930s. Thus the 'confusion' that puzzled fashion writers in the 1970s, with the apparent end of an orderly evolution of one style out of another, is explicable in terms of postmodernism.

Fredric Jameson explained this in terms of the way in which 'modernist styles . . . become postmodernist codes. . . . If the ideas of a ruling class were once the dominant (or hegemonic) ideology of bourgeois society, the advanced capitalist countries today are now a field of stylistic and discursive heterogeneity without a norm' (Jameson, 1984: 65). But for Jameson, unlike Baudrillard, the pluralism of postmodernist codes represents a *compulsory* confusion, and this, for him, exemplifies a sensibility in which all sense of development and history is lost, so that the jumble of stylistic mannerisms becomes as 'schizophrenic' as the consumer culture which produced them; the promiscuity of contemporary modes is just part of the fragmentation and depersonalisation of postmodernity. Insofar as recent fashions have relied heavily on 'retro-chic', the recycling of the styles of the recent past, this too fits with Jameson's description of the postmodern, with its reliance on pastiche or 'parody without laughter'.

Pastiche and the retrieval of styles from the past were, however, a feature of fashion long before postmodernism appeared. Christian Dior (1957) believed that until designers such as Madame Vionnet introduced revolu-tionary new techniques of cutting into fashion design in the early twentieth century the shapes of garments changed only very slowly, an impression of change being created rather by the use of superficial decoration and stylistic motifs often rifled from the past. The Victorians incorporated all sorts of historical styles into their fashions, and equally drew inspiration from abroad and from popular culture. The frogged, rather masculine Garibaldi jacket became a fashionable female garment after the Italian nationalist fled his native country; late eighteenth-century 'Dolly Varden' hats followed in the wake of Charles Dickens' *Barnaby Rudge*. In the Edwardian period Liberty, a London store that specialised in fashionable forms of what was known as 'aesthetic dress' (based on the ideas of the Pre-Raphaelites), advertised evening gowns in a variety of 'historical' styles – Egyptian, medieval, Elizabethan and Madame de Pompadour – in its catalogues. Even in the 1950s, a period that has retrospectively been invested with a seamlessly perfect style, ambience and ideology, the reality was more complex. For example, the British musical *The Boyfriend*, first produced in 1955, inaugurated a rash of pastiche 1920s fashions in a period normally located at the apex of modernity. It was in 1954 that the Diaghilev exhibition took London by storm; and in 1956 Liberty relaunched their original William Morris designs for fashion and furnishing fabrics – all these events anticipating recycled motifs we now think of as more characteristic of the late 1960s and the 1970s.

Jameson nevertheless finds a specific quality in contemporary as opposed to historical re-creations of the past. What he terms nostalgia mode 'was never a matter of some old-fashioned "representation" of historical content, but approached the "past" through stylistic connotation, conveying "pastness" . . . connotation as the purveying of imaginary and stereotypical idealisties' (Jameson, 1984: 67).

Hal Foster, too, argues that the nineteenth-century use of styles from the past at least involved some sense of protest:

> What . . . does this 'return' imply if not a flight from the present? Clearly, this was the thrust of eclectic historicism in 19th-century art and architecture (especially British): a flight from the modern – in its romantic form, from the industrial present into a preindustrial past; in its neoclassical (academic) form, from lived class conflict to the ideal realm of myth. But then this flight expressed a social protest, however, dreamy; now it seems symptomatic of sheer *post-histoire* escapism. (Foster, 1985: 122–3)

Yet Proust, writing of the fashions of 1912, already could see no meaning in the fashions of the day:

> All the hats now were immense, covered with all manner of fruits and flowers and birds. In place of the beautiful dresses in which Madame Swann walked like a queen, Graeco-Saxon tunics, pleated à la Tanagra or sometimes in the Directoire style, accentuated Liberty chiffons sprinkled with flowers like wallpaper. . . . And seeing all these new components of the spectacle, I had no longer a belief to infuse into them to give them consistence, unity and life; they passed before me in a desultory, haphazard, meaningless fashion, containing in themselves no beauty. (Proust, 1981: I, 460)

A sense of the loss of meaning is already present, then, in the high modernist *À la recherche du temps perdu*, and, set against Proust's insightful comments on the subjective quality of our aesthetic judgements, Jameson's lament for the loss of norms is revealed as romantic and nostalgic, although what past he is longing for is never made clear, whether it is the orderliness of liberal bourgeois society or the unrealised collective purpose of a socialism infused with functional aesthetic values. Perhaps neither.

In the 1970s Kennedy Fraser, fashion correspondent of the *New York Times*, described the irony of retro dressing in terms consistent with Jameson's:

> Clothes came to be worn and seen as an assemblage of thought-out paradoxes, as irony, whimsy, or deliberate disguise. Thrift shop dressing carried it all to its ultimate. We took to clothes for which we had spent little money, which didn't necessarily fit us, and which had belonged in the past to some dead stranger's life. Behind the bravado . . . there may have lurked a fear of being part of our time, of being locked into our own personalities, and of revealing too much about our own lives. (Fraser, 1985: 238)

Above all, she suggested, these fashions expressed detachment. The 'bravado' came from the sense that to wear second-hand clothes that maybe looked strange, untidy or eccentric was somehow radical, yet it involved a disavowal of any 'mistakes'. In any case, the clothes cost almost nothing, so mistakes were never costly.

For Kaja Silverman, on the other hand, retro was an important counter-cultural mode, a 'sartorial strategy which works to denaturalise its wearer's specular identity, and one which is fundamentally irreconcilable with fashion' (Silverman, 1986: 150). Far from destroying the past, or merely constructing a stereotypical 'pastness', 'it inserts its wearer into a complex network of cultural and historical references'. It is precisely its masquerade quality that has radical potential.

Negrin has noted that Silverman was only one of several feminists writing in the 1980s who argued for 'forms of dress which highlight the constructed nature of the body and self identity' (Negrin, 1999: 100). This was an unsurprising reaction to a widespread feminist rejection of fashion. In *Adorned in Dreams* (Wilson, 1985), one of my main purposes was certainly to question the contradictory attitude of the women's movement towards fashion, dress and appearance. At that time there was a mandatory denial of interest in one's appearance, yet in practice most feminists, in Britain at any rate, took a good deal of trouble in order to achieve the required degree of vaguely Pre-Raphaelite dishevelment or businesslike butchness. For, as Meaghan Morris pointed out, we really *cared* about style:

> We hear a lot these days about superficial style-obsessed postmoderns: but . . . we're the ones, after all, who installed a ruthless surveillance system monitoring every aspect of style – clothing, diet, sexual behaviour, domestic conduct, 'role playing', underwear, reading matter . . . interior decoration, humour – a surveillance system so absolute that in the name of the personal-political, everyday life became a site of pure semiosis. (Morris, 1988: 179)

I also wished to assert the importance of dress as a serious social phenomenon, worthy of sustained study. This was quite aside from any connection with postmodernism, yet fashion did at the time seem to fit rather well with the developing postmodern discourse. As Andreas Huyssen suggested:

> Postmodernism operates in a field of tension between tradition and innovation, conservation and renewal, mass culture and high art . . . a field of tension which can no longer be grasped in categories such as progress vs. reaction, Left vs. Right, present vs. past, modernism vs. realism, abstraction vs. representation, avant-garde vs. Kitsch. (Huyssen, 1986: 48)

The fact, he suggests, that such categories have broken down creates a crisis, which includes a crisis of representation. And postmodernism is the representation of this crisis. Huyssen in fact seeks to save postmodernism from its own ambiguity by making it the site from which the Others may speak. Alternative marginal movements, he believes, can create a 'postmodernism of resistance' as opposed to 'anything goes' postmodernism. Translated to the field of fashion, this would seem to support alternative, counter-cultural fashions as, indeed Kaja Silverman argues. Yet it would be equally possible to argue that postmodern eclecticism destroys any perspective from which a fashion could truly be defined as counter-cultural, precisely *because* 'anything goes' in a wholly relativistic postmodern realm.

In 'denaturalising the wearer's specular identity' contemporary fashions arguably have liberating potential. They refuse the dichotomy nature/culture. Fashion in our epoch denaturalises the body and thus divests itself of essentialism. This should be liberating for women, since essentialist ideologies have been oppressive to them. Fashion often plays with, and playfully transgresses, gender boundaries, inverting stereotypes and making us aware of the masquerade of femininity. Fashion exends art into life and offers a medium across the social spectrum with which to experiment.

Yet the way in which 'dress becomes a parodic play in which the body of the wearer is denaturalised' (Negrin, 1999: 100) does not exhaust its possibilities. Negrin argues that this is to *reduce* fashion to image and self-identity to appearance, and merely to replicate the priorities of the fashion industry. However, it is not clear why it is necessary to yoke together the idea of a constructed body and identity with the corollary that this *necessarily implies* that dress becomes 'parodic play'.

There certainly are playful and celebratory aspects to dress (although 'playful' and 'celebratory' are not coterminous) – although these may have been overemphasised in the 1980s in an attempt to escape a perceived feminist puritanism. In the heyday of 'second-wave feminism', moreover, dress could still signal rebellion, but by 1990 prescriptive feminism, at least in the area of dress, had largely disappeared and a wider public had been familiarised with lipstick lesbians, fetish dressers and Madonna as a feminist glamour icon, new stereotypes that had pretty much displaced the old caricature of the hairy feminist in dungarees. In general, moreover, it has become clearer since the early 1980s that what Quentin Bell (1947) called 'outrage' in dress has largely ceased to function as a form of rebellion, since it no longer shocks anyone (not in any western metropolis, at any rate). Perhaps global warming has something to do with it, but every summer men and women wearing a minimum of clothing propel their pierced and tattooed bodies through the supermarket without anyone even noticing them, let alone feeling shocked. There *are* forms of dress that remain sharply contested – the veil, for example, about which there is neither a feminist nor a religious consensus. Yet in general it seems less relevant in the year 2000 than it seemed in the early eighties to stress the way in which dress can play with gender and masquerade, and to emphasise that aspect of dress to the exclusion of all others would, in any case, always have been one-sided – indeed Judith Butler's (1990) insistence on the *wholly* parodic and masquerading nature of gender was always problematic and she herself has modified her earlier positions on this.

Dress and adornment, in fact, are never 'only' matters of image. Clothes relate intimately to the body and construct the way one experiences it at any given time. Not only is fashion the form in which the body manifests itself, as Silverman argued, it is also one of the forms in which social relations manifest themselves; it is also part of material culture. In suggesting, therefore, that the only alternative to a functionalist attack on fashion is its valorisation as play, Negrin's argument is itself very one-dimensional. She follows Hal Foster in arguing that it may now be more important to struggle against the notion of 'woman as artifice' than that of 'woman as nature', but while this is an interesting point, it is still important to bear in mind that genetics and evolutionary psychology are today (in their more populist versions at any rate) reasserting the primacy of 'nature' over 'nurture' so to point to the constructed nature of gender remains necessary.

It still seems meaningful to discuss certain art-works, films and architecture – and fashion – in terms of postmodernism as a range of styles, although Jameson's pastiche, eclecticism, 'nostalgia mode' and 'retro chic' have been questioned. Whether, as Negrin suggests, there is a distinctive 'postmodern feminism' seems less clear. It is certainly the case that within cultural studies recent feminist thinking, as Lynne Segal has pointed out, 'has encouraged us to aspire to' the flaunting of 'diverse pleasures, entitlements and self-questioning . . . (often, disconcertingly, in line with late capitalist consumerism)' (Segal, 1999: 232). This is not, however, the totality of feminism. Nor are there certain subjects that are inherently 'postmodern'. Fashion as a material practice, as an industry, as a source of meaning and as the vehicle of complex ideologies is much too important to be consigned to that particular pigeon-hole.

Finally, to debate fashion within the context of postmodernism now seems constricting. Even at its most empty, most postmodern criticism and theory surely never, as Negrin contends, equated self-identity unproblematically with one's style of presentation (although Baudrillard may be an exception), and certainly did not 'accept this uncritically'. On the contrary, much postmodern theory has been a long-drawn-out lament that catalogued the ills of postmodernism while lacking the inspiration of any visionary or utopian alternative. Yet the explanatory potential both of postmodern pessimism and of its 'playfully' optimistic alternative face has now been exhausted, and, in a new century, it is 'well an old age is out, and time to begin a new'.

PART TWO

6

THE SPHINX IN THE CITY
RECONSIDERED

Honoré de Balzac's *Illusions perdues* is the tale of a youthful poet and aspiring genius, Lucien de Rubempré, who travels from the provinces to Paris thirsting simultaneously for artistic recognition and social success. Initially driven to despair by a hopelessly unfashionable provincial appearance, he is prepared to run up debts, to lie, cheat, betray and fall fatally under the influence of the demonic Vautrin, homosexual, criminal and double agent, in order to make his mark upon the urban stage. Such is the potency of the spell cast by 'beauty, success and the city'.

In Balzac's world, a fashionable appearance was an essential component in the achievement of success. Although the origins of the western fashion cycle could be traced to the courtly life of France and Italy, it was in the cities that the western fashion cycle really took off. Richard Sennett has suggested that the early modern city was a stage, with fashion the essential prop for theatrical identities which were worn like masks. The expansion of urban life in the wake of the industrial revolution brought about a change: appearances now became 'direct expressions of the "inner" self . . . guides to the authentic self of the wearer', and fashionable dress gave 'clues to private feeling', although at the same time dress actually became more uniform, so that henceforward it would be from the tiny details of costume that a person's identity would be deciphered (Sennett, 1974: 163).

This may have been true for the fashions established by the nineteenth-century bourgeoisie, but in the twentieth century fashion as theatrical display reappeared in the styles created by minority groups such as British Teddy boys, hippies, Punks and the gay 'clones' of the 1970s, while contemporary dress incorporates the whole range from the urban industrial uniform of Gap and DKNY to the flamboyance of subcultural styles. My interest in the culture and representation of urban life, explored in *The Sphinx in the City* (Wilson, 1993), arose from this seductive view of the city as the crucible for the development of fashion, and in particular of fashion as, eventually, a form of popular culture. To explore the way in which fashion evolved through its relationship with the urban was to develop a view of urban life as social spectacle, and of the metropolis as a magnet not only for the social, sexual and artistic aspirations of the rising middle classes, but also of the excluded and the disreputable – adventurers in the milling world of eighteenth-century commerce and nineteenth-century capitalism. From this perspective the city was a vast department store of mass consumption. It was also a spectacle to be consumed – and that spectacle could include the lost, the disreputable and the damned.

To discuss urban space in terms largely of consumption is, of course, to present a very partial view. In the 1970s a powerful tradition of Marxist research had focused on the ways in which cities are shaped by the imperatives of capital. This perspective had shown how municipal housing, redevelopment, planning permissions and road schemes were undertaken in the pursuit of profit rather than in the interests of the millions who live in cities. The fiscal crisis of American cities in the 1960s and 1970s had grimly demonstrated how the flight to the suburbs of the middle classes had undermined the tax base and created wastelands, ghettos and no-go areas, even as the pincer movement of gentrification squeezed working-class families and the poor out of their familiar neighbourhoods. David Harvey (1973) and Manuel Castells (1978) in particular had subjected the class and racial divisions of urban space to a scathing analysis and exposed the ways in which capitalist industry, enterprise and investment had churned up roads, destroyed mixed neighbourhoods and working-class strongholds, created bleak industrial zones, built ethnically segregated 'project' wastelands and torn down precious buildings, all in the interests of capital accumulation. Yet the Marxist analysis of the powerful forces that were shaking cities to their foundations was so irresistible that it could appear to become deterministic, while the call for social justice increasingly sounded as little more than a desperate hope in the face of the juggernaut of capital.

Criticism of these powerful critiques also came from those who felt they were over-generalised. Some urbanists argued that the concentration on macro-imperatives of space lacked an appreciation of the particularities of place. In the early 1980s a move away from Marxist class analysis opened the way for an exploration of urban space as an inherently contradictory and multifaceted phenomenon, and as a subjective experience as well as an objective socio-economic formation. In Marshall Berman's *All That is Solid Melts Into Air*, this constituted a reinterpretation rather than a rejection of Marxism. Berman followed Marx in celebrating as well as criticising the vortex of modernity in nineteenth-century Paris and Moscow, and in mid-twentieth-century Brooklyn and the Bronx:

> Marx is evoking and enacting the desperate pace and frantic rhythm that capitalism imparts to every facet of modern life. He makes us feel that we are part of the action, drawn into the stream, hurtled along, out of control, at once dazzled and menaced by the onward rush . . . exhilarated but perplexed; we find that the solid social formations around us have melted away. (Berman, 1983: 91)

At the same time he raised the question whether 'Marx's own analysis of the dynamic of modernity' did not ultimately undermine 'the very prospect of the communist future he thought it would lead to' (Anderson, 1984: 100), concluding that 'Marx's dialectic of modernity [might re-enact] the fate of the society it describes, generating energies and ideas that melt it down into its own air' (Berman, 1983: 114) – the consumptionist rage for novelty and change might persist unaltered, as destructive to socialism as it had ultimately been to capitalism. Perry Anderson, on the other hand, argued that in 'a genuinely socialist culture' – a 'free community of equals' – the insatiable search for the new, 'defined simply as what comes *later*', would be replaced by a culture in which the different was multiplied 'in a far greater *variety* of concurrent styles and practices . . . a diversity founded on the far greater plurality and complexity of possible ways of living. . . . The axes of aesthetic life would . . . run horizontally, not vertically' (Anderson, 1984: 113).

A certain pluralist variety has actually come to pass among the very inequalities of a postmodern urban realm described with both horror and fascination by Fredric Jameson. Jameson wrote of the way in which 'urban squalor can be a delight to the eyes, when expressed in commodification, and . . . an unparalleled quantum leap in the alienation of daily life in the city can now be experienced in the form of a strange new hallucinatory exhilaration' (Jameson, 1984: 76). This was an admission that there could even be an unpleasant illicit thrill in the visible cheek-by-jowl coexistence of groovy excitement and intense squalor, the pleasure/danger knife-edge of the city – a dubious neo-bohemianism exploited in some of the most controversial films of the 1980s, for example *Dressed to Kill*.

A strong critique of redevelopment persisted, for example in Neil Smith's account of the 'Battle of Tompkins Park' on the Lower East Side (Smith, 1992). However, this was to some extent overtaken by the ambiguity of the whole postmodernity debate, in which some contributors focused deliberately on the city as a space of consumption, welcoming gentrification and the expansion of leisure spaces and entertainment. Some postmodernists substituted for the alleged Marxist determinism of social injustice and capital accumulation the fatalism of nostalgia and the fascination of cities in decline, aware, as Balzac had been in the 1820s, of how the cruel juxtaposition of poverty and wealth, beauty and ugliness, undeniably adds to the feverish excitement captured by Jameson.

An interest in city life as an aesthetic experience was linked to the importance of autobiographical writing as part of the new urban literature. Berman's book is one important example of this; Iain Sinclair (1997) and François Maspero (1994) have likewise explored the relationship of identity and self to the urban landscape, while Richard Sennett began a primarily theoretical book, *The Conscience of the Eye* (Sennett, 1993), with a description of the walk he often took from his Greenwich Village home up to Fourteenth Street. The rediscovery of Walter Benjamin's work since the 1970s influenced this trend, which is consistent with the wider popularity both of biography and of autobiography in recent years – a general turn towards 'the personal' in an epoch in which the authority of objective theory has been repeatedly questioned.

Just as the divisions between theory and more personal forms of writing were breaking down in the 1980s, so the many conferences and writings on 'the city' challenged the divisions between subject disciplines, bringing together artists and planners, novelists and reformers, journalists, performers and activists. 'The city' became a huge, and often amorphous, portmanteau subject. Ed Soja wrote an essay entitled 'It All Comes Together in Los Angeles' (Soja, 1989), but in a much bigger way it all came together simply in 'the city' or 'urban space': postmodernity, sexuality, representation, community, identity, urban politics and economics, not to mention cyberspace and global communications. Writing about urban space seemed to offer unmatchably rich possiblities: it could be both sensual and intellectual, visual and discursive. The city was *cool*; it was glamorous. It was also everything. With the waning of Marxist analysis, 'the city' could become an alternative form of 'totality' without actually being one, a world that included politics, gender, ethnicity, poverty, eroticism, consumption, history, heritage, art and mass culture. You could talk about anything under this grand umbrella without having even to make a gesture towards fitting it into the dominant theory, because there was none, since 'totalising' theories were rejected. Fierce debates between proponents of different postmodernities nevertheless continued, and insofar as they encompassed discussions of the postmodern city or urban realm, they partially occluded a much more longstanding debate.

This was the debate between pro- and anti-urbanists, which had been well under way in the nineteenth century, if not before, indeed Raymond Williams (1975) argued that it could be traced back at least to the seventeenth century in Britain. *The Sphinx in the City* originated as a contribution to this debate, suggesting that urban life had historically offered women more opportunities than rural life. These opportunities were often tantalisingly unfulfilled, offset by counter-influences of exploitation, exclusion and a harsh sexual morality; nevertheless, urbanisation provided one plank in the gradual emancipation of women. Today the distinction between town and country, the provinces and the metropolis is less stark than formerly, class divisions have widened with monetarism so that the lives of different classes and groups of women have less in common today than at any time since 1945, and it is difficult to talk about women as a single group. Nevertheless, rural life is arguably still even more restrictive and lacking in opportunity for the poor (of both sexes) than life in cities.

Against this it has been argued that a majority in Britain and other western countries are voting with their feet; those who can are leaving the big city centres and moving to small towns, suburbs and villages, in order to escape the perceived dangers of crime and pollution, expensive housing and poor education for their children. There is a popular belief that life for children in the countryside is safer and healthier, that somehow you 'cannot' bring children up in the big city. This belief was poignantly expressed by a bereaved parent in Dunblane, the small Scottish town in which sixteen schoolchildren and one of their teachers were murdered by an insane gunman; the grieving father wept as he described how he and his family had left Glasgow in order to 'get away from crime'. This faith in the safety of country life, understandable though it is, may be partly an illusion: rural life, just like urban life, is much better for the rich than for the poor, and inequality remains an overwhelmingly more important source of division than the country/town divide.

The argument is also made that since the majority reject urban life, to celebrate or promote it is 'elitist', the response of 'well-tended cosmopolites' (Lebas, 1996), members of a privileged group who alone have the financial means to take advantage of the delights of city living. This is a form of argument that has often been deployed within feminism and more generally on the Left as a critique of opponents who nevertheless *share* a broadly similar political perspective – middle-class intellectuals and radicals sensitive to their own status in relation to the disadvantaged for whom they claim to speak. But the vision of the average academic as a well-heeled cosmopolitan seems rather bizarre, suggesting someone out of Tom Wolfe's *The Bonfire of the Vanities* or Jay McInerney's *Brightness Falls* – Manhattanites losing their grip while earning million-dollar salaries, rather than middle-range university lecturers. In Britain at least, academic life has declined in status, with many lecturers approximating more to a 'lumpen intelligentsia' than an affluent *über*-class, rich in cultural but not in economic capital; while the genteel poverty of many women academics aligns them more closely to a long fictional line of women, such as the heroine of Charlotte Brontë's *Villette* or the protagonist of Dorothy Richardson's autobiographical novels of Edwardian bohemian life, than to hot-shot lawyers and junk bond dealers dining in the top ten New York restaurants. Of course white middle-class women are unimaginably 'privileged' by comparison with the world's poor – of both sexes; but to focus on the relative privilege of this particular group is, whether unintentionally or not, to distract attention from the much greater inequalities which make far more difference globally.

The logical conclusion of the many attacks over the years on 'white middle-class feminists and/or socialists' could be that they should just shut up. 'Privilege' delegitimates their opinions, since they do not speak from a position of oppression (although most of them are salary earners, many are women and some are non-white). But it is utterly perverse to argue that in some form of liberal self-abasement, those with the possibility of voicing a critique of existing society should abstain. For that is the most substantial privilege we enjoy – of having a voice, of being heard, even if only or largely in the restricted circles of the university. Even if one takes the view that dissidents are allowed a voice as a form of safety valve in capitalist society, the possibility of speaking brings with it the responsibility to do so. To remain silent would be to abrogate responsibility. The task is rather to find a language in which to express our critique of contemporary society and aspirations for a better one. Disagreement is fine, and can be constructive, provided, that is, that it is used to find ways if possible of resolving differences of strategy and analysis in pursuit of a wider shared goal.

Today, all agree that cities need to be revitalised, improved, cleared of crime and traffic congestion; there is little agreement as to how these goals are to be achieved, however. Nineteenth-century urban planners demanded reform, argued that social justice required a planned city based sometimes on utilitarian principles of surveillance, hygiene and labour discipline, sometimes on socialist principles of redistribution. But after the advances of large-scale planning in the mid-twentieth century, disillusionment set in. In 1961, Jane Jacobs, in *The Death and Life of American Cities*, famously attacked the whole rationale of planning, and argued for the natural development of intimate city neighbourhoods as opposed to the megalomania of vast municipal housing estates. Neither she nor her disciple Richard Sennett in *The Uses of Disorder* (Sennett, 1970) admitted that the absence of regulation and large-scale planning do not invariably lead to the proliferation of Greenwich Villages and the preservation of traditional mixed neighbourhoods; they took a resolutely anti-statist stand in calling for the public sector to abandon its overweening, as they saw it, architectural and social engineering interventions in urban life.

It is true that in some British cities after the Second World War an infernal alliance between municipal government and property developers resulted in the barbaric destruction of city centres such as Bradford and Newcastle; on the other hand, in some parts of London, for example in Camden, it was municipal policies of compulsory purchase of old properties for public housing in the 1970s that preserved parts of the district both from wholesale gentrification *and* from massive redevelopment. In any case municipal planning is not to blame for the logic of capital, which lays waste in its own fashion and is distinct from the planning and architectural mistakes of the 1950s and 1960s, disastrous though these often were. Municipal planning wanted to destroy the slums and give people decent housing and a pleasant, healthy environment safe for children. That was an honourable goal. Planning was needed to rid cities of slums and rack-rent private landlords. Planning was necessary to get filthy industrial sites away from the houses surrounding them.

Planning nevertheless brought serious disadvantages. It was not simply that municipal housing schemes reproduced zoning dogmas which separated homes from city centres, shopping and entertainment as well as from factories; it was not simply that they followed architectural ideologies such as the Garden City or the Le Corbusierian tower block, both of which were ultimately anti-urban. Nor was it simply that municipal landlords could be authoritarian and incompetent. It was also the loss of the unplanned, of atmosphere and the excitement of the city as spectacle.

To some the celebration of the exciting dangers of the city, or at least of its amorality, amounts to little more than the aestheticisation of the misery of others. It smacks of the *flâneur*'s essential voyeurism, even narcissism, it

is the discourse of the privileged, and negates the authentic experience
of ordinary people. Yet planners and reformers do not represent those
mythical 'ordinary people' either, for when the masses do speak up for
themselves they may voice sentiments of which the experts thoroughly
disapprove: 'ordinary people' may turn out to be racist tenants' associ-
ations, or mothers' groups who want the death penalty for paedophiles.

In Chapter 1 I discussed the tensions between those who have celebrated
mass culture and those who have denounced it, and tried to move towards
an analysis that avoids such stark extremes. Similarly, there are urbanists
who have avoided both the Scylla of facile celebration and the Charybdis of
over-zealous welfarism, transcending the dichotomy between pleasure and
danger, safety and risk, and refusing the false choice between the spectacle
of glitter and glamour and the sterile white world of utopia. Kevin Robins
(1995), for example, has pointed out that aggression and antagonism are
inescapable features of civic life. A key figure in urban culture, he suggests,
is the stranger; the city is a place to which many different strangers come
and encounters between strangers are not always friendly. Even if individuals are not personally hostile, the more negative urban literature has
repeatedly invoked a notion of the crowd as a dangerous entity pregnant
with collective hostility and always threatening loss of control and the
inauguration of a reign of disorder. The crowd becomes a kind of unnatural
force of nature, the ruled threatening the rulers like a flood, a hurricane or a
fire. Robins explores the way in which the appearance of the stranger
equally threatens the existing order, thus calling up the fear that is also
expressed in fear of the crowd. The stranger is not formless and chaotic,
like the crowd; on the contrary, he sharpens the identity of the established
resident, but often in a paranoid fashion.

As Robins points out, the usual reaction by architects and urbanists to
the perceived chaos and disorder of cities has been precisely the opposite:
not to embrace, but rather to seek to extirpate disorder, responding with
plans for totally ordered and orderly cities based on pure rationalism.
Indeed, this is part of the long tradition of utopian writing. Robins argues
that this kind of rationalism is a defective response to urban disorder, since
it denies, suppresses or ignores our emotional and unconscious reactions to
every aspect of urban life. Urban life in its very being is a continual
interaction of rational and irrational, order and disorder, harmony and
friction. What he calls the urban regeneration agenda is, therefore, merely
'the acceptable face of rationalism', and fails to deal with the problems of
the disorder its vision of harmony confronts. Rationalism in this sense is a
kind of perfectionism, the idea that the good city is one in which all
problems have been eliminated.

Yet for Robins neither aggression nor rationalistic perfection need be the
end-point. Quoting Georg Simmel, he suggests that the newcomer brings
'new and vitalising qualities into urban culture', and that the diversity of
communities and the encounters of strangers offer opportunities to work
through hostility and arrive at dialectic and creative change.

Both in *The Sphinx in the City* and in the following chapter, I try to argue against what I have always experienced as a too monolithic feminist account of women's subordination and victimisation, as has also, for example, Mica Nava in a number of essays. This may create the false impression that I am unwilling to acknowledge the extent of women's disadvantaged situation and special difficulties when living in cities. In fact, like many writers, I am simply struggling with the chasm between what is and what we desire; and hoping that urban difference and diversity can exist without division, pleasure without danger, and glamour without inequality. Perhaps this is too optimistic. So often – in discussions of pornography, sexuality, fashion and now urban life – it seems as if I have belonged to that beleaguered group of socialists and feminists forever walking the tightrope of the elusive 'third way', searching for compromise between two incompatible perceptions: the sometimes dour leftist apocalypse of a carceral capitalism from which there is logically no escape, and the alternative, a seemingly rather frivolous insistence on pleasure.

Yet, however difficult, it is essential to hold those incompatible views in tension. To deny that there are any pleasures to be had in capitalist society is to depart too radically from the perceptions of most of those around us. It is only by recognising and analysing those pleasures and their source that we can develop a view of something that might be better.

7

THE INVISIBLE *FLÂNEUR*

The relationship of women and cities has long preoccupied reformers and philanthropists. In recent years the preoccupation has been inverted, the Victorian determination to control working-class women replaced by a feminist concern for women's safety and comfort in city streets; but whether women are seen as a problem of cities, or cities as a problem for women, the relationship is perceived as one fraught with difficulty.

With the intensification of the public/private divide in the industrial period, the presence of women on the streets and in public places of entertainment caused enormous anxiety, and was the occasion for any number of moralising and regulatory discourses in the nineteenth century. In fact, the fate and position of women in the city was a special case of a more general alarm and ambivalence which stretched across the political spectrum.

It is true that some – predominantly liberals – expressed an optimistic and excited response to the urban spectacle. Perhaps not surprisingly, it was those who stood to gain most from industrial urbanisation whose praise for it was the strongest: the new entrepreneurs of the rising bourgeois class. For them the cities, above all the great city, the metropolis, offered an unprecedented and astonishing variety of possibilities, stimuli and wealth. The development of a consumer and spectacular society on a scale never previously known represented opportunities for progress, plenty and a more educated and civilised populace. So went the liberal argument (see Vaughan, 1843).

Hostility to urbanisation was more likely to come from the two opposite extremes of the political spectrum (see Lees, 1985). On the left, Engels was deeply critical not only of the slum and factory conditions in which the majority had to survive, but equally of the indifference and selfishness with which people behaved in crowds where no-one knew anyone else. By contrast with an implied natural order of things, the new urban forms of human interaction had about them 'something repulsive, something against which human nature rebels', for urban life encouraged 'the brutal indifference, the unfeeling isolation of each in his private interest' (Engels, 1962: 56). The utopian socialism of William Morris led him to denounce the dirt and poverty of the industrialised town; he advocated a return to medieval village architecture and an Arcadian way of life in which women would be once more safely ensconced in the domestic sphere (Morris, 1986: 234–5). Morris's vision is in many ways an attractive one, but that it is still received so uncritically, for the most part, indicates the continuing strength of left-wing romantic anti-urbanism (and covert patriarchalism).

Rightwing critics of urban life similarly harked back to an organic rural community. They feared the way in which the break-up of tradition in cities led to the undermining of authority, hierarchy and dignity; the menace of the cities included not only disease and poverty but, even more threateningly, the spectres of sensuality, democracy and revolution.

One particular cause for alarm was the way in which urban life undermined patriarchal authority. Young, unattached men and women flocked to the towns to find more remunerative work. There, freed from the bonds of rural social control, they were in danger – it was felt – of succumbing to temptations of every kind: immorality, illegitimacy, the breakdown of family life and bestial excess appeared to threaten from all sides. What was perhaps almost worse was that in the rough and tumble of the city street and urban crowd, distinctions of rank of every kind were blurred.

In particular, female virtue and respectability were hard to preserve in this promiscuous environment. 'Who are these somebodies whom nobody knows?' famously enquired William Acton (1968) in his survey of prostitution, published in 1857, and prostitution was the great fear of the age. Evangelical reformers of the 1830s and 1840s wrote impassioned tracts in which they described this, the 'great social evil', as a plague that was rotting the very basis of society, and they campaigned for its complete eradication. Significantly, they frequently linked prostitution to the ideals of the French Revolution. Prostitution was not only a real and ever-present threat to morals; it was also a metaphor for disorder and the overturning of the natural hierarchies and institutions of society. Rescue, reform and legislation were to rid the cities of this frightful menace (see Walkowitz, 1980).

The pioneer of investigations into prostitution was the French bureaucrat Alexandre Parent-Duchâtelet, whose survey of the problem as it manifested itself in Paris appeared in 1836. He favoured regulation of a positively Foucauldian kind, arguing that each prostitute must have her dossier, and that the more information could be gathered about each individual, the better she was known by the state, the easier would become the task of surveillance:

> Public women, left to their own devices and free of surveillance during the anarchy of the first years of the first revolution, abandoned themselves to all the disorders which, during this disastrous period, were favoured by the state of the society; soon the evil became so great that it excited universal outrage, and . . . in 1796 the municipal authorities ordered a new census . . . registration was always considered the most important means of arresting the inevitable disorder of prostitution. Is it not in fact *necessary to get to know the individuality* of all those who come to the attention of the police? (Parent-Duchâtelet, 1836: 266–7, my italics)

Alain Corbin (1986) has drawn out the way in which Parent-Duchâtelet's writings articulate a contradictory ideology of prostitution. In this ideology the prostitute's body is putrefying, and infects the social body with corruption and death, yet at the same time it is a drain which siphons off that which would otherwise corrupt the whole of society. In order for the prostitute/drain to perform her function without contaminating everything else, bourgeois surveillance and regulation were to bring the brothel within a utilitarian regime of control.

Parent-Duchâtelet's perspective was distinct from that of the British evangelical clergymen and philanthropists, his stance closer to that of the physician William Acton. By the 1850s Acton was arguing for the regulation of prostitution from a worldly and cynical perspective far different in tone from that of the evangelical Christians.

In Britain an intense struggle developed between those who favoured more stringent regulation and those who objected to it. The regulation of prostitutes could all too easily develop into the regulation of all, particularly all working-class, women. Josephine Butler undertook her campaign against the Contagious Diseases Acts (from 1864) on civil liberties grounds, and partly because women who were not prostitutes could so easily fall foul of the new ordinances and find themselves subject to arrest and the humiliating and hated internal examinations with the 'steel penis' (the speculum) (Butler, 1896). Judith Walkowitz (1980) has argued that the very existence of these Acts resulted in the increased separation of prostitutes from other women – and that thus the regulation of prostitutes contributed, if not to the creation, certainly to the exacerbation of the evil it was intended to restrict.

The prostitute was a 'public woman', but the problem in nineteenth-century urban life was whether every woman in the new, disordered world of the city, the public sphere of pavements, cafés and theatres, was not a public woman and thus a prostitute. The very presence of unattended – unowned – women constituted a threat both to male power and a temptation to male 'frailty'. Yet although the male ruling class did all in its power to restrict the movement of women in cities, it proved impossible to banish them from public spaces altogether. Women continued to crowd into the city centres and the factory districts.

The movements of middle-class women were more successfully restricted. The development of the bourgeois suburb as a haven of privacy and gentility was particularly marked in Britain, serving to 'protect' middle-class women from the coarseness of the urban crowd, and these women, even in a city such as Paris, where the exodus to the suburbs did not occur in the same way, were closely guarded. In British society it was the young marriageable woman under thirty years of age who was most rigorously chaperoned; married women, governesses and old maids had rather more – if hardly flattering – freedom (Davidoff, 1973).

Bourgeois men, on the other hand, were free to explore urban zones of pleasure such as – in Paris – the Folies Bergères, the restaurant, the theatre, the café and the brothel, where they met working-class women (whereas in London men congregated in the masculine clubs). The proliferation of public places of pleasure and interest created a new kind of public person with the leisure to wander, watch and browse: the *flâneur*, a key figure in the critical literature of modernity and urbanisation.

In literature the *flâneur* was represented as an archetypal occupant and observer of the public sphere in the rapidly changing and growing great cities of nineteenth-century Europe. He is an almost mythological or allegorical figure, who represented what was perhaps the most characteristic response of all to the wholly new forms of life that seemed to be developing. This response was one of ambivalence.

The origins of the word *flâneur* are uncertain (Ferguson, 1994); the *Nineteenth-Century Encyclopaedia* Larousse suggested that it may be derived from the Irish word for libertine. The editors of the *Encyclopaedia* devoted a long article to the *flâneur*, whom they defined as a loiterer, a fritterer away of time, associated with the new urban pastimes of shopping and crowd-watching. They suggested that he could exist only in the great city, the metropolis, since provincial towns would afford too restricted a stage for his strolling and too narrow a field for his observations. They also commented that although the majority of *flâneurs* were idlers, there were among them artists, and that the multifarious sights of the astonishing new urban spectacle constituted their raw material.[1]

By the mid-nineteenth century the *flâneur* was a recognised figure in Paris. However, an anonymous pamphlet published in 1806 may be the earliest reference to this urban individual. It describes a day in the life of 'Monsieur Bonhomme', a loiterer of the Bonaparte era, and clearly set out in this pamphlet are all the characteristics later to be found in the writings of Baudelaire and Benjamin (Anon., n.d. [1806]).[2]

No-one knows, states the anonymous author of this pamphlet, how M. Bonhomme supports himself, but he is said to be a rentier, seemingly set free by his unearned income from familial, landowning or mercantile responsibilities to roam Paris at will. He spends most of his day simply looking at the urban spectacle; he observes in particular new inventions, for example he stops in the Place Louis XV 'to examine the signals of the marine telegraph, although he understands nothing about them', and he is fascinated by the many new building works getting under way. Public clocks and barometers regulate his routine – an indication of the growing importance of precise time-keeping, even for one who was under no regimen of paid labour – and he passes the hours by shopping or window shopping, looking at books, new fashions, hats, combs, jewellery and novelties of all kinds.

A second feature of M. Bonhomme's day is the amount of time he spends in cafés and restaurants; he chooses establishments frequented by actors, writers, journalists and painters, that is, his interests are predominantly in the arts. During the course of the day he picks up gossip about new plays, rivalries in the art world, and projected publications, and his eager anticipation of the Salon exhibitions of painting is mentioned several times.

Third, a significant part of the urban spectacle is the behaviour of the lower ranks of society, for example he watches soldiers, workers and 'grisettes' at an open-air dance. Fourth, he is interested in dress as a vital component of the urban scene. Fifth – and less characteristically – women play but a minor role in his day. He notices an attractive street vendor and hints that she may be engaged in prostitution on the side, but there is a silence on the subject of his own erotic life. On the other hand a woman painter is mentioned, and the shouts of the manageress of the restaurant he patronises indicate her role as overseer; these observations implicitly bearing witness to the many women painters still active at this period, and to the important role played by women in the catering trade (possibly partly because of the conscription to the army of male cooks, bakers and waiters).

Particularly striking is M. Bonhomme's marginality. He is essentially a solitary onlooker, activated, like Edgar Allen Poe's 'Man of the Crowd', by his fleeting, but continuous and necessary contact with the anonymous multitude. In his resolution 'to keep a little diary recording all the most curious things he had seen or heard during the course of his wanderings, to fill the void of his nocturnal hours of insomnia', is the germ of the *flâneur*'s future role as writer; it also hints at the boredom and ennui which seem inescapably linked to the curiosity and voyeurism which are also so characteristic. Here, then, the mid-nineteenth-century *flâneur* appears fully formed in the much earlier context of post-revolutionary Parisian society: a gentleman, a remittance man, he is subtly *déclassé*, and above all he stands wholly outside production. He heralds the society of consumption.

Siegfried Kracauer and Walter Benjamin wrote of the emergence of the *flâneur* in terms similar to each other, although Kracauer emphasised more strongly the economic determinants of the role. He argued that the 1830s and early 1840s saw the age of the 'classic bohemia' in Paris, and defined the bohemian as a student, living in his garret while planning to become a great writer or artist. Many of these students formed relationships and lived with young women from a humbler background, the 'grisettes'. Kracauer (1937) argues that the bohemians came from the lower middle class or petite bourgeoisie of artisans and clerks, and that bohemia went into decline with the development of industrial capitalism, when this class was squeezed into extinction as factories replaced workshops and the world of Louis-Philippe was replaced by the Second Empire of Napoleon III, the ultimate society of the spectacle.

Kracauer made a radical distinction between this student bohemian and the *flâneur* of a later date. The dandies who took possession of the Maison D'Or and the Café Tortoni in the 1830s and 1840s formed another distinct category. The street, especially the Boulevard des Italiens, in which the Café Tortoni was situated, was the centre of fashionable public life, and along it loitered the dandies, the bohemians and the courtesans – but also the population at large. 'Innumerable curious sightseers strolled through these streets on Sundays,' asserts Kracauer, who claims that:

> All classes of the population received a common and uniform education in the streets . . . their real education. Workers, laughing grisettes, soldiers, the petty

bourgeoisie, who have few opportunities for strolling and gazing at shop windows during the week . . . all took the opportunity of gazing their fill on Sundays. (Kracauer, 1937: 23)

This special form of public life was played out in a zone that was neither quite public nor quite private, yet which partook of both: the cafés, the *terraces* and the boulevards, also in Benjamin's arcades, and, later, the department store and the hotel. These were commoditised spaces in which everything was for sale, and to which everyone had relatively unrestricted entry, yet they endeavoured to re-create the atmosphere of the salon or the private house. Here, the glamorous (or would-be glamorous) section of society was at home; the crowds came to stare, but also to mingle with them. The society which thus constituted itself as a spectacle was a society of outsiders, and the boulevards and cafés offered, as Kracauer puts it, a homeland for these individuals without a home.

Kracauer, like Benjamin, emphasises the commercialisation and commoditisation of two areas: writing and sexuality. Urban industrial life generated a demand for new forms of writing – the *feuilleton*, the magazine article. It gave birth to a new kind of literature, a journalistic record of the myriad sights, sounds and spectacles to be found on every corner, in every cranny of urban life. This was as much the case in Britain as in France. It was an inquisitive, anecdotal, ironic, melancholy, but above all voyeuristic literature. As Dickens' friend George Augustus Sala wrote, 'The things I have seen from the top of an omnibus! . . . Unroofing London in a ride . . . varied life, troubled life, busy, restless, chameleon life. . . . Little do you reck that an [observer] is above you taking notes, and, faith, that he'll print them!' (Sala, 1859: 220).

Kracauer locates the genesis of the new journalism in the revolution brought about by the publisher Émile de Girardin, who commercialised the press. 'Newspapers had hitherto been purely political organs, with circulations restricted to small groups of readers sharing the same views. Small circulations meant high subscription rates, and newspapers had to charge their readers 80 francs a month in order to be able to exist at all' (Kracauer, 1937: 66). Girardin charged only 40 francs for his paper, *La Presse*, but accepted far more advertising, which was easily obtained because of its expanding circulation. This, however, had the further result that the papers (as others followed suit) became less political, catering rather to a demand for entertainment in the form of amusing articles about everyday life, gossip, and, before long, the serialised novel, such as Eugène Süe's *The Mysteries of Paris*. These developments in turn increased the demand for journalists (Kracauer, 1937: 66–7).

Kracuaer describes the convergence on the boulevards and in the cafés of the upper-class dandies and the new journalists, arguing that these groups were in many ways similar. Both rejected conventional society. Yet both were also dependent on it. As a result their attitude towards it was cynical or ironic rather than passionately oppositional. Their blasé attitude – the attitude Georg Simmel saw as typical of urban life – was the attitude of

men who have been bought; for, while critical of the philistinism of bourgeois society they were paid to entertain the very philistines they sometimes
despised and sometimes hated.

Kracauer argues that sexuality was likewise commercialised as the
grisettes, who had simply lived as unmarried companions with their lovers
were replaced by the 'lorettes' (so called because they lived in the Notre
Dame de Lorette district), who exchanged sex for money on a less emotionally committed basis: 'although it was necessarily only the favoured few
who succeeded in scaling the giddy heights to which the great courtesans
belonged, there were nevertheless a number of honourable intermediary
stages, and those who belonged to the boulevard rank and file had climbed
quite a considerable portion of the ladder' (Kracauer, 1937: 72). Whether
such a schematic distinction between the grisette and the lorette can really be
made seems rather doubtful, especially since the grisette was something of a
literary myth, but women who lived by their wits and their sexuality certainly
played an important role in the Second Empire, often acting as negotiators,
Kracauer claims, in the orgies of speculation and stock-market madness
characteristic of Louis Napoleon's reign.

During the Second Empire Paris became an even more dazzling spectacle
than it had been in the 1830s, and in this Paris the *flâneur* replaced the
bohemian, or so Kracauer suggests, although again this clear-cut distinction
cannot in my view be substantiated. For Kracauer, however, the difference
between bohemian and *flâneur* was the difference between romanticism and
cynicism. For him the *flâneur* is the ultimate ironic, detached observer,
skimming across the surface of the city and tasting its pleasures with curiosity
and interest. Walter Benjamin wrote of the way in which the *flâneur* as artist
'goes botanizing on the asphalt' (Benjamin, 1973: 36); he is the naturalist of
this unnatural environment.

Marcel Proust had already lighted upon the metaphor of the naturalist,
comparing Marcel, the eponymous narrator of *À la recherche du temps
perdu*, to a botanist. This comparison is made on the occasion when Marcel
observes a chance encounter between two homosexuals (both of whom he
already knows socially without realising, until this moment, the nature of
their sexual inclinations). He likens the unexpected meeting of the two men
to the conjuncture of a rare kind of bee with the equally rare orchid which
needs its visit in order to be fertilised. Although both are known to the
narrator, the two men are strangers to each other and from utterly different
walks of life, and when they come face to face the scene seems, to Proust, to
be 'stamped with a strangeness, or if you like a naturalness, the beauty of
which steadily increased' (Proust, 1981: II 627). This is similar to the way in
which the *flâneur* viewed the multitudinous encounters that occurred every
day and thousands of times over in the streets of the great city – and indeed
it was the growth of urban life that made possible the very emergence of the
homosexual identity.

It is this *flâneur*, the *flâneur* as a man of pleasure, but more, as a man
who takes visual possession of the city, who has emerged in feminist debate

as the embodiment of the 'male gaze'. He represents men's visual and voyeuristic mastery over women. According to this view, the *flâneur*'s freedom to wander at will through the city is an exclusively masculine freedom, which means that the concept of the *flâneur* is essentially and inescapably gendered. Janet Wolff (1985), for example, argues that there could never be a female *flâneur*; the *flâneuse* was invisible; or, rather, did not exist, while Griselda Pollock (1988) writes of the way in which women, middle-class women at least, were denied access to the spaces of the city, even a successful painter such as Berthe Morisot most often taking as her subject-matter interiors and domestic scenes instead of the cafés and other sites of pleasure so often painted by her male colleagues.

Yet these distinctions, like Kracauer's, may be too rigid. Griselda Pollock and Janet Wolff concede that some women at least were permitted access to certain parts of the essentially masculine public domain, but Wolff argues that nevertheless 'the ideology of women's place in the domestic realm permeated the whole of society' (Wolff, 1985: 37). To say this is, however, automatically to accept at face value and on its own terms the nineteenth-century ideological division between public and private spheres. But in practice the private sphere was *also* (and still is) a masculine domain; although the Victorians characterised it as feminine, the domestic interior was organised first and foremost for the convenience, rest and recreation of men, not women, and feminists have argued that the private sphere has usually been women's workplace rather than their refuge. Moreover, the bourgeois home was not a particularly safe haven for the working-class women, domestic servants, who were trapped within it. On the contrary, it was an 'ideal location' for sexual attacks across class boundaries:

> In the attics, basements and backstairs of the Victorian home, that haven of peace and security, housemaids were in permanent contact with a male population whose intentions were often bad . . . while the mistress was at church or on a walk, the big houses of the rich murmured with illicit desires and furtive ambushes. (Barret-Ducrocq, 1991: 47, 49–50)

Janet Wolff maintains that women were wholly excluded from the public sphere:

> The experience of anonymity in the city, the fleeting, impersonal contacts described by social commentators like Georg Simmel, the possibility of unmolested strolling and observation first seen by Baudelaire, and then analysed by Walter Benjamin, were entirely the experiences of men. By the late nineteenth century, middle-class women had been more or less consigned (in ideology if not in reality) to the private sphere. The public world of work, city life, bars, and cafés was barred to the respectable woman. . . . (By the end of the nineteenth century shopping was an important activity for women, the rise of the department store and of the consumer society providing a highly legitimate, if limited, participation in the public. But of course, the literature of modernity . . . [was] not concerned with shopping.) (Wolff, 1990: 58)

So perhaps it doesn't then matter if women are stared at, harassed or actually attacked in public spaces, because 'in ideology' they're still at home anyway.

To substantiate her view, Janet Wolff cites Thorstein Veblen (1957), who viewed bourgeois women as vehicles for 'conspicuous consumption'; they were the chattels of their husbands, who consumed vicariously through them. The amazingly elaborate way in which they dressed, in particular, he felt, constructed them as 'signs' for their husbands' wealth. As was noted in Chapter 5, he had been influenced by the arguments of the dress reform movement, which rejected fashionable dress on the grounds that it was ugly and unhygienic, unhealthy and restricting; but, writing in 1899, Veblen was already out of date, since these radical ideas were influencing mainstream fashion. Women's fashions were following those of men. Just as men had adapted sporting wear into an urban uniform at the beginning of the nine-teenth century, so now women were adopting the 'coat and skirt', a style originally designed for riding, for city wear (and in the twentieth century Chanel and others were to work this into a universally accepted fashion for women).

It is not always clear whether Janet Wolff perceives the *flâneur* as a gendered concept, or as a descriptive account, or whether it is both, and it may not be legitimate to counter her interpretation of an ideology by recourse to empirical fact. Alain Courbin implies that such a strategy is *not* legitimate: 'Images and schemas rather than collections of monotonously repeated arguments or denotative discourses should be our object of study' (Corbin, 1986: 210); in other words we are confronted by representations and these are impossible to counter by means of material evidence, trapped as we are in 'the ultimate labyrinth – history' (Buci-Glucksmann, 1986). Yet the distinction Janet Wolff draws between 'ideology' and 'reality' raises serious problems. Ideology, it is implied, bears absolutely no relation to 'reality', and conceivably all women could venture out onto the streets yet still could be 'in ideology' confined to the home. Ideology thus becomes a rigid and monolithic monument of thought, and by an inversion of reflexionist theories of ideology, instead of ideology mirroring reality, reality becomes but a pale shadow of ideology, or parts company with it altogether. Such an approach is unhelpful to the political cause of feminism, since it creates such an all-powerful and seamless ideological system ranged against women, and one upon which they can never make any impact.

Griselda Pollock insists on a similar radical division between the 'mental map' of ideology and the 'description of social spaces', although there 'was none the less an overlap between the purely ideological maps and the concrete organisation of the social sphere' (Pollock, 1988: 68). Thus the desperate dash for freedom from Althusserian concepts of base and superstructure has ended up in an idealist realm of Hegelian pure thought or spirit.

The feminist historian Mary Poovey, on the other hand, recognises the ways in which ideologies and experiences slip and fluctuate together. She believes that in nineteenth-century England 'representations of gender constituted one of the sites on which ideological systems were simultaneously constructed and contested'. They were 'sites at which struggles for authority occurred':

> To describe an ideology as a 'set' of beliefs or a 'system' of institutions and practices conveys the impression of something that is internally organised, coherent and complete. . . . Yet . . . what may look coherent and complete in retrospect was actually fissured by competing emphases and interests. . . . The middle-class ideology we most often associate with the Victorian period was both contested and always under construction; because it was always in the making, it was always open to revision, dispute, and the emergence of oppositional formations. (Poovey, 1989: 2–3)

Janet Wolff is inaccurate in arguing that by the closing years of the nineteenth century middle-class women had been 'more or less' consigned to the home, since this was the very period when they were emerging more and more into the public spaces of the city. With the growth of white-collar occupations for women, there was a need, for example, for eating establishments where women could comfortably go on their own. The lack of these in London had long been keenly felt. In 1852, one observer had noted that working-class women did frequent public houses – places in which no middle-class person of either sex would have felt comfortable. By the 1870s guidebooks were beginning to list 'places in London where ladies can conveniently lunch when in town for a day's shopping and unattended by a gentleman' (quoted in Thorne, 1980: 25). Restaurants as we know them were much more common in Paris than in London, but by the 1860s were springing up in the British capital too. Crosby Hall, Bishopsgate, opened in 1868, employed waitresses instead of waiters, and 'made special provisions to ensure that women felt comfortable there' (Thorne, 1980: 40). These provisions included the installation of women's lavatories with female attendants. Thereafter the number of eating establishments grew rapidly, with railway station buffets, refreshment rooms at exhibitions, ladies-only dining rooms and the opening of West End restaurants, such as the Criterion in 1874, which specifically catered for women. By the end of the century, Thorne points out, Lyons, the ABC tea-rooms, Fullers tea-rooms, vegetarian restaurants, and the restrooms and refreshment rooms in department stores had all transformed the middle- and lower middle-class woman's experience of public life. While it would be possible to argue that these expanding provisions indicate the extent of the problems faced by women in negotiating public space, they hardly support the view that women were 'invisible', for even if they were secluded and separate in their own restaurants, this was only because they were 'out and about' in the first place.

Nor was shopping invisible in the literature of modernity. The commoditisation of which Benjamin wrote in the early nineteenth-century arcades was all about the availability of goods to buy and the compulsion to look at them. Zola, Proust, Dickens, Dreiser and many others recorded this aspect of urban life, which evidently fascinated them even when it appalled. Shopping and/or window shopping constructed the identity of the *flâneur* as far back as M. Bonhomme.

Benjamin was also acutely aware of the sexualisation of the city and the links between sexuality and the sale of goods. In her discussion of 'Modernity and the Spaces of Femininity', Griselda Pollock (1988) is concerned with representations in the art of Édouard Manet and his contemporaries of a proletarian or *demi-mondaine* female sexuality by painters who predominantly came from a superior social class. Many of the locations these painters recorded were sexualised public places in which lower-class women sold their bodies directly or indirectly to bourgeois men. Respectable middle-class women were rigorously excluded from such locations.

Griselda Pollock writes from within a theoretical tradition that has emphasised the importance of the 'male gaze': 'the gaze of the *flâneur* articulates and produces a masculine sexuality which in the modern sexual economy enjoys the freedom to look, appraise and possess' (Pollock, 1988: 79). This theoretical position rests on the psychoanalytic approach of Jacques Lacan. Feminists influenced by Lacanian psychoanalysis

> have been particularly concerned with how sexual difference is constructed . . . through the Oedipal process. . . . For Lacan, woman cannot enter the world of the symbolic, of language, because at the very moment of the acquisition of language, she learns that she lacks the phallus, the symbol that sets language going through a recognition of difference; her relation to language is a negative one, a lack. In patriarchal structures, thus, woman is located as other (enigma, mystery), and is thereby viewed as outside . . . male language. (Kaplan, 1984: 321)

The male gaze is constructed as voyeuristic, but it does not simply represent conscious desire and potential mastery; its unconscious significance is to 'annihilate the threat that woman (as castrated, and possessing a sinister genital organ) poses' (Kaplan, 1984: 323).

This position offers little in the way of a theory of change, yet although many feminists approach it with ambivalence, it has gained a perhaps surprising domination over feminist art history, film theory and literary criticism. The use of a Lacanian perspective represented, among other things, a reaction against the vulgar reflexionism of seeing art as simply a mirror of reality, but the shift to the opposite extreme has been such that it has gone beyond a recognition that our knowledge of reality is always constructed through discourse and representation to a determinist, indeed fatalistic, idealism in which 'reality' is meaningless; and ironically, a theoretical position derived from Lacan, who argued for a split and unstable subjectivity, has resulted in the creation of a theoretical Medusa's head, whose look petrifies everything, and fixes women forever in the stasis of otherness, turned to stone by the Male Gaze.[3] We might have expected an emphasis on signifying practices and representations to have resulted in a fluid universe of shifting meanings (like the urban spectacle itself). Instead the opposite has happened and the Lacanian discourse has reinforced, indeed replicated, the ideology it was meant to deconstruct.

Debates among feminists seem often to begin as differences of emphasis and end as polarised antagonisms. Although we know that the world is turned upside-down when viewed through a gendered lens, by this time we also know that not every feminist sees the same scene through her spectacles, nor does every feminist have the same prescription.[4] Janet Wolff, Griselda Pollock and I would all, I imagine, agree that women were exploited and oppressed in the nineteenth-century city, and my points of difference are partly matters of emphasis, although there are two more fundamental underlying disagreements: over the usefulness or not of Lacan, discussed above; and whether urban space is so fundamentally constructed by gender difference that women are not simply disadvantaged but representationally excluded or even extirpated, or whether, rather, the city is a contradictory and shifting space which can be appropriated by women.

It is also a matter of emphasis whether one insists on the dangers or the opportunities for women in cities. It depends on what is being compared with urban women's lives. In the nineteenth century and today opportunities were vastly affected by class and ethnicity; if, on the other hand, we compare the life of urban working-class women with what they had left behind in the countryside, we may well conclude that the cities opened a vista of opportunities. One study of divorce in France at the end of the eighteenth century suggests that the reason divorce was more common in cities was because women had a wider choice of alternative forms of financial support (paid work) and a wider range of alternative housing than in rural areas (Phillips, 1980). They were still poor and disadvantaged, but less poor and disadvantaged than their sisters in the countryside. They were, on the other hand, worse off than the men of their own class. The majority of women led insecure lives at best, lives usually of grinding poverty; according to one study there were 60 per cent more female than male paupers in Paris in the 1870s (Leroy-Beaulieu, 1873). Yet most became wage labourers, and this offered a potential vestige of freedom denied the rural woman worker embedded in the family economy.

There existed also intermediate social zones inhabited by women of indeterminate class, who were sometimes able to escape the rigid categories into which society tried to force them. The women of the English Pre-Raphaelite circle were of this kind – although it is important to remember that they were far from typical in Victorian society. Elizabeth Siddall figures in Pre-Raphaelite legend as Dante Gabriel Rossetti's muse, and the epitome of a style of femininity celebrated by the group. In fact, she too was a painter, although her attempts to succeed in this male-dominated calling were fraught with difficulty, disappointment and the condescending patronage of her lover and of John Ruskin. William Morris's wife, Janey, and his daughter Mary both worked in subordination to him in his business, although his daughter was responsible for the embroidery section, in charge of a cohort of women workers; and Morris was sadly tolerant of Janey's relationship with Rossetti. The lives of these women bore no very close relationship to the accepted picture of Victorian society as one in which women were at all times rigidly policed and controlled, and one in which a departure from convention was irreversible and fatal (see Marsh, 1985; Marsh and Nunn, 1989). Indeed, William Acton (1968) himself acknowledged that prostitution was but a passing phase in the lives of many women, and one that by no means usually ended in disaster, disease and death. Indeed, for him, that was one of the most troubling aspects of the 'great social evil' – that fate did *not* appropriately punish its practitioners.

So, while it would be unwise to generalise from the varying fates of these women, the feminist analysis of the Pre-Raphaelite representations of them in art at the very least underplays or misses a whole range of inconsistencies and contradictions. No matter how carefully these are acknowledged, the psychoanalytic study of 'regimes of meaning' (Pollock, 1988),[5] dependent upon largely unconscious processes – the study of woman as sign – too often ends with the reduction of woman to sign, devoid of agency.

Janet Wolff's claim that there were no *flâneuses* also disregards the women writers of the nineteenth century. Admittedly they had greater difficulty than men in following their calling, one solution to this being the adoption of a masculine identity. George Sand famously adopted male attire in order to be able freely to roam the streets. Delphine de Girardin, a successful novelist, poet and playwright under her own name, adopted a male pseudonym for the column she wrote in her husband's newspaper, but its content might have been written by any Parisian *flâneur* – although the identity of its author was well known, and from time to time she devoted the column to overtly feminist polemic.

We should therefore be very careful not to overemphasise the passivity and victimisation of nineteenth-century women, and we should not assume that the clear line of demarcation which the bourgeoisie attempted to draw between public and private, as between the virtuous and the fallen woman, was as definitive as it was meant to be. Ideological discourse, from Hegel right through to Mrs Beeton's *Book of Household Management*, continually reworked the ideologies of women's role and separate spheres, so that philosophy itself was gendered, yet in attaching so much weight to these constructions we lose sight of women's own resistance to and reworking of these systems of thought.

While middle-class women were represented as passive icons of femininity, working-class women were often described a wholly unfeminine. The pamphlets and reports of philanthropists and reformers, which were literary representations as well as polemics, characterised them as violent, wild and bestial. They were insolent and defied the observers' codes of morality. 'Their carelessness, their frivolity, their audacious impudence are tirelessly catalogued. These indomitable, intoxicated furies seem to fear nothing and nobody' (Barret-Ducrocq, 1991: 31). Having for the most part no 'private sphere' to be confined to – their homes in the slums being so vestigial – they thronged the streets, and this made them appear as a major threat to bourgeois order. To read the journalism of the mid- to late-nineteenth century is to be struck by their presence rather than their absence.

Even these women did not inhabit the streets on the same terms as men, however, and many of them may have engaged in prostitution at some point in their lives. Perhaps the prostitutes were even the working-class *flâneuses*, since they were often represented as the female equivalent of the *flâneur*, just as the grisette was the counterpart to the bohemian. These pairings, however, occlude the differences in economic status as well as being somewhat mythical.

The significance of the prostitute was certainly as the representation of the sexualised woman; but prostitution was also a metaphor for the whole new regime of nineteenth-century urbanism. Both Baudelaire and Benjamin viewed the metropolis as the site of the commodity and of commoditisation; and prostitution symbolises commoditisation, mass production and the rise of the masses, all of which phenomena are linked for Benjamin:

> Prostitution opens up the possibility of a mythical communion with the masses. The rise of the masses is, however, simultaneous with that of mass production. Prostitution at the same time appears to contain the possibility of surviving in a world in which the objects of our most intimate use have increasingly become mass produced. In the prostitution of the metropolis the woman herself becomes an article that is mass produced. (Benjamin, 1985: 40)

Contemporary critics have taken Benjamin to task for equating women with sexuality, and for identifying women as the 'problem' of urban space (Gilloch, 1996). Benjamin certainly takes as his starting point Baudelaire's assumption that woman *is* the site of sexuality, although he is not a miso-gynist on the Baudelairean scale. In Baudelaire's writings women represent the loss of nature that appeared as a key feature of urbanisation. The androgynous woman, the lesbian, the prostitute, the childless woman, all arouse both new fears and new possibilities, raising questions – even if they provide no answers – as to the eroticisation of life in the metropolis. Benjamin is well aware that Baudelaire 'never once wrote a prostitute poem from the perspective of the prostitute' (Benjamin, 1985: 42). Adrienne Monnier, he points out, believed that women readers disliked Baudelaire, whereas men enjoyed his work, because 'to the men he represents the depiction and transcendence of the lewd side of their libidinal life, or redemption of certain sides of their libidinal life' (Benjamin, 1985: 44).

As Susan Buck-Morss has pointed out, Benjamin follows Baudelaire in objectifying the prostitute, and, in emphasising the 'heroism' of 'unnatural' types of urban womanhood, he surrounds them with the isolating aura of bourgeois tragedy. For him, as for Baudelaire, the prostitute remains the 'other' (Buck-Morss, 1986). His observations betray a nostalgia for lost naturalness at times (it is the artificial disguise of cosmetics that renders women 'professional'); and in writing of the lesbian as unnatural, sterile, masculine, he perpetuates a stereotype – although, more interestingly, he sees her masculinity as a protest, itself 'modern', against technological urban civilisation.

Nevertheless, it is illuminating to read the Benjamin/Baudelaire com-mentary as an attempt to explore just what were the consequences for sexuality of the expanding metropolis and its new urban forms. It had consequences for masculinity as well as femininity.

The interpretation of the *flâneur* as masterful voyeur underplays the financial insecurity and emotional ambiguity of the role. True, the role was open only to a narrow segment of the population – educated men (and was thus a class-bound as well as a gendered concept, as Griselda Pollock (1988) points out); but it often led to poverty and obscurity. An excessive emphasis on 'the Gaze' occludes – ironically – the extent to which the *flâneur* was actually working as he loitered along the pavement or delved into the underworld of the 'marginals'. It also obscures the enormous anxiety which the discourse on the *flâneur* expresses.

The *flâneur* characteristically appears as marginal. Baudelaire aligned himself with all the marginals of society, with the prostitutes, the ragpickers, the drunkards. This was not just the usual identification of a 'lumpen' intelligentsia with its underclass counterpart, it was rather that Baudelaire anticipated Benjamin in interpreting the society in which he lived in terms of an overwhelming commoditisation. The whole society was engaged in a sort of gigantic prostitution; everything was for sale, and the writer was one of the most prostituted of all, since he prostituted his art. Such a view implies that this 'art' is sacred, it relies on ideas about genius and the superiority of the artist; but it also reflects the real insecurity and poverty of the nineteenth-century freelance, and the desperation experienced, or certainly expressed, by many of Baudelaire's contemporaries and friends.

For Benjamin, the unease of the *flâneur* expresses a more generalised insecurity and diseased consciousness. He described the metropolis as a labyrinth. The over-used adjective 'fragmentary' is appropriate here, because what distinguishes metropolitan life from rural existence is the continual brushing against strangers and the experience of observing bits of the 'stories' men and women carry with them, without ever knowing their conclusions, so that life ceases to form itself into continuous narrative but becomes instead a series of anecdotes, dreamlike, insubstantial or ambiguous. Meaning is obscure, committed emotion cedes to irony and detachment. The fragmentary and incomplete nature of urban experience generates its melancholy: a sense of nostalgia, of loss for lives never known, of experiences that can only be guessed at.

Benjamin interprets Baudelaire's obsession with 'spleen' as a pointer towards the deeper meanings of the urban spectacle and the *flâneur*'s apparently inconsequential existence. At the heart of Benjamin's meditation on the *flâneur* is the ambivalence towards urban life already mentioned, a sorrowful engagement with the melancholy of cities. This melancholy seems to arise partly from the enormous, unfulfilled promise of the urban spectacle, the consumption, the lure of pleasure and joy, always destined to be somehow disappointed, or else undermined by the obvious poverty and exploitation of so many who toil to bring pleasure to the few.

Benjamin's critique identifies the 'phantasmagoria', the dream world of the urban spectacle, as the false consciousness generated by capitalism. The crowd may look but not touch, yet this tantalising falsity – and even the very visible misery of prostitutes and the homeless – is aestheticised, and overcomes the observer like a narcotic dream. Benjamin expresses a utopian longing for something other than this urban dream labyrinth. Indeed, utopianism is more generally a key theme of nineteenth- and twentieth-century writings about 'modern life'. In Max Weber, in Marxist discourse, in the writings of postmodernism, the same theme is found: the melancholy, the longing for 'the world we have lost', although what it is that has been lost is no longer clear. Strangely, the urban scene comes to represent utopia and dystopia simultaneously.

For Benjamin the *flâneur* is not only economically insecure, nor does he represent simply the general angst of modernity. He is also sexually insecure. The labyrinth not only describes a mood; it has a specific sexual meaning: male impotence. It is, suggests Benjamin, 'the home of the hesitant. The path of someone shy of arrival at a goal easily takes the form of a labyrinth. This is the way of the [sexual] drive in those episodes which precede its satisfaction' (Benjamin, 1985: 40). The voyeurism encouraged by the commoditised spectacle leads to the attenuation and deferral of satisfaction. This, too, relates to Baudelaire's 'spleen', a mood or temperament that determines his vision of the city. Gambling, wandering and collecting are all activities, suggests Benjamin, waged (or wagered) against spleen – but unsuccessfully, for the *flâneur*'s routines are repetitive and monotonous, and, as Benjamin ominously observes: 'for people as they are today there is only one radical novelty, and that is always the same: death. Petrified unrest is also the formula for the image of Baudelaire's life, a life which knows no development' (Benjamin, 1985: 40). The *flâneur*'s endless strolling is an example of 'eternal recurrence', the eternal recurrence of the new, which is 'always ever the same'. And the monster at the heart of the labyrinth is the Minotaur, the monster waiting to kill. Baudelaire's spleen is a kind of death: 'male impotence – the key figure of solitude' (Benjamin, 1985: 40).

If, therefore, there could never be a female *flâneur*, it would be because the *flâneur* himself never existed, since he was but the embodiment of the special blend of excitement, boredom and horror evoked in the new metropolis, and the disintegrative effect of this on the masculine identity. He turns out to be like Poe's 'Man of the Crowd', in being a figure of solitude who is never alone, and who, when singled out, vanishes. He is a figure to be deconstructed, a shifting projection of the angst of modernity rather than a solid embodiment of male bourgeois power. Benjamin likens him to 'the idler whom Socrates engaged as his partner in discussion in the Athenian market place. . . . Only there is no longer a Socrates and so he remains unengaged. And even the slave labour has come to an end which guaranteed him his idleness' (Benjamin, 1985: 47). He floats with no material base, living on his wits, and, lacking the patriarchal discourse that assured him of meaning, is compelled to invent a new one.

The *flâneur* therefore represented not the triumph of masculine power, but its attenuation. A wanderer, he embodied the Oedipal under threat. The male gaze failed to annihilate the castrate, woman. On the contrary, anonymity annihilates *him*. His masculinity is unstable, caught up in the violent dislocations that characterised urbanisation. In Baudelaire, desire is polarised between perversity and a 'mystical consummation', a split still considered to be the key to Victorian sexuality (but which has not been overcome). The split is constitutive of male impotence; and the metaphors of stone and petrifaction in Baudelaire's poetry hint at this ruin of desire (Buci-Glucksmann, 1986: 226).[6]

The turbulent metropolis in the industrial period is a 'transgressive' space, which 'dislocates established frontiers and forces apparent opposites together in thought' (Buci-Glucksmann, 1986: 221). It is the *mise-en-scène* of the disintegration of masculine potency. It is an agoraphobic, giddy space, productive of hysteria, terror. The image of the labyrinth conceals this other way of experiencing the threat of urban space – as too open, causing whomsoever ventures into it to become totally destabilised. Agoraphobic space tempts the individual who staggers across it to do anything and everything – commit a crime, become a prostitute. It is the location of the *acte gratuite* and of the Dadaistic attack on meaning.

The only defence against transgressive desire is to turn either oneself or the object of desire to stone. One such attempt may be the representation of women in art as petrified, fixed sexual objects. Another is the transformation of the masculine self into its own object of desire. This is the project of the dandy, who also in the process turns himself to stone.

It is the *flâneur*, and not his impossible female counterpart, who is invisible. He dissembles the perversity and impossibility of his split desires, attempting an identification with their object, and wrenching his 'heroism' out of this defeat: 'The pageant of fashionable life and the thousands of floating existences – criminals and kept women – which drift about the underworld of a great city . . . prove to us that we have only to open our eyes to recognise our heroism' (Baudelaire, 1992: 107).

The heroism, for both sexes, is in sheer survival. It lies also in the ability to perceive and understand the beauty and individuality as well as the ugliness and melancholy of urban life. The act of creating meaning, seemingly so arbitrary, is heroic in itself. The zealous reformers saw themselves as heroic in daring to plunge into the hell of the slums, but ultimately more truthful – and thus braver – was the disturbed glance of the *flâneur* as he stoically recorded what he saw and acknowledged in his own person the challenge to patriarchal thought and existence constituted by the city of modernity.

Notes

1. The entry is headed *flâneur/flâneuse*, but refers exclusively to the masculine throughout the article. A second meaning of *flâneuse* is noted: the name of a reclining chair, illustrated in the entry, its name presumably an allusion to the idleness of its occupant.
2. My thanks to Tony Halliday for drawing my attention to this pamphlet.

3. Susan Buck-Morss (1986) has pointed out that the image of the Medusa's head is frequently used to refer to the castrating potential of the urban woman, and especially the woman of the revolutionary crowd. See also Hertz (1983). There is a feminist tradition of the subversion of this image: see Cixous (1980).

4. Ocular imagery, in fact, is one example. In postmodern discourse there has been much criticism of the overvaluation of the visual, the visual terrorism of modernism being held to be one of its major crimes. Doreen Massey, for example, has written:

> It is now a well-established argument, from feminists, but not only from feminists, that modernism both privileged vision over the other senses and established a way of seeing from the point of view of an authoritative, privileged and male position . . . the privileging of vision impoverishes us through deprivation of other forms of sensory perception. (Massey, 1991: 45)

Luce Irigary made a similar point in *Speculum of the Other Woman* (1985). Martin Jay, however, writes, in the context of a discussion of the work of Michel Foucault, of 'a discursive or paradigm shift in twentieth-century French thought in which the denigration of vision supplanted its previous celebration'. He suggests that

> it may be time to begin probing the costs as well as benefits of the anti-ocular counter-enlightenment. Its own genealogy needs to be demystified, not in order to restore a naive faith in the nobility of sight, but rather to cast a little light on the manifold implications of its new ignobility. (Jay, 1986: 196)

The feminist critique of vision and its 'mastery', aligning it simplistically with the masculine, is part of this new problem rather than the solution of an old one, and seems a rather rebarbative extension of the domain of the politically correct.

5. This is not to deny Griselda Pollock's sensitive analysis in its own terms of representations of Elizabeth Siddall in the chapter here referred to: 'Woman as Sign in Pre-Raphaelite Literature: The Representation of Elizabeth Siddall'.

6. Buci-Glucksmann suggests that there is a partial convergence of Benjamin's analysis of Baudelaire with Lacanian thought.

8

THE INVISIBLE *FLÂNEUR*: AFTERWORD

Sometime in the mid-1980s cultural sociologists and critics discovered and became fascinated by the *flâneur* as a key figure of modernity. Just why this was so is not clear. It may have had to do with the parallel interest developing at the same period in the sociology of consumption, with a more general interest in the nature of the postmodern city, and with the revival of city centres through culture and the growth of tourism. In 1994 the publication of *The Flâneur*, edited by Keith Tester, signified a high point of interest, but not even the insightful and informative articles in his collection could resolve the ambiguity of the elusive loiterer, nor explain his revived popularity.

If the *flâneur* himself was mysterious and ambiguous, the interest contemporary critics took in him was ambivalent. Academic writers seem unsure, or disagree, whether the *flâneur* belongs to the past or still exists today. Some writers have celebrated the *flâneur*, others have seen this figure as merely a narcissist, a privileged bourgeois who functions to endorse and even celebrate the commodification of urban existence. To the first group, to observe the passing crowd, to loiter in shops and cafés, to explore forgotten corners of cities, is to uncover the secret of urban modernity, but to the second it merely reveals its meaningless banality.

For Baudelaire, the *flâneur* is a poet, who by reason of his vocation triumphs over the spectacle of the crowd in giving it meaning (Tester, 1994: 4–5). Yet the literary success of *flânerie* was due to the nineteenth-century *feuilleton* and its main literary form was not poetry but a journalism that peaked, according to Peter Fritzsche (1996), in popularity in turn-of-the-century Berlin (see also Sprengel, 1998).

Some writers suggest that there can still be *flâneurs* in contemporary cities. For them shopping malls and theme parks, especially but not exclusively Disneyland and Disney World, become locations for the new *flânerie*. Yet many urban theorists discuss these contemporary spaces in overwhelmingly negative terms. Postmodern pessimists feel that the individuals trapped in West Edmonton Mall or the Epcot Center lose any sense of mastery over the environment. These are certainly not poets, or even journalists, but seem to writers such as Zygmunt Bauman to be cultural dupes or dopes, described by the visiting sociologist with fascinated horror:

The pursuit of aimless leisure here approaches the surreal. . . . West Edmonton . . . is not such much a shopping city as a fully integrated consumer fantasy that succeeds in being mindlessly mellifluous, utterly ridiculous and absolutely out of this world. . . . The pleasure is in being part of a quietly lunatic alternative universe where the thin line that divides shopping from entertainment . . . [is] almost totally erased. (Bauman, 1994: 150–1)

In the 1970s the French critic Louis Marin (1977) described Disneyland as a 'degenerate utopia'. Commentators such as Umberto Eco in *Travels in Hyperreality* (Eco, 1986) and Jean Baudrillard in *America* (Baudrillard, 1988) responded to these spaces with, at best, satirical cynicism. This is the gaze of the European *flâneur* as he views the weird eccentricities and vulgar excesses of American culture. In this respect, it is the commentator alone, not the tourist hordes, and certainly not the indigenous population, who qualifies as *flâneur*. The shopping mall or the theme park could nevertheless provide a contemporary setting for his or her activities; indeed, against those who argue that the *location* for *flânerie* has disappeared, proponents of the idea that the activity continues claim that these new sites correspond to the nineteenth-century street.

Susan Buck-Morss goes further, suggesting that the activities of the zapping radio listener, the television watcher, the Internet surfer and the package tour tourist are those of the latter-day *flâneur*. She finds 'traces of *flânerie*' in many of the activities of mass society, particularly in the 'merely imaginary gratification provided by advertising, illustrated journals, fashion and sex magazines, all of which go by the *flâneur*'s principle of "look but don't touch"' (Buck-Morss, 1986: 105).

There are also artists for whom *flânerie* is the raw material of all their work. The novelist Iain Sinclair is one example, especially in his non-fiction exploration of London, *Lights Out for the Territory* (Sinclair, 1997).

Yet the ambiguity of the *flâneur* is as striking as ever. It is still uncertain whether she or he is simply strolling, loitering and looking (window shopping) or whether these activities must be transformed into a representation – journalism, film, novel – in order to qualify as *flânerie*. Women are especially caught in this ambiguity. When I suggested that nineteenth-century prostitutes might be considered as the *flâneuses* of their time I was being (intentionally) provocative, and one telling argument advanced against this view was that prostitutes are not strolling and observing, but are *working*. Some feminists have taken this argument further and pointed out that even as shoppers women are working rather than simply loitering and observing. That the 'classic' male *flâneur* might also be working – in the sense of collecting material for his writing or painting as he strolled the streets – is seen as somehow different from the activities of women, whether prostitutes or housewives. There is a further ambiguity in that whereas the window shopping and strolling of the *flâneur* seems partly to qualify because it is vaguely sexualised, the overtly sexual activities or intentions of the prostitute do not, perhaps for the very reason that they are *insufficiently* ambiguous.

So confusion remains whether the *flâneur* is redeemed by his dedication to *creative* work, or whether we include the activities of the tourist in the category. What seems to be excluded is the purposeful walking of office workers, housewives and others whose passage through the streets is utilitarian, a necessary journey, rather than an end in itself. Even this, however, seems implicitly to become pedestrian *flânerie* in Michel de Certeau's essay 'Walking in the City', when he describes the 'language' of the routes taken by individuals through the city labyrinth (Certeau, 1984).

The debate whether women are excluded from the role of *flâneur* by reason of their gender may be unresolvable because the disagreements between feminists stem from divergent philosophical and/or political positions. An interesting recent collection of essays about women in the Weimar period comes little closer to a conclusion than earlier debates, although it produces rich new material in support of both sides of the argument (Ankum, 1997). This argument goes beyond questions concerning the meaning of shopping and strolling. The Lacanian theory of the male gaze, most famously developed by Laura Mulvey (1975), but widely adopted by feminist art and film critics, has been extraordinarily and rather bafflingly influential. Perhaps the explanation is that the theory provides rich possibilities for perceptive and elaborate interpretations of cultural products, on the one hand, and subjective experience, on the other. Yet it reduces feminist theory to an account of female subjectivity, and, in political terms, a pessimistic one at that. The Lacanian room, or labyrinth, has no exit, and the political goals of equality and justice become meaningless and irrelevant in the light of the gendered construction of the unconscious. The ultimate truth is a gendered, binary psychic universe. It follows that the main political consequence of Lacanian theory (if, indeed, it can be described as political) is a continual reworking and dwelling on the ways in which femininity is endlessly reconstructed and reproduced, and a resolute pessimism in terms of the possibility of external change for women. Insofar as the analyses of Griselda Pollock and Janet Wolff conform to this theoretical framework in their work on women painters and the impossibility of the female *flâneur*, they are thus, for all their virtues, overdeterministic and ahistorical. For them, on the other hand – and for many feminists – analyses such as my own, which emphasise the more optimistic aspects of historical change for women, seem like, and may even be misread as, a denial that women are oppressed at all (Wolff, 1994: 135), which was never my intention. I have always taken it as too obvious even to mention that women are not equal with men, either in the nineteenth century or today. Professional women on high salaries are obviously better placed than working-class or unemployed women, and also have better life chances than working-class men – or, for that matter, than the majority of men from ethnic minorities. Even these women, however, are not equal with the men of their own class, and they are still at risk of violence from 'men in general'. Gender, class and ethnicity intersect in complex ways. Yet it is still true that, worldwide, men own 90 per cent of the wealth, and women do 90 per cent of the work. A gender hierarchy existed in the nineteenth-century western city and persists to this day, even if in an altered form.

It is not this obvious point that divides feminists. As I suggested in the previous chapter, the differences seem to lie in the weight attached to change. Janet Wolff has discussed Gwen John's life as an example of the gendered nature of female artists' lives. It would certainly be difficult to deny that women artists in Paris then had greater difficulty than their male colleagues in achieving recognition and being taken seriously. In artistic, as in more conventional circles, women were perceived as inferior in every way, and Janet Wolff's description of Gwen John's life as an artist in Paris in the early years of the twentieth century, her concern with her appearance, and her exposed situation as a single woman in the street, in cafés and in department stores, emphasises the negative aspects of these pursuits and positions them as different aspects of her oppressed existence (Wolff, 1994).

Yet by 1900 there did at least exist a colony of independent women artists in Paris. They were gaining access to the various training schools for painters and sculptors, made significant contributions to modern move- ments in art, and in some case enjoyed considerable success, although they continued to be marginalised by critics and dealers (see Garb, 1994; Perry, 1995). There is also more than one way of interpreting Gwen John's own remarks about her sorties into the streets and cafés of the city. Alicia Foster (1999), for example, interprets her attitude to dress more positively. I do not see how it betrays feminism to emphasise the hopeful aspects of a changing situation, rather than forever insisting on the negative and unchanging aspects of male prejudice and psychic formation. Perhaps Zygmunt Bauman's course is the most reasonable; he sees the identity of *flâneur* as having moved from masculine to feminine: '*flâneurisme*'s modern/ postmodern history may be, with but a little stretching, told as one of the feminisation of the *flâneur*'s ways' (Bauman, 1994: 47).

One final point, however, should be made. The male gaze concentrates on women who are young and are constructed as sexually desirable. This is a heterosexual discourse. Women could escape 'the Gaze' if they were old or if they forwent the masquerade of womanliness. Old women and drably dressed women do become invisible, and in that invisibility – intended, whether consciously or not, as annihilation – there is a kind of negative freedom; but also a kind of social extinction.

An example of this freedom in practice was the life and work of the German graphic artist Jeanne Mammen in 1920s Berlin. The Weimar 'New Woman' with her short hair and boyish figure was an ambiguous and contested figure. Mammen recorded in her illustrations of Berlin life both 'the ambivalence of the women promenading the boulevards' and the alliances made by these women with one another – women as friends, *surviving* in the city. She herself made maximum use of her own freedom:

[She] travelled through the wealthy west and poor east of the city, through pubs, seedy bars and dance halls, the pleasure centres of the rich, the demimonde and the underworld. Her own freedom of action is almost on a level with that available to

9

LOOKING BACKWARD

Urban Nostalgia

Ay, in the very temple of delight
Veil'd Melancholy has her sovran shrine.

John Keats, 'Ode on Melancholy'

For a few years in the 1960s I left London to live in the Midlands city of Leicester. To return thirty years later in very different circumstances, to address a conference, naturally awoke a sense of the past and of change. More unexpectedly, I experienced a feeling of warmth towards a city I had disliked and where I had not been happy. Indeed, the visit was more than a trip to a no-longer-existing past. It was also an encounter with a long-vanished self. And it was filled with a sense of nostalgia.

This ghost of my past self was someone I did not wish to meet again. Then I had been a social worker in a group of academic sociologists, a hanger-on, dissatisfied with work to which I was unsuited, a resentful victim of low self-esteem. I had blamed Leicester for my frustration. Place and mood had reinforced each other, as they often do. I had felt myself marooned in the Midlands, and had longed to escape. To one who had always lived in a vast metropolis, Leicester had seemed small and suffocating.

Yet this feeling was not entirely subjective, for in the early post-war period Leicester was an archetype of provincial life. It proudly publicised itself as the richest city in Europe. It was rich because it had one of the highest rates of female employment in Britain, and probably in Europe, in the knitting, textiles and typewriter factories. In other words, its 'wealth' was working-class, or rather the then much-discussed working-class affluence of fat wage packets but little capital accumulation.

'Affluent' as it was, Leicester had pockets of poverty, notably the notorious Braunstone Estate, frequently visited by social workers. This was a vile example of the 1920s planning fashion for municipal estates built on garden suburb lines. By the 1960s it had degenerated into a place where weeds and couch grass had replaced lawns, where old-fashioned prams had been abandoned, bent and screwed up like enormous dead spiders, and where mothers used to speak darkly of 'the Cruelty'. The Cruelty was a person, a large, bluff, breezy NSPCC inspector.

In the popular sociological language of the period, Braunstone was a subculture, but in retrospect it seems an extraordinarily unthreatening place, bearing little resemblance to the current stereotype of the sink estate populated with crack dealers, lone mothers and roaming gangs of hot-rodders. There was poverty, and no doubt 'cruelty' and petty crime in Braunstone, and there were national panics about juvenile delinquency and rising crime rates, but by comparison with today Braunstone seemed a subculture at ease with itself, calm and complacent.

Perhaps it was just part of Leicester's dullness that it couldn't even produce any decent deviants. Thirty years previously J.B. Priestley had visited the place and had commented on its blandness:

> The citizens, who are proud of the place, boast that it is one of the cleanest manufacturing towns in this country, and they are quite right: it is. They also boast that it has a very enterprising town council, and I have no doubt that it has. . . . It is comparatively prosperous. You feel almost at once that it is a very worthy borough that is deservedly getting on in the world. But it is hard to believe that anything much has ever happened there. . . . The town seems to have no atmosphere of its own. I felt I was quite ready to praise it, but was glad I did not live in it. There are many worse places I would rather live in. It seemed to me to lack character, to be busy and cheerful and industrial and built of red brick, and to be nothing else. (Priestley, 1977: 115)

In the 1960s Priestley's condescending account still fitted. Low-profile immigrants from the Baltic states had settled there after 1945, and by the sixties there was a large Asian community in the city, but this hardly affected the perceived homogeneity of the place. Leicester was *too* homogeneous. A city that appears not to change seems stagnant.

The historian J.F.C. Harrison implied as much when he made a return visit to the Leicester he'd known as a child in the 1920s:

> The trams were missing . . . (what a grinding and squeaking they had made as they negotiated the right-angle bend into East Park Road). . . . It was a strange feeling: the names of the streets were the same and brought back memories. . . . I felt a bit like Rip Van Winkle. The newsagents and sweet shops were still much as before, but the names above them were Indian. The women wore saris below their coats and anoraks. . . . It would be an exaggeration to say that this added an exotic touch; at the most it modified the outward signs of a typical English, lower middle-class district. (Harrison, 1995: 8)

It may, however, have been because of its very homogeneity that Leicester featured in so many post-war British fictions, a series of 'angry young man' novels whose theme was the longing to escape. The hero of C.P. Snow's novel sequence *Strangers and Brothers* was nurtured in and rebelled against Leicester. William Cooper's autobiographical novel was even entitled *Scenes from Provincial Life*. Philip Larkin, who worked at the university library for a number of years, judged this to be 'the great Leicester novel' (Motion, 1993: 238), but Cooper's star has waned, and it now seems doubtful if there could in any case even be such a thing as the *'great'* Leicester novel. If there were it would more likely be the best-known British campus novel of the 1950s, Kingsley Amis's *Lucky Jim*, published in 1954. Malcolm Bradbury, too, was inspired by Leicester to write a university novel, the 1959 *Eating People is Wrong*.

It is hard to understand how so boring a city could have inspired so much fictional creativity, but to reread these novels is to understand why. Then one realises that not just Leicester, but *Britain itself* was (or seemed) astonishingly monotone then. No wonder Leicester became the archetype for a bleak world of aesthetic impoverishment, mental desperation and erotic deprivation. The austerity of the time, at least as described, was only partly alleviated by a sense that the protagonists of these books were engaged in a serious existential search for the moral meaning of life – and *Lucky Jim* lacked even that redeeming feature. It made me laugh aloud when I had read it, aged nineteen, but my rereading revealed it as a veritable compendium of anti-intellectual, anti-artistic and woman-hating attitudes. They had seemed quite normal in the 1950s.

Contemporary Leicester has clubs, bars and restaurants in abundance, but in the 1950s it was not unusual in *lacking* cafés, music venues and shops taken for granted by even the most impoverished student of today. There were only pubs *anywhere*, apart from the oases provided by coffee bars (Malcolm Bradbury's hero makes a daring sortie to the only Leicester coffee bar, a dimly lit roomful of doomy poseurs). This was just how things *were* when Harold Macmillan was telling the British people they'd never had it so good; and while the pay packets of the workers got fatter, a sometimes philistine yet earnest intelligentsia groped fitfully towards hedonism through the thick penumbra of a decaying puritanism.

Leicester in the 1960s was caught in that transitional moment. It was in the process, perhaps without fully realising it, of abandoning John Major's nation at ease with itself. What that Conservative Prime Minister mis-remembered as a world of moral certainty and quiet contentment in the 1950s was becoming in Leicester around 1965 a hesitancy. There was a final abandonment of those provincial, puritan values as Britain moved, with something between a sidle and a lurch, towards the frivolity of the fully consumerised society.

The hero of Bradbury's *Eating People is Wrong*, equated puritanism and provincialism, yet although he at first seemed to dismiss Leicester out of hand – 'there were, indeed parts of the town in which one felt a real sense of place; but most of the time one felt a sense of anywhere' (i.e. nowhere) – he elsewhere acknowledged Leicester's confidence and civic splendour, created in 'a riot of Victorian self-help':

> It was sheer Tawney: religion and the rise of capitalism. . . . As business and non-conformity boomed, the former market town had erected Victorian Gothic churches, a Victorian Gothic town hall . . . a temperance union hall, a mechanics institute, a prison, and a well-appointed lunatic asylum. (Bradbury, 1959: 19–20)

(The asylum later housed the university in its early years.)

Returning to Leicester, it was possible for me too to be more responsive than in that other, earlier life to the charm and graciousness of the red brick of the Victorian monuments and the Edwardian suburbs with their shrub-beries, lawns and memories of moral solidity, civic responsibility and paternalism. Even though many of them had ceased to be family homes, to become instead university and business offices, they still spoke of that lost 'provincial life', in an age when the word 'provincial' has lost much of its resonance.

The contrast between provincial and metropolitan – which was the central theme of many a nineteenth-century hero's narrative – no longer inspires. Who is not clothed today in the blasé attitude which, for Georg Simmel, characterised only the urban dweller? Balzac's Lucien de Rubempré felt like 'a frog at the bottom of a well' in his home town of Angoulême, but today a changed sense of space and distance has muted this contrast.

The 1959 film of another provincial novel of the 1950s, John Braine's *Room at the Top* (1957), reinforces the feeling that a whole separate provincial English world, the world of the proudly, resolutely *local* Midlands or Northern industrial city, has disappeared, or been transformed beyond recognition. To Braine's hero, Victorian Bradford symbolised what seemed like the permanence and power of the elite he aspired to join. Yet even as he plotted his rise to power, urban planners were seized with a thirst for change and the modern, believing their large-scale demolition and reconstruction would solve social problems and usher in a new era of leisure and consumption in a shiny new environment. The new city centres were to be both classless and modern. The dark splendour of Bradford's city centre was to be replaced by the flat blandness of New Town modernity.

The post-war rebuilding of the Birmingham Bull Ring was another example of this, publicised as a miracle of the modern age. The glossy leaflets distributed when it opened described 'stiletto-proof' flooring and the revolutionary benefits of air-conditioning, which would allow visitors to leave their 'top coats' at the door. The merits of 'continental' restaurants were detailed, along with the ease of travel by escalator, while the introduction of Muzak – said to be 'the end product of twenty-five years research experience' – would, it was claimed, when piped through the halls, create a 'warm, gay and welcoming atmosphere'. Later, there was even a Cliff Richard film about this reconstruction, in which Sir Cliff played the part of a property developer and sang a song which went: 'Now I believe that you're a tough town and that's the way I like 'em,/Concrete City I'm not that easily thrown' (Adams, 1995). That, however, was in the 1970s, after disillusionment had set in, when everyone knew about the Poulson/T. Dan Smith corruption scandal in Newcastle, when empty office blocks had become eyesores, and when tearing town city centres had ceased to be fashionable.

In the 1990s the 1960s revamp of the Bull Ring was in its turn scheduled to be torn down and replaced by a more traditional (read 'heritage') version of the city centre. Then it became fashionable, paradoxically, to feel almost as nostalgic about the bright, modernist optimism of the 1960s as about nineteenth-century Paris or Jane Jacobs' Greenwich Village. Once an experience is safely in the past it may be invested with a charm it lacked at the time.

However, as in Birmingham, nostalgia is still more likely to take concrete form in re-cobbled precincts evocative of pre-industrial city centres than in the shape of post-war modernity. Patrick Wright (1985) has analysed this British (but not exclusively British) obsession with national heritage as an 'accommodation of Utopia'. 'It borrows many of the trappings of the English utopia (of Arthurian legend, of Blake and Samuel Palmer, of Morris and the Pre-Raphaelites) but it stages utopia not as a vision of possibilities which reside in the real . . . but as a [separate] realm existing alongside the everyday' (Wright, 1985: 78). The result is not memory, but amnesia as the reconstitution of the past somehow effaces its actuality.

This suggests that there may, then, be a difference between memory and nostalgia. My only visit to Leicester between the 1960s and 1995 was to view the Biba exhibition in 1993. This re-created the Biba boutiques of the late sixties as well as displaying her fashions, so emblematic of the period. There were also Biba boxes, cosmetics and ceramics for sale. The rooms were crowded with middle-aged women walking round with their friends and exchanging memories, and the visitors' book was crammed with long autobiographical extracts, most of which played variations on the theme of the golden sixties. Fashion, simply because it is so ephemeral, is particularly apt to produce feelings of nostalgia, and often that sense of quaintness which seems essential to the feeling. It is possible to smile indulgently at a former self who actually wore mini skirts and feather boas, armholes so tight they gave you chest pains, collars as large as spaniels' ears, and sleeves that vied in volume with those of any bishop.

In other words, there is a subtle disavowal at the heart of nostalgia. This may be the reason for the lurking moral ambiguity that surrounds it. It is likely to be disparaged – we 'wallow' in nostalgia, which suggests it is perceived as sentimental and self-indulgent. On the other hand, the *Shorter Oxford Dictionary* defines nostalgia as a translation of the German *Heimweh* or homesickness, 'a form of melancholia caused by prolonged absence from one's country or home'. Yet this seems inadequate. It gestures to the need for a sense of belonging and familiarity, of identity and roots, but it doesn't capture the ambivalence of nostalgia.

Raphael Samuel has suggested that one legacy of Romanticism is the way in which 'memory and history are so often placed in opposite camps'. Memory, he says, has been constructed as 'subjective, a plaything of the emotions, indulging its caprices, wallowing in its own warmth; history, in principle at least, was objective, taking abstract reason as its guide and submitting its findings to empirical proof' (Samuel, 1994: ix). Nostalgia conforms to this configuration of memory as the province of feeling rather than thought, and may be denigrated for this reason – that it dispenses with a (pseudo-?)scientific rationalism in favour of the truth of feeling.

In 1930s a French historian gave a paper at the Musée Carnavalet, in the Marais district of Paris. He said:

> We are almost at the World's end here in this district of the 'Marais' – the marsh – now so deserted by society, so plebeian and commercial, but which for all its social degeneration has a beauty and poetry that have survived the upheavals of the past 30[0?] years. It is the remnant of a Paris where silent and provincial corners still exist. Where there are grass-grown streets, flanked by mansions that were not built yesterday – the mansions of the old aristocracy, full of memories. (Gillet, 1930: x)

This passage is strongly scented with nostalgia. There is an even greater sense of nostalgia for today's reader, since now it is known that the Marais declined still further after 1945. It only just missed having its square, and its seventeenth-century *hôtels* completely destroyed and redeveloped in the 1960s, and has survived, not as a 'lost corner' of Paris with artisans' *ateliers* and local residents, but as the heart of gay chic and gentrification.

The dominant feeling in Gillet's comments is, however, not a sense of loss, but a sense of pleasure, a pleasure due to the ambivalence of nostalgia. Perhaps ambivalence is not quite the right word for this sense of having an inherently contradictory experience. The author, a Parisian, delights in the un-Parisian nature of this corner of his capital city, a city that, it turns out, is simultaneously a modern capital and a provincial town. At least, it can contain within its modernity an encapsulated experience of another and opposite mood, of provincial melancholy and marginality. The *flâneur* who strolls through this Marais of 1930 can thus imagine that he at one and the same time inhabits an historical past of seventeenth-century grandeur and a present day of dereliction, where the past is, as it were, in disguise, incognito. He can also experience provincial melancholy without unpleasant consequences, since he is not actually living in the provinces. He can enjoy the ghosts of the *ancien régime* while continuing to be a modern citizen in a republic. He can enjoy the present through the lens of the past, and the past through the lens of the present. This may come dangerously close to the sentimentality of vicarious experience without responsibility, but differs both from that and from any sense of pure loss. It is a liminal experience, on the threshold where past meets present. It is a heterotopic experience, which contains within it mutually exclusive emotions.

Nostalgia, therefore, is not exclusively or even primarily about a sense of loss. In their study of Sheffield after the closure of the steel industry, Ian Taylor and Ruth Jamieson demonstrated how advertisements – for beer, for example – played on a memory or invocation of the lost steelworkers' community, its manliness and power, its harshness and yet, in a sense, its joyfulness. They showed, too, how the lives of at least some young men in 1990s Sheffield enacted a strange parody of the ethic of male comradeship and mutual support essential in the tough and dangerous world of the steel mills. Young men still needed the loyalty and trust of their group, only now their lives were organised round petty crime and drugs. What had changed was the economic bargain whereby men had supported women and children; this was replaced by overt expressions of hatred for women and alienation from children (Taylor and Jamieson, 1997: 152–80). The advertisements for beer were perhaps nostalgic, but the anger and grief expressed by the older members of the community at the devastation around them were emotions very different from nostalgia. Nostalgia is never angry. That is perhaps why it may be like Wright's accommodation with utopia.

There is a moral ambiguity about nostalgia. It is a strange emotion. It endows something old and familiar, something that may now exist only or almost only in memory, with a beauty it may never have possessed at the time. Rather than being a longing for the past, or for somewhere far away, it is a re-creation of a past or a place that never was. Wright's 'national heritage' idea of city centres expresses a desire to return to the pedestrian city of the past, even to the industrial city of the nineteenth century, so reviled at the time – but it is unlikely that we should appreciate that past if we were returned to it. We should like to see the Victorian Greek Revival public buildings of Bradford rise again in all their former glory (and that would certainly be an improvement on what replaced them). But who would wish to return to the stifling snobbery and hypocrisy of the Bradford of *Room at the Top*? Who today could bear the Leicester endured by Bradbury, Cooper and Larkin – and even more by Larkin's lover, Monica Jones, so cruelly caricatured by Amis? The 1950s may have seemed peaceful, but beneath the placid surface seethed boredom inflamed by sexual repression, which found an outlet in self-conscious nastiness, while the anti-feminism of the period forced women into hateful choices. Few would really want to go back to all that. Similarly, on my return to Leicester I could afford to acknowledge the expansive solidity and calm of the city in the sixties *because* I was no longer a sulking social worker caught at the wrong end of the different 'liberated' sexism of that period.

Nostalgia is an accommodation with change. To revisit a city after many years was to be made abruptly aware of change, of the tortoise-like process of slow erosion that normally goes unnoticed to those who tread the same streets day after day.

Yet the refusal of change is one of the agendas of the long tradition of utopian writings. Patrick Wright sees utopia 'as a vision of possibilities which reside in the real', but there is another view, explored by Françoise Choay (1997), the utopian wish to 'stop history'. Everything must change – once – but then nothing must change ever again, because everything is already perfect. Cities have featured as templates of the perfect society in many utopian writings, and a contemporary sense of loss in relation to actual cities may be bound up with a subliminal collective awareness of a cultural vision of the perfect city. But whether perfection locates itself in the past or in the future, it makes it almost impossible to accept the messy present. It is therefore not surprising if the vision of the perfect city has frequently, if paradoxically, led to the kind of anti-urbanism found, for example, in William Morris's *News From Nowhere*.

Even a bad past may be retrospectively idealised, for both good and bad reasons: bad because the past can become a lie, but good because it has become part of an individual's accepted identity. Nostalgia may, like utopia, 'stop history', fixing a past as we should like it to have been. At the same time the pleasurable aspect of nostalgia may be in part due to our measuring of the distance we have come. This need not necessarily even be in the sense of progress or improvement, but simply in the sense of experiencing the reality of change, the passage of time, and the existence of that great hinterland of 'lost time' that somehow still lives within us.

At its most rewarding this may become the Proustian understanding, not of the remembrance of things past, but of the retrieval of the past, a movement whereby we also reappropriate the present by understanding and acknowledging that past. Only by not just remembering but by confronting and reinterpreting the past was Proust's hero, Marcel, able to fulfil his destiny. Only by engaging with the changing fabric of the city and by acknowledging change as both loss and enrichment can we adequately approach the experience of living in urban space, without being caught between utopia and decay. When I lived in Leicester I hated it, but in looking back I can recognise both its attractions and my own faults, which I projected onto the city.

Nostalgia, finally, may be a passive emotion. It may bind us insincerely to a touched-up past, a 'national heritage' version of reality. On the other hand nostalgia may produce an awareness that can help us to move beyond it into an acceptance of and an active engagement with the inevitability of change.

10
WRITING THE ROMANCE OF THE SUBURBS
A Review of Literature

The earliest English suburbs were coeval with the industrial revolution. John Nash's Park Village West by Regent's Park in central London, an example of English picturesque style, dates from the Regency period, like his similar model village at Blaise Castle near Bristol. In Park Village West, Nash designed narrow, winding roads flanked by spacious houses whose quaint details, such as gothic turrets, crenellation and dormer windows, lent variety. The almost maze-like layout meant that the whole development 'unfolds itself gradually to the spectator', an example of the use of concealment and surprise, a characteristic carried on into later suburbs (Richards, 1946: 7).

In the mid-nineteenth century, prosperous families retreated to the suburbs to escape the noise, smells, dirt and coarse crowds of the industrial city. The Victorian suburb also expressed their aspiration to aspects of aristocratic lifestyle: the country house, surrounded by park land – in this case a large garden – and the horse and carriage. These early suburbs provided a domestic haven, extending the domestic interior as a realm for the 'angel in the house', the wife and mother. Yet the association of the suburb with conventional bourgeois values was not then as fixed as it was later to become; one of the most distinctive London suburbs of the late nineteenth century was Bedford Park at Turnham Green, which, with its Norman Shaw architecture and Queen Anne-type houses, quickly became a chosen retreat for members of the aesthetic intelligentsia.

The Garden City ideal promoted by Ebenezer Howard and first realised at Letchworth in Hertfordshire, north of London, influenced the design and layout of later suburbs, but J.M. Richards, writing in 1946, explored a fundamental distinction between the Garden City and the suburb. The Garden City, he maintained, is not anarchic enough and is dominated by the expert, whereas the suburb is 'the one hideout of the amateur, on whose participation a living tradition must always depend' (Richards, 1946: 66). The Garden City was planned as a perfect whole; it was indeed an utopian idea; it was meant to be a complete city in itself, although freed from all the baneful aspects of urban life, in particular vast size.

The suburb represented a different ideal and had a different purpose. Nevertheless, the winding roads and culs-de-sac of the Garden City, and its reworking of rural styles in architecture, was influential in the design of suburbs. These stylistic features were also evident in the municipal suburbs laid out by the London County Council shortly before the First World War, for example at White Hart Lane in Tottenham and Oak Village in Acton.

Efficient public transport systems and cheap workmen's fares were in place by the last decade of the nineteenth century. This enabled working-class families to move from city centres to the terrace housing that was erected around city centres. However the heyday of the traditional, privately built and privately financed suburb was the period between the First and Second World Wars, especially the decade from 1928 to 1939. In London this was when 'Metroland' was built, a world of suburbs quite distant from the centre of the capital, with speculative housing built on cheap land made accessible by the tentacles of the underground railway system. The peculiarities of the economy at this time resulted in exceptionally low labour and raw material costs, combined with unusually low interest rates. At the same time skilled workers and white-collar workers who continued in employment, particularly in the Midlands and the South of England, actually saw their incomes rising in real terms. It was possible to buy a house in the suburbs for as little as £600; a small down-payment and low weekly mortgage rates made a house of one's own for the first time an achievable dream come true.

Architects and planners committed to the Modern Movement, however, subjected the suburbs to a stinging attack, deeply hostile both to the unplanned ribbon development of the typical suburb and to its characteristic architecture. The epithet 'suburban' rapidly became a term of abuse. It was used to indicate not just poor design, but also narrow, lower middle-class morality, an exaggerated concern with domestic cleanliness, conformity to vulgar, conservative taste in interiors and a snobbish 'keeping up with the Joneses'. The Modern Movement had come to dominate architectural thinking and ideology, and modernists brought the full force of their loathing and outrage to bear on the new, semi-detached suburbs.

Paul Oliver (Oliver, Davis and Bentley, 1981) has identified three distinct strands in the attack on the suburbs. First, there was the attack on the whole idea of the suburb. Critics argued that the suburb was destroying the very countryside to which the suburban dwellers were so keen to have access. It was also a non-place, a dormitory for downtrodden office workers who were forced to travel long distances every day to work. It was further denounced as a feminised and trivialised world that emasculated its menfolk who worked long hours in order to maintain ugly, vulgar houses and domestic interiors; the taste displayed by the suburb was fundamentally defective. Within this comprehensive hatred of the suburb there were more specific objections: to the quality of the housing that was being built; and to the rambling and unimaginative layout of estates, which were often monotonous as well as being barren of amenities such as shops and adequate transport, but particularly of places of entertainment and any sort of night life.[1]

A series of BBC radio talks in 1933, 'Design in Modern Life', included the first ever broadcast discussion of modern architecture, and was afterwards published in the BBC weekly magazine, *The Listener*. This talk championed modernism, arguing that 'the next step in the design of dwelling units must be the block or group of dwellings with every centralised service which the sharing of costs makes economically possible' (quoted in Oliver, Davis and Bentley, 1981: 40). In 1940 the influential planner Tom Sharp published *Town Planning*, which made similar arguments. He argued that the suburb was an escape from reality, individualistic and selfish, especially when what was needed was not the suburban sprawl that was destroying the countryside, but the redemption of the towns (Sharp, 1940: 40–5).

The extensive bombing of British cities during the Second World War focused the attention of planners and architects on what might be done after the ending of hostilities, when towns would have to be rebuilt. Many of them saw it as a great opportunity for the Modern Movement. Bombing had already destroyed many ugly Victorian industrial urban centres; rebuilding would be essential, opening the way for utopian modernist cities that would also eradicate 'suburban sprawl'.

The Modern Movement continued to dominate after 1945, and the 1950s and 1960s became the epoch of the tower block. Although the tower block has recently been to some extent rehabilitated, it came to symbolise the failures of modernism. Typical of this phase of modernist thinking was the estate of blocks of flats for 10,000 tenants built in Roehampton, West London, by the London County Council in the 1950s. Roehampton was itself a middle-class suburb, far distant from the centre of London, and local residents protested at the plans to move so many poorer Londoners into this exclusive district.

The London County Council architect William Howell, whose inspiration was Le Corbusier's *Radiant City* and *unité d'habitation*, appears to have wanted to create a city centre within the very suburb he abhorred, for he wrote:

> We went to Roehampton thinking we had a certain mission: we felt this would turn the tide back from the suburban dream . . . a return to the excitement of the city . . . this is what we must do; we don't want to rush out and live in horrid little suburbs and semi-detached homes. . . because we felt it discarded the positive things from the city and got very little in exchange. We saw this in terms of the fact that we wouldn't want to go and live there because everything from the bright lights to the art galleries, the continental restaurants, in short 'life', the things one goes to the city for – it didn't seem to be happening in the suburbs. (Oliver, Davis and Bentley, 1981: 19–20)

Yet some years before, a challenge to confident assumptions of this sort had come from an unlikely champion: J.M. Richards, shortly before he became editor of the *Architectural Review*. This was unexpected because the *Architectural Review* was the voice of the Modern Movement at the time.

The Castles on the Ground (Richards, 1946) was written while its author was still on active service in the Middle East at the end of the Second World War. It was much more than an architectural treatise. It was at one level a nostalgic evocation of 'home', a romantic re-creation of the author's own past as well as of a distant, almost dreamlike place. It was also a serious investigation of popular taste. In it Richards attempted to tease out the specific and unique subjective qualities of the 1930s suburb. He identified its central 'puzzle' as its contradictory quality of being in 'bad taste' and yet appealing to a substantial majority, but he did not dismiss nor patronise the taste it exemplified. Instead he tried to analyse its appeal.

The suburb was, he suggested, 'neither the town spread thin nor the country built close, but a quite different type of development with its own inimitable characteristics'. It succeeded because the suburban home was 'each Englishman's idea of his own home, except for the cosmopolitan rich, a minority of freaks and intellectuals and the very poor'. Even for the very poor 'it is what they would dream about if anyone could dream about what they have never known and if the fight for existence allowed time for much dreaming' (Richards, 1946: 31). Many architects believed that the unique architectural synthesis, the eclecticism, of the suburb was its most disastrous quality, but for Richards this was its chief virtue. For the suburb was

> an ad hoc world, conjured out of nothing. . . . The town evolves its shape from its function, from streets and squares and traffic intersections, and the grouping of buildings; and the country from the adaptation of natural landscapes to human purposes. But the suburb is not primarily a mechanism, nor is it in any sense a modification of something previously existing; it is a world peculiar to itself and – as with a theatre's drop scene – before and behind it there is nothing. Hence the scenic nature of its appearance. (Richards, 1946: 37)

As the embodiment of a dream, Richards felt that the suburb did have a certain utopian quality, but that it was unlike both the literary utopias and the actually existing garden cities in being unplanned and spontaneous. It gave those who lived in it a sense of belonging to a sympathetic world and 'an opportunity of making out of that world something personal to themselves . . . an outlet for their idealistic and creative instincts. The suburb therefore shuts out an unkind world, and to that extent is negative in being escapist' (Richards, 1946: 37).

The Castles on the Ground contained detailed and loving descriptions of every aspect of the suburban scene – the Art Deco Odeon cinemas, the neo-Georgian parades of shops, the advertisements for Ovaltine, the interiors of dairies and cafés. Richards also analysed instead of merely denouncing the architecture. It was, he suggested, a mixture, a compromise between fear of non-conformity and the urge to live fantastically. It bore witness to 'the human vagaries which are the foundation of architectural richness' (Richards, 1946: 192).

The 1930s suburb, in other words, expressed a human desire for self-expression and variety, but combined with a need for security and predictability. 'In a world made unsafe for self sufficiency, suburban architecture can be described as an attempt to create a kind of oasis in which every tree and every brick can be accounted for, to exclude the unpredictable as far as possible from everyday life' (Richards, 1946: 36).

Richards believed, furthermore, that there was something specifically English about the suburb, partly because of the importance of the garden. He suggested that the suburban house and garden formed two parts of a single whole, with the characteristic French windows opening on to the back lawn as a permeable boundary between the two. Richards was appreciative of the decorative themes of the suburban house – touches of Art Deco, stained glass, fake Tudorbethan beams – for even if imitative and hackneyed, they were sincere in what they expressed. By contrast, precisely the fault of the Modern Movement was that it was at some level inauthentic.

For within his celebration of the suburb Richards embedded a critique of modernism. Modern architecture, he suggested, was in danger of making

> the mistake of allowing itself to become a specialised art that can only be appreciated by the minority. For a minority art is a closed art, closed to the warming influence of popular enthusiasm and understanding. It also tends to be dogmatic and to lack the common touch that should enable it to reflect those human vagaries which are the foundation of architectural richness. (Richards, 1946: 37)

More serious even than this dogmatism, he argued, was the way in which the Modern Movement aimed to express utopian socialist ideals, and to represent a socialism already achieved when no such socialist utopia actually existed 'on the ground'. In other words, if the suburb was one kind of dream world, modernism was another, social, or, rather, *socialist*, dream world, and, insofar as it was architecturally represented by actual projects, this modernist socialist utopia was more of a chimera than the suburb. The suburb conformed to actually existing conditions, whereas modernist projects were in a sense false in purporting to give people something that in fact it was not giving them and could not, in the circumstances of the time, give them. Modernism's utopianism was a false promise, impossible of fulfilment.

This being the case, the 'man in the street' was

> following sound instincts in refusing to welcome modern design in all its purity and discipline. If he did so he would be entering a fool's paradise, since he would only find himself enjoying the shadow of the modern world without its substance – the substance being, of course, its economic benefits. (Richards, 1946: 64)

The project of creating socialist housing enclaves in the middle of a capitalist society was doomed to failure.

This did not mean that Richards totally endorsed suburban taste. In a sly swipe at its values he suggested that the dominant aesthetic tastes in any society were always those of the nation's leaders. Suburbia, therefore, was merely 'the preferences of the business class . . . writ large' (Richards, 1946: 59). This modern bourgeois taste was conservative.

The pre-war suburb may have had an imaginative, utopian appeal, but it also provided the nuclear family of the period with many substantial advantages, as J.F.C. Harrison has described. His family moved from inner Leicester to the suburb of Evington in 1936. There,

> a bathroom and indoor lavatory, a front door that no longer opened directly onto the street, a garden with a lawn and flowerbeds – these were things which transformed the quality of family life . . . there were other delights . . . a bay window looking onto the front garden, the leaded lights in the front door, the gleaming white tiles and chromium taps in the bathroom. (Harrison, 1995: 50)

Harrison recognises that the venom directed at the suburb was a covert attack on those who lived in it, an attack on lower middle-class culture in general. He acknowledges nevertheless that although the inter-war suburb was a pleasant place in which to live, and, in particular, provided an exceptionally safe and free environment for children, its culture was indeed inward-looking, narrow and politically conservative. 'Habits of reading were strictly utilitarian: "Is John doing anything?", "No – only reading a book."' (This from his mother, who had been a school teacher.) But ultimately he defends the semi-detached house against its detractors, taking issue with the way in which

> for Orwell, Priestley and leftish writers generally [in the 1930s] it stood for petty bourgeois mediocrity. Yet for millions of ordinary people it was a great step forward. . . . As a form of popular housing it was [an] ideal family house and it allowed for individual tastes and preferences. Pride of possession was fostered and an Englishman's semi-detached house was indeed his castle. (Harrison, 1995: 58)

Harrison suggests, as an historian, that the lower middle-class world of the pre-war suburb has been neglected, dismissed as a part of history too uninteresting to study, but in the 1980s and 1990s several writers did explore the culture of the suburbs. It was probably no accident that as early as 1973 Richards' *The Castles on the Ground* was reprinted, for this was when, in the wake of disillusionment with the tower block, local authorities were discovering rehabilitation, and private developers and architects were discovering postmodern eclecticism.

In 1981, *Dunroamin: The Suburban Semi and its Enemies* was a combative and polemical contribution to the debate. This book seemed in harmony with the early Thatcherist period, when council housing in Britain was being enthusiastically sold off. It was a spirited defence of the thirties suburb and its individualism. It also mounted an intemperate attack on all aspects of the 1930s Modern Movement. The authors of *Dunroamin* dismissed modernism as one long sneer at the petite bourgeoisie, an expression of arrogance and paternalistic elitism, based ultimately on snobbery and self-interest. Its authors claimed that the real reason for the resentment of architects towards the suburbs in the 1930s was that the suburban house was designed not by architects but by builders, and thus threatened both the aesthetic domination of architects and their livelihood. Furthermore, architects could not bear the intrusion of the lower orders into the hitherto exclusive region of *their* suburb, that is, the upper middle-class suburb of the Edwardian period.

Yet – as is frequently the case when the politically correct slur of 'elitism' is deployed – the *Dunroamin* authors applied double standards. They denounced the hostility of the modernists towards the suburb as mere snobbery, but at the same time applauded the aspirations of the new owners of the semi-detached houses along the arterial roads. These new home-owners, however, were just as snobbish, bent on putting a distance between themselves and the municipal housing estate or the mean streets from which they had escaped. Paul Oliver and his co-authors were, however, fully in tune with the 1980s in rejecting the collective ideals of public housing in their defence of suburban individualism.

Nevertheless, behind the polemic there was a nostalgia and an affection for the suburb. Richards, Harrison and Paul Oliver and his co-authors all themselves grew up there, and their texts, interesting in research and polemical terms, are also exercises in remembrance. It may be significant that the imaginative rehabilitation of the suburb is confined to the 'classic' suburb of the 1930s. No comparable literature yet exists that explores the suburbs of the 1980s and 1990s with their rows of identical dwellings of raw red and yellow brick and their new interpretations of old vernacular tropes.

There is no 'magic' or dreamlike quality about these contemporary suburbs, it seems, whereas in retrospect the suburbs of the 1930s have a strangely magical, even surreal, atmosphere. Some have become run down, but many, more peaceful and empty even than in their heyday, seem more prosperous than ever. Many of the enclosed front gardens of Edgware and Bromley have been paved over and turned into carports for classy BMWs and Volvos. In some districts wealthy immigrant families have displaced the aspiring white-collar workers of an earlier period. In others, an ageing population of long-term owners, pensioners now, have difficulty in main-taining their properties. The suburbs of the 1930s are still there, but they are not the suburbs with which the writers discussed above engage with such nostalgia. So, in analysing the 'rise' or heyday of the British suburb, historians and sociologists have embalmed it, and, in celebrating the world of their parents, have, intentionally or not, revealed it unequivocally as a world we have irretrievably lost.

The culture as well as the architecture of the suburbs has been rehabili-tated in recent years. David Chaney (1997) argues that suburban culture embodies utopian aspirations and romantic notions of authenticity. Roger Silverstone (1997) has noted how the search for privacy and the expansion of consumer culture have made of the suburban home a source of individual rather than family and/or class identity formation. Gary Cross

(1997), on the other hand, believes that the suburban way of life has been largely destroyed by consumerism and the long hours of work required to pay for more and more material goods.

Interest in suburban culture may be seen as part of a wider revisionist agenda in cultural and media studies. James Curran has noted the significant contribution of this 'new revisionism' in rejecting the 'elitist pessimism' that was most forcefully expressed by the Frankfurt School of culture critics, in particular Theodor Adorno and Max Horkheimer. 'A key formative influence in this shift,' Curran points out, was Pierre Bourdieu, who 'showed that there was a close correspondence in France between socio-economic position and patterns of taste in art and music. Cultural and aesthetic judgements, he concluded, had no absolute, universal validity but were merely ways of defining, fixing and legitimating social differences' (Curran, 1996: 270).

As discussed in Chapter 1, this influential view has led to a thoroughgoing relativism, or, some would say, 'cultural populism' (McGuigan, 1992), to such an extent that it has become difficult to discuss cultural works in aesthetic terms at all – or has simply seemed irrelevant to do so. The rehabilitation of the suburbs may be seen as part of this trend, one of many attempts to surmount social prejudice and snobbery in order to investigate the meaning of taste(s).

There is a feminist dimension to cultural populism, which has championed just those feminine activities and aspirations that generations of male designers (as it is assumed) sneered at. Judy Attfield, for example, has described the way in which in post-war Britain the New Towns, designed for the most part by architects schooled in the Modern Movement and committed to functionalism, became the site of aesthetic battles between the tastes of the designers and that of the tenants. In Harlow, for example, 'a censorious account of "mistakes" made by tenants appeared in a 1957 review of "Furnishing in the new towns" by *Design* magazine':

> They fight shy of open-plan living . . . there is a strong tendency to shelter behind net curtains. Large windows are obscured by elaborate drapes and heavy pelmets, by dressing table mirrors and large settees. Corners are cut off by diagonally placed wardrobes and sideboards. By careful arranging and draping, the open plan houses are being closed up again, light rooms are darkened and a feeling of spaciousness is reduced to cosy clutter . . . in achieving cosiness they are completely at variance with the architects' achievements in giving them light and space. (quoted in Attfield, 1989: 219)

The modernists of *Design* magazine could not understand that many families just *prefer* clutter, and that minimalism is difficult to live up to, especially if there are children around the house. Yet the devotion of the architects to light and space was perfectly sensible. Even if they did not take into account the desire for a privacy that open-plan living frustrated, it does not follow that their original ideas were wholly misconceived.

The championing of popular taste in support of a 'feminist' agenda that celebrates *any* predominantly feminine activity is taken to self-parodying lengths in Alison Clarke's attempt to recast the 1950s Tupperware party as an example of women's empowerment:

> Women were unified in their desire not just for material luxuries, but for a sense of belonging. Becoming a [Tupperware] dealer or manager meant having a large network of social relations, extra money and standing in the community. Far from construing post-war women as 'domestic and quiescent', Tupperware and its potent articulation of material culture and social relations, operated as a blatant promotion of ambition and control. (Clarke, 1997: 149)

That there might have been other and more far-reaching forms of empowerment for housewives in the 1950s than selling plastic containers at commercial 'parties' seems not to have occurred to Alison Clarke. The defenders of audience research have always argued that audiences subvert mass culture, reworking what they see and listen to in oppositional ways, resisting ideological domination. However, as Curran pointed out, this occludes the possibility that there might have been other better, greater, more inspiring films, books, music and television that audiences could have watched. He suggests that the 'tacit system of valorisation based on audience pleasure' should be viewed with reserve. 'Even the most creative audiences can be confined – "Soap operas allow women viewers to take pleasure in the character of the villainess, but they do not provide characters that radically change the ideology of femininity"' (Curran, 1996: 270–1). To defend the culture of the suburbs on the grounds of the Tupperware party's proto-feminist potential is an extreme example of the tendency to which Curran rightly objects.

Another and more promising understanding of the suburb is the discovery of its 'darker' side. There is a fascination in the discovery that about 90 per cent of Punk bands came from the suburbs. The suburbs are no longer seen as anonymous, boring and conformist. In the new myth, suburban couples take part in wife-swapping parties. Bored suburban housewives become part-time sex workers. The suburb is the haunt of the paedophile, even the mass murderer. Terrorists hide out there. The neo-fascist who in 1999 bombed a Bangladeshi restaurant in London's East End, a street in Brixton where mostly Afro-Caribbeans live, and a Soho gay pub was living in the London suburbs. Artists and eccentrics, however, live there too, in flight from the phoney bohemianism of the haunts they once colonised but which have now been gentrified: in the 1990s Chris Cutler, formerly of the avant-garde band Henry Cow, moved to Thornton Heath, an outlying South London suburb, finding it more authentic than the inner city (Wright, 1995), while novelists such as Hanif Kureishi and Susan Hill have explored the eccentricities and rich diversity of the suburb.

Meanwhile the classic suburbs of the 1930s have become living museums of Art Deco. They have become dream worlds in which, in imagination at any rate, we slip into the past. Theirs is a *mise-en-scène* of nostalgia, and the suburb, at least as re-created culturally, represents a reassuring, safer world in which 'we' were less postmodern, more secure.

Note

1. This essay does not attempt to deal with the extensive American sociological literature published after the Second World War, in which a wholescale *social* attack on the suburb was launched. This literature included bestsellers such as Richard Gordon et al., *The Split Level Trap* (1964), John Keats, *The Crack in the Picture Window* (1956), William Whyte, *The Organization Man* (1956) and Betty Friedan, *The Feminine Mystique* (1963).

11

LIVING DOLLS

I want to be a machine

Andy Warhol

The forecourt of the Beaubourg was pale with cold this January afternoon. The cobbled square sloped upwards and away from the massed pipes, tubes and escalators of the Centre. Every movement stirred the frozen air around us, gripped us, slowed us down, but it hurt even more to stand still. Feet and fingers ached with cold. Our breath made empty speech balloons of foggy whiteness

He stood near the top of the slope. At a safe distance from him a little knot of onlookers huddled and stared. He exhaled nothing, no cloud of breath escaped his lips; so this *he* must surely be – a doll, a statue, a clockwork figure, an *it*. We huddled in our thick furs, but he never shivered in his thin jacket. He was a men's outfitters' dummy from the 1950s in a flimsy fifties suit, white shirt, dark tie and lace-up shoes, with hair slicked into short back and sides, and a tanned, clean-cut face, smooth as plaster. He carried a small attaché case. He was a piece of kitsch sculpture.

Suddenly his arm jerked up, he executed a half turn, brought his attaché case to the horizontal position, supported it with his other hand and snapped open the locks to display the contents of his briefcase (a notebook, some sandwiches). He took a few steps down the slope, paused, took up his petrified position again, then waltzed into a new series of clockwork movements. The effect was uncanny, exciting. It was thrilling, even euphoric, to watch so perfect an imitation of lifeless lifelikeness. Yet at the same time we felt cheated that the moving statue was not a living doll, but only a performer. Frozen to the cobbles and compelled to stare, we watched the endless sequence over and over again. 'Do it again!' we wanted to shriek, like children. He did, anyway.

The relentless repetition of this imitation of life eventually grew tedious, and we wandered away towards one of the old market cafés and a *croque monsieur*. Yet we continued to cast backward glances at the mechanical figure, who still stiltedly jerked and turned, and we felt somehow baffled, unsatisfied yet bewitched by his mysterious performance.

Two and a half years later: the tourist season in Florence. They still sell (as new) black and white postcards from the fifties – of the Piazzale Michelangelo with girls in circular skirts, who stand posed like something out of *L'Année dernière à Marienbad*, or shots of the Piazza della Signoria parked with a few 'vintage' cars. In the evenings the Piazza is crowded with American teenagers, with hippies, with a youthful international soldiery of pleasure seekers. There are guitarists who sing the songs of the sixties, 'Blowin' in the Wind' and 'Yellow Submarine'. There are fire-eaters, sword-swallowers and jugglers on this hot night, as there were in the Beaubourg forecourt in January.

Near the entrance to the square the largest crowd encircles two performers. A woman dressed as a man stands behind a hurdy-gurdy. 'He' wears a waistcoat, shirtsleeves rolled up, dark striped trousers, a trilby pushed to the back of his head and a bow tie; a figure from the slums of the twenties, Chicago, Naples, Petticoat Lane, anywhere, an old-fashioned organ grinder. Instead of a monkey, a giant doll flops at his feet, arranged so she leans against the organ. He stands her upright, balances her on her feet, sets her head and arms in place, and winds her up. Then he wearily turns the organ handle and the plaintive music begins. The big-boned doll with her plaits and apron and ballet shoes turns slowly round, her arms move up and down, her head jerks left and right. The crowd watches silent and motionless. The doll dances slowly and clumsily in time to the tinny music the organ grinder laboriously cranks out. When finally it ends he sits the doll down once more, her arms now holding her apron wide, and waits.

The silence continues. Then gradually, grudgingly, notes and coins drop into the doll's wide-spread apron. The organ grinder stands impassive, leaning against his machine, and puffs a cigarette as he watches and waits, while the doll sits rigid, smiling blankly, open armed. In the silence a note flutters down, then another. The crowd waits, resentful, withholding.

A man leans down and flaunts a large note, holding it just out of reach of the doll – nearer, pulled away, nearer again. Dead silence. The tension grows. He waves it under her nose again. She droops immobile. A third time – and she cracks and snatches it, laughing, but defeated. The spell has been broken. The crowd moves reluctantly away. The man has spoilt it by bringing it to an end. Yet there is also pleasure in the doll's defeat.

The crowd drifts away, and the buskers have vanished, as if it had been a dream. Perhaps they are travelling through Italy, wandering performers, itinerant players, as though it were still the nineteenth century. They may be lovers, perhaps he beats her, perhaps she is always the organ grinder's doll, perhaps they live out a master–slave existence.

At the bottom of the escalator in London's Bond Street Underground station there's a small, brightly lit concourse with short corridors leading to the platforms on each side. At the foot of the up escalator a life-size Action Man twists and jerks. He wears a combat jacket, camouflage trousers tucked into boots, leather gloves and a balaclava helmet. The creepy bit is that he has a plastic mask instead of a face. The crowds coming out of the passage confront him suddenly and unexpectedly as they turn towards the moving stairway. From the mouth of the opposite platform passengers waiting for their train watch mesmerised. Some go on watching even when their train arrives, riveted by the twitching, epileptic Action Man and his effect on the passengers leaving their train on the opposite side.

This was the unofficial performance art of the 1980s. These performance artists flourished at a time when intellectuals and journalists were discovering postmodernism, and they've largely vanished now that, although postmodernism is still with us, we talk about it less. We have come to take is as much for granted as the air pollution city dwellers have learnt to live with. We breathe in postmodernism without even noticing it.

The art of these human dolls is a form of alienation whereby a living human being re-creates herself or himself as a thing. Yet to the audience the performance must appear ironical, containing its own commentary on commodification, alienation and dehumanisation. At the same time the performer's masquerade as an inanimate being glorifies the alienation it mocks, for the art – the perfect imitation of a mechanised object, necessitating rigid control over one's own body – is a triumph of mind over matter. It is also heroic, for the living doll endlessly exposes itself to the ambivalent sadism, the gleeful indifference of the crowd, forever repeating the exaltation of a secular martyrdom, an aesthetic consummation that is forever only foreplay.

These performing figures build on memories of kitsch and the popular, and the performance evolves as an avant-garde pastiche of mass culture. Ambiguously it plays with the surfaces and appearance of retro or schlock, in a ritualised repetition of gestures, a cycle of fetishised postures, an artistic repetition compulsion that has no resolution.

Harder to explain than the performer's pleasure in this ritual so carefully rehearsed is the compulsion to watch that grips the audience. The experience is simultaneously compulsive and wearisome. Passers-by can't tear themselves away, and at the same time, because there's no conclusion, the audience finds the spectacle tedious and even irritating, becomes caught up in ambiguity and hesitation, whether to stay and watch some more, when to go, what's the point.

This ambivalence is very different from the unmixed pleasure with which we would watch an acrobat or rejoice in the skill of the dancer or musician. It equally lacks the cynical respect with which we respond to the tricks of the conjuror or fire-eater, when we know a deceit is being perpetrated but nevertheless enjoy the skill whereby we are deceived. At least in such performances there is a beginning, middle and end. The narratives of the living dolls, by contrast, are opaque and uncertain in meaning. What does it mean? Does it mean anything? Sure, the audience flings money at them, but the Beaubourg tailor's dummy did not even bother to pick up the coins, and would have continued to drill and jerk had the square been completely empty.

We watch the living dolls with reluctant addiction and with feelings both unpleasant and magical. The impossible idea of humans being turned into dolls is a theme of horror literature, creepily explored, for example, in a forgotten novel, *The Doll Maker*, by 'Sarban'. In this novel, as in the film *The Stepford Wives*, it is men who turn women into dolls, killing them in the name of love. It may therefore be that for women the uncanny death-in-life feeling of the living doll performers has some unconscious resonance with fear of men's 'love' when it becomes a murderous form of oppression and control. 'Love' in this sense turns women into dolls who suffer a kind of petrifaction or living death. Yet the men in the audience are equally mesmerised.

A different but related theme is that of the doll that comes alive in order to kill human beings. This is the theme of Freud's famous essay 'The Uncanny'. In it he took the example of E.T.A. Hoffman's tale 'The Sandman' to demonstrate the association of these themes with the compulsion to repeat – the persistent re-enactment of past unresolved conflicts in the present, a neurotic symptom whereby what cannot be resolved must be endlessly repeated. These half-mysterious street performances, then, may be cultural repetition compulsions. The repeated movements, the cyclical nature of the act, reflect the satisfaction/frustration of the compulsion to repeat – a compulsion that never succeeds in resolving the buried conflict, but merely re-enacts it in a disguised form. The repressed only returns, it is never transcended.

Freud explained the buried conflict as the fear of castration, but entwined in the tales of living dolls and humans turned to statues is the fear of death itself. Hence the relief of the audience when the masquerade breaks down and the doll is reassuringly unmasked as a living person after all. Yet there is also unpleasure and disappointment in this denouement, as if we wanted the illusion to continue, wanted the person to be, really, a doll, wanted the magical, not the 'real', not because we want the living to be dead, but rather because we want the doll to come alive – a common enough childhood fantasy, as Freud observed.

That would be the simple desire for the triumph of pleasure principle over reality, or magic over brute fact. In fact, the mixed feelings of the audience suggest that there is more to it than that, and that the living dolls arouse some collective repressed ambivalence in the onlookers that is hard even to name.

Each living doll is a tic on the face of the city, found either in public spaces where people rushing by are stopped in their tracks and given a shock, or else, more often, in the public squares, gardens and piazzas created for leisure. With their desperate semaphore of gestures they mutely sign anxieties we cannot even name, in spaces of anomie where shopping is disguised as recreation.

Their performances can only achieve the full effect in the anonymity of the crowd. The performance is instant. The living doll appears as if by magic and afterwards disappears as quickly. It banishes all fear by being neither dead nor alive, and in this way has made itself safe from the dangers of the city. It expresses the feeling of semi-euphoria, of slightly dream-like disassociation, that sometimes invades the individual drifting along in the crowd. The living doll is like Poe's 'Man of the Crowd', a restless wanderer, seeking to exorcise some guilt, seeking to escape, yet finding its being only in the crowd. The living doll, too, lives only in the crowd; it is the gaze of the crowd that gives it its life. There must be an audience; the doll must be watched in order to exist.

And it's unclear, undecidable, whether its cult of self-transformation into a work of art is the supreme alienation or whether it's the supreme transcendence, the triumph of performance over our living, incoherent flesh. Or perhaps it enacts the repetition compulsion of consumerism, the game in which everything changes, but is always repeated and always the same.

12

BRICOLAGE CITY

Myths of Brighton

The sound of seagulls. I remember the taste of salt on my lover's skin,
lying in our bedsit room, after one hot day on the beach, summer 1955.
Life was sweet.

Anon, *Daring Hearts*

A 1954 history of Brighton (Gilbert, 1954) referred to it as 'ocean's bauble',
and that would be one way of imagining it: as a glittery, crystalline,
opalescent jewel at the end of the road from London, a magic piece
of flotsam thrown up on the south coast seashore. It is not a particularly
small town – in the fifties it was one of the thirty largest in Britain – but
it seems small, or at least compact. At the same time it carries a much
larger load of representational baggage than other cities of similar size; it is
larger than the sum of its parts, for it is more than a resort, it is a myth, a
myth of English excess and hedonism, constructed partly from its contrast
to its opposites: to Middle England, Suburbia and utilitarian Chapel
morality.

In the seventeenth century Brighthelmston had been a flourishing fishing
town, but in the early eighteenth century was in decline, partly because of
the incursions of the sea. It was given a new lease of life when in 1754 Dr
Richard Russell arrived to put into practice his theories about the benefits
of salt water for the treatment of diseases of the glands. Patients were
advised to drink the water as well as taking hot salt baths. Soon sea
bathing, too, became popular, and the fishing families found more lucrative
employment in organising the bathing huts which were wheeled down to the
water's edge so that their occupants could climb out and venture into the
waves. The Countess of Huntingdon brought her sickly son to Brighton in
the hope that sea bathing would improve his health, and in 1783 the Prince
of Wales visited his uncle, the Duke of Cumberland, who had a house on
the Steyne.

This visit inaugurated Brighton's transformation into a fashionable
watering spa and pleasure resort. It was soon being organised along the
lines of inland spas such as Bath and Tunbridge Wells, with a Master of
Ceremonies, assembly room, parade, band, circulating library and theatre.
Both sunny and 'bracing', it was protected from cold winds by the surrounding chalk hills of the Downs. These provided opportunities for riding
excursions, but the great place to be seen was on the promenade or Front,

where the daily parade on horseback or in open carriages was the social climax of the day.

The coming of fashionable society resulted in a rapid and magnificent architectural flowering. The residential areas of Kemptown and the Brunswick Terrace area in Hove date largely from the reign of George IV rather than the Regency; indeed the fashion for neo-classical buildings lasted in Brighton until the 1850s (Dale, 1967). The architect chiefly responsible for the crescents and squares was Charles Augustus Busby, who established himself in Brighton in 1822 in partnership with the father and son team, Amon and Amon Henry Wild. Busby despised the work of architects such as Robert Adam with his predilection for Roman and even Egyptian motifs, and favoured instead a pure Greek revival style.

The grandiose stucco sweep of the Kemptown crescents and the squares and terraces on the Front at Hove bear witness both to this stylistic purity and to the new and old money of the Regency, which, a little like the Thatcherite 1980s, was a culture both raucous and reactionary. John Nash's Brighton Royal Pavilion, that kitsch and camp and cardboard monument to eclecticism, postmodern *avant la lettre*, playfully referenced Britain's imperial role, with its Gujarati gateway (actually built much later), its minarets and towers. Some of its turrets and chimneys were damaged in the great gale of 1987; they were restored in plastic, and it shows – in fact since it has been cleaned the whole building looks fake. But that is as it should be.

The British Royal Family's recent problems of divorce and mistresses have been likened to similar royal conflicts in the Regency period; but there are wider similarities between the two periods, both struggling with a revolution in industrial production. The early years of the nineteenth century were marked by riots and by their violent suppression, by attacks on civil liberties and 'Jacobins', and eventually in many cases by disillusionment on the part of radicals with the turn taken by the French Revolution. Working-class dissent had yet to gain legitimacy and the organisation later provided by the trade unions and the Labour Party. The similarities should not be overstated, but in the 1980s striking miners and poll tax rioters saw their opposition once more delegitimated as the parameters of permissible dissent appeared to narrow, while leftwing disillusionment was again widespread. As the gap between rich and poor widened, the rich flaunted their wealth and the New Right presided over social and moral as much as economic deregulation. This continued throughout the 1990s. The Pavilion's *faux* Chinese interiors would have delighted the Regent Princes of the late 1990s, Geoffrey Robinson or Derry Irvine, and it became one of the sets for Ian McKellen's film of *Richard III*. This updated Shakespeare to a fascistic 1930s, which also had a contemporary relevance.

It was due to the Prince Regent that Brighton became so fashionble, yet it attracted writers and artists as much as high society luminaries. Henry and Hester Thrale and Fanny Burney stayed there towards the end of the eighteenth century; painters revelled in its clear light. It was never a one-dimensional resort.

The letting of furnished lodgings to fashionable visitors meant new sources of income for the residents. It was already a service town, with work for domestic servants, chefs, actors, musicians and other entertainers. As a fashionable resort it also attracted hangers-on of all kinds, adventurers, prostitutes and quacks as well as bona fide doctors.

This may account for one aspect of Brighton's peculiar attraction; that it was at one and the same time a place for pleasure, fashion and the social spectacle, yet was health promoting. Virtue coincided with pleasure. Schools and churches sprang up alongside the theatres and hotels. Transgression and piety went hand in hand. The Victorian churches built by Father Wagner and his sons as monuments to High Church Anglicanism stood for 'what used to be called the London, Brighton and South Coast Religion, i.e. beautiful ceremony, singing and furnishings' (Dale, 1967: 46). They were as much a part of nineteenth-century Brighton as the gin palaces and hotels.

Queen Victoria visited Brighton several times in the early years of her reign, but she and Prince Albert disliked the Pavilion and soon deserted Brighton in favour of Osborn on the Isle of Wight. Brighton, while still fashionable, began gently to decline, although it had a master of ceremonies until 1855. However, by this time the railway, which came to Brighton in 1841, had given the town a new lease of life of a rather different kind. The old civilities of the watering spa were being swept aside by the beginnings of holidaying for the many, at least in the summer. The fashionable upper-class visitors now came for the 'season' in the winter months.

Dickens described a bleak and dismal Brighton in *Dombey and Son*, in which he banished poor little Paul Dombey to a cheerless boarding school in one of Brighton's hilly back streets, flinty, chalky and sterile. He dwelt on the pious and cheeseparing aspect of the many establishments that catered to the school and holiday trade, and the respectability that wafted especially from the Hove side of the town. Yet in the same years the population was doubling, and the weekly arrival of the Sunday excursionists from London not only brought flourishing music hall and other entertainments along with large numbers of public houses and taverns, but aroused fears that the town would be flooded with prostitutes, and that there would be a disregard for the appropriate observance of the religious aspects of Sunday. This was notwithstanding Brighton's reputation as a centre of High Church worship; indeed many of the crowds who came down for the day were members of the London Jewish communities, for whom Sunday, not being their Sabbath, was a convenient day for rest and relaxation.

In the 1860s one anonymous writer described a rackety and vulgar town with many depressing boarding houses managed by women whom he categorised as either 'vultures' (openly stingy) or 'crocodiles' (more guileful), presiding over lodgings garnished with broken furniture, antimacassars and ugly ornaments – an enduring caricature. The visitors were a motley,

Dickensian crew of the genteel poor who had seen better times, and *nouveaux* vulgarians:

> Pork pie hats, from which tresses flow behind, caught up in nets, are stuck jauntily on their heads; jackets in which they thrust their hands (like saucy schoolboys) fall back to discover waistcoats like men's; but fortunately . . . from the waist down they are dressed as women, and ample skirts stick out with indignant protest at any too near an approach to Balmoral boots laced with red ribbon. . . . The sunset, or some other glowing influence has become fixed upon their cheeks, and altogether, what with their bearing of insouciance and their unfeminine independence of style, and the total absence of quiet, modest bearing in every movement and gesture, they present an example of the English girl of the nineteenth century which I would rather that a foreigner . . . should not behold. (Anon, 1862: 17)

But while the wealthy paraded up and down the promenade, the housing built for the influx of service personnel, and later for railway workers and their families, had already sunk into slums and squalor. The first slum clearances took place in the 1870s, but conditions did not improve. The artist Eric Gill, who was brought up in the Preston Road area in the 1880s, described it as 'a shapeless mess . . . a congeries of more or less sordid streets growing like a fungus wherever the net of railways and sidings and railway sheds would allow' (quoted in Gilbert, 1954: 73).

The 1930s suburbs testify to the growth of twentieth-century Brighton as a dormitory town for commuters to London. This had actually started long before. As early as 1823 William Cobbett had written of the stock jobbers who 'skip backwards and forwards on the coaches and actually carry on stock jobbing in Change Alley although they reside in Brighton'. At the mid-century, another author wrote of the London merchant who 'goes backwards and forwards to his marine villa with more ease and in as little time as he formerly occupied with driving to Norwood or Hampstead' (quoted in Gilbert, 1954: 65).

The local authorities of Hove and Brighton undertook many housing developments in the twentieth century, one of the earliest and most praised being Moulsecoomb, designed by Professor Adshead after the First World War and modelled on Garden City principles. It was to be a 'garden suburb by the sea', but by the time two little girls from the estate were murdered in a local park in 1986 it had long become run down and dilapidated.

In a gruesome twist, Katrina Taylor, one of two little girls used in a police reconstruction of this crime, was herself murdered ten years later. She had been 'struggling to bring up her baby daughter and fund her £200 a week heroin habit,' reported the *Observer* newspaper (Thompson, 2000: 12), but became caught up in a minor drugs war. This was part of Brighton's 'seamy underbelly' – at the end of the century there was 'a dramatic increase in burglaries, muggings and shootings'.

Brighton had always had a sleazy underside, and poverty in Brighton was as perennial as the rakish charm and the excitement of the place. Much of the employment in the town was seasonal work in service trades that were always relatively poorly paid. At the time of the 1971 census, Brighton was equal third with Liverpool in the league table of cities with the highest proportional take-up of free school meals. Of the worst towns in Britain, it was the eleventh highest in terms of children in care, eighth for infant mortality, fifteenth for unemployment, seventeenth for one-parent families and twenty-fifty in terms of lack of basic housing amenities such as a bathroom. In addition 25 per cent of Brighton's population was of pensionable age. This profile made it more like a northern industrial or post-industrial town than a typical south of England city (Queen's Park Rates Book Group, n.d. [1983?]: 91). Unlike the squalor of industrial towns, though, Brighton's poverty was not recognised. Yet there had always been a suspicion that the neo-classical frontages of Kemptown and Hove were made of plywood, the painted face of a macaroni, a swell, a Cyprian, hiding a sordid reality of graft, greed and down-and-out desperation. Yet the contrasts, half-hidden, hinted at rather than in the open, give Brighton an edge, a glint of cruelty behind its smiling face.

The popular Brighton of the late Victorians and the Edwardians lives on in the ghost of the crumbling West Pier and the still lively Palace Pier. Day-trippers still walk gingerly along the duckboard catching a glint of the water underneath, and the tinny music churns out and the gamblers punch desperately at the fruit machines, while boys stand transfixed in front of the violent world of virtual shoot-outs and motor races.

The rowdy, cheap world of the funfair at the end of the Pier had always contained an undercurrent of violence. To children today the ghost train is just a joke and only slightly scary, if at all. Yet it was in this very ghost train that the man who masqueraded as Colley Cibber was murdered in *Brighton Rock*, its tawdry thrills adding to the banal finality of that little lamented death.

The Big Wheel and the Dodgems bring out the aggressive rather than the spooky side of seaside fun. A third machine – more like an instrument of torture – straps the pleasure seekers into two long rows of chairs, then hurls them up into the sky, suspends them upside-down for an endless minute, turns them again on its spit, and reverses them once more as screams and heartless music mingle in the salty air. This mechanical dinosaur, lifting them high and shaking them in its jaws, seems to issue a threat, a subliminal reminder of the danger beneath the laughter, the water beneath the rotting duckboards, the scream behind the smile. That scream is repeated endlessly by the cold-eyed gulls that never cease to shriek as they circle overhead. Yet their cries are more melancholy than vicious, the cries of abandoned lovers and nostalgic pleasure-seekers fallen on hard times.

If the Palace Pier is reminiscent of cockney fun at the turn of the century, of music hall humour and coarse laughs, that all turned to something sadder and more sinister in the world of the twenties and thirties embalmed along the coast. This was a Brighton made famous by Graham Greene and Patrick Hamilton. This was the gangsters' Brighton of razor fights at Kemptown races – although that came to an end with the big murder trial in 1936. The more enduring aspect of the Greene – and even more of the Hamilton – myth was seediness. These chroniclers of the depressive ambience of the 1930s explored the collapsing lives, the blackmail, poisonings and despairing hatred hidden within the big, decaying houses of the hinterland behind the Front, with their dirty lace curtains and adulterous weekends. This myth has something to do with the way Brighton was always a city for marginal occupations, for transients; beloved by students, actors, alternative journalists, fortune-tellers and ex-army types down on their luck. This was a Brighton where the line between residents and visitors was blurred, at least superficially, with seasonal workers, seasonal residents, the retired and the 'resting'; a place where identities could be fudged and hidden.

In 1994 the critic John Carey attacked Greene, among others, in a populist polemic full of loathing for what he perceived as the contempt displayed by leftwing intellectuals for 'ordinary people'; but the elitism, if such it was, of Greene's attitude, does not explain its power as a myth. It was in the austerity years of the 1940s, just after the end of the Second World War, that *Brighton Rock* was made into a seedy British version of *film noir*. It explored the desperate Brighton of the anti-hero, Pinky, and his small-time gang, the slum Brighton of the little back streets with their decaying fishermen's cottages and the coarse, jolly Brighton of the Pier and the pubs. Lastly there was a glimpse of the posh but not very pukka Brighton of the hotel lounges and cocktail bars, the Brighton of bookies and gamblers and *nouveaux riches*. The film expressed one of the moods of post-war Britain, starved of consumer goods and longing for some fun, and perhaps it also functioned as a film about the Home Front in wartime and just after, as much as one about Brighton as a specific place. But why the desperation behind the booze and the fumbled kisses touched, and goes on touching, a nerve is harder to understand. (A later film, Neil Jordan's *Mona Lisa* in the 1980s, envisaged Brighton more as a kind of utopia in which fatal acts had no consequences, and the sea beckoned like a vista of opportunities.)

A faded, genteel thirties has lasted until the present day along the coastline towards Beachy Head, and in the opposite direction towards Portslade and Worthing. There are Tudorbethan beams and pebbledash; there are houses like ocean-going liners, with porthole windows, rounded corners to walls washed white, and flat roofs and railings like a promenade deck; there are sunburst gates and dormer windows, bungalows and diamond-leaded window panes. There was also at one time the Ocean View Hotel, perched on the slope of the Downs with its name in big letters, as if this were Hollywood, but converted beyond the Art Deco hall doors into an old people's holiday home, as institutional as any of the gloomy Victorian lodging houses described by Dickens and others.

Further along, and in an even more commanding position, at Saltdean, the Royal National Institute for the Blind building presents a triumphal monument to modernism, with glassed-in stairway and curving wings. It's bleak and isolated and all in the middle of nowhere. This makes it strange and even forlorn, emblematic of the fate of modernism – to be left high and dry, its triumph undercut by those who prefer the kitsch, the cosy, the comfortable, who prefer the Saltdean oval Lido and semi-detached Moderne.

Embassy Court in Hove is another monument to modernism, a concrete ziggurat, but a monument less to the thirties than to the fifties, when it signified showbiz glamour. Rex Harrison and Kay Kendall stayed here, and they weren't the only ones. Now the rust is bleeding down from the metal window frames, the grimy windows are half-covered with fusty curtains, there are satellite dishes and mouldy carpet and the smell of decay; but in its time it was part of the world that was opening out as rationing ended, as Princess Margaret wielded her cigarette holder, as Sir Bernard and Lady Docker climbed into their gold-plated limousine, and as the film stars came to Brighton. Tommy Trinder, Max Miller and Gracie Fields lived in Brighton then, as did Anna Neagle and Herbert Wilcox, Hermione Baddeley and Laurence Olivier. There was even a small film studio after 1952, which turned out shorts and documentary films (Chapman, 1996). This Brighton lives on in some of the pubs and antique shops in the Lanes, and above all in the fish restaurants. Wheeler's has disappeared from Soho, but it still thrives in Brighton, as does English's oyster bar with its red brocade and velvet. There you can see couples straight out of the 1950s: she plastered with make-up and wearing a big-brimmed hat and a pale mink coat as if they were the latest thing; he red-faced in blazer and flannels, with a Brylcreem hairstyle and a paisley handkerchief to match his tie.

There was also a Brighton of artists and a colony of writers. Yet Brighton did not seem to know where it was going after the war. Both Hove and Brighton councils became vandals rather than saviours. Gloucester Place was pulled down to make way for a telephone exchange and a cinema. At one time Hove council even wanted to pull down Brunswick Square to facilitate the creation of a thirty-foot-wide dual carriageway along the front. In central Brighton large parts of the North Laine with its old cottages and narrow streets were seen as ripe for redevelopment, since its housing had deteriorated. Well into the 1970s it was under threat, and seemed likely to be turned into a gigantic car park.

The neo-classical Bedford Hotel, Dickens' favourite, and designed by Thomas Cooper, who was also responsible for the imposing town hall, was pulled down in 1964. It was also during the early 1960s that Churchill Square was developed as a concrete shopping precinct. This became a draughty wind-tunnel, bleak and unattractive. In the mid-1990s this monument to post-war brutalism was due for demolition in its turn. By the year 2000 it had become a warmer, funkier, more enclosed shopping mall, and the familiar chain store branches were joined by newer, slightly smarter ones. But this wasn't Brighton, it was anywhere.

The local authorities were not entirely or even primarily to blame for the destruction of many of the old Brighton buildings. To a large extent they followed prevailing tastes. John Betjeman recalled that when he first visited Brighton in 1918, 'Kemptown was regarded as seedy [and] . . . stucco was regarded as false' (Betjeman and Gray, 1972: 5). Only with the publication in 1935 of a social history of Brighton by Osbert Sitwell and Margaret Barton did the revival begin of interest in and appreciation of the neo-classical stucco of Hove and Kemptown. After 1945 the Regency period became fashionable. In 1951 a Regency exhibition was held there to celebrate the Festival of Britain and the first efforts to restore the Pavilion were being made.

In the 1980s unemployment and homelessness hit Brighton. Researchers continued to express anxieties about the future of the town, although new forms of employment were coming to the coast. Banking and finance services relocated to the area; the opening of Gatwick Airport in 1958 gave a boost to the conference and exhibition business, and the University of Sussex and Brighton Polytechnic were flourishing. These did not necessarily help the poor. It became a place of 'London prices, Brighton wages' (Burchill, 1999: 2). Indeed, the class divide widened, here as elsewhere. As London house prices continued to rise, Brighton attracted even more commuters and permanent residents. The café where homeless and mentally disturbed customers had once found a safe haven in the North Laine was gentrified, and new shops replaced the old warehouses and stores in Kensington Gardens.

Brighton was still a centre of bricolage, however. The post-industrial economy is all about the recycling of possessions, and in Brighton this was brought to a fine art. There seem always to have been more Oxfam shops and second-hand clothes dealers there than in other towns, shops smelling of used textiles and filled with old ladies' fur coats and leftovers from the early seventies. The days are long gone when you could find a Utility suit or a thirties frock in these emporia of lost lives, but the students and designers of the 1990s seized on the batik dresses and cheesecloth blouses, purple polyester flares and plastic shoes with square toes and heels (McRobbie, 1989b). There are also used saucepans, electrical gadgets that no longer function, and dog-eared volumes of Catherine Cookson and Jeffrey Archer. This is a whole other (nether)world of pleasures and anxieties, of breakdown and bricolage, of the accumulation of personalised oddments, the refuse of the consumer world, the 'Other' of the bright, smart chain stores up on the Western Road. To rifle through the bricolage of Brighton is to find the eternal mysteriously in the ephemeral. These plates and frocks and faded best-sellers have lost their original purpose, but await a new one, as yet undefined.

The researchers who wrote of Brighton's social problems, the radicals who tried to organise the poor, and the councillors who worried about Brighton's future and tried to shape it into respectability and prosperity were doing what they had to do, yet partly missed the point. Brighton would lose its personality if it were shaped too much away from eccentricity and the marginal. For it is not only eccentric styles and the bricolage of living that have always flourished in Brighton. It has been a home for eccentric beliefs and bricolage of the mind as well. The spiritualists and tarot card readers might have seemed like just another tawdry facet of the world of the Palace Pier and the tinny merry-go-round. But the popular world of the sea-front Gypsy Petulengro and Madame Sosotris finds an echo in the Brighton backland of New Agers and hippie mysticism, cults and strange rituals. It is not so surprising that pagans, white witches and Goths are drawn to Brighton when you remember that an ancient tradition of sacred sites lies buried deep below the stucco and bungalows: the prehistoric religious sites of the Downs.

Brighton is a junk shop of broken ideas and recycled theories – recycling of the mind as well as of the broken coffee-grinders and crimplene suits in Oxfam. Loiterers rifle through the second-hand books and records not so much for something to buy as for something to believe. Nothing has ever been too strange to find a haven among the boarding houses and rented rooms, the holiday flats and grandiloquent squares.

A place for exiles – Prince Metternich retreated to Brighton in 1849: Louis-Philippe paid a brief visit soon after. A place for deviance – Oscar Wilde and Bosie stayed here in the 1890s. A place for the high-wire balancing act of walking the fine line between outrage and martyrdom, defiance and victimhood – it is a place above all for gays. There are no overt homosexuals in *Brighton Rock*, which in one way is rather surprising, for queers, queens and gays discovered the city long ago. Seaside resorts have always been an ideal location for sexual minorities, drawn to these places where carnival reigns, where morals are relaxed and there are opportunities for masquerade and mischief. In the 1950s Brighton was probably the gayest town in Britain:

> It was the *freedom* in Brighton. There were so many gay people and they seemed to be accepted and there were clubs for gay people . . . ohh, wonderful! It was absolutely Mecca because it was very gay then. Brighton's gay now but it was very very gay then. (Brighton Ourstory Project, 1992: 13)

A local newspaper headline of the period predicted that Brighton would be 'a gay town from now on' – presumably no double meaning was intended, since 'gay' did not replace 'queer' as a term for homosexuals until Gay Liberation. In the early sixties, though, Brighton *was* gay in the future sense of the word. It boasted, among other attractions, a club with red Regency flock wallpaper and candelabra wall lights, where a famous literary queen (famous especially for his weekly column in a mass-market women's magazine) held court and bowled his audience over with his camp quips.

By the 1970s gays were very out in Brighton. No more bitchy camping in dusty little clubs, now it was Gay Liberation, with well-advertised discos and a demonstration every weekend. In the eighties they were more subdued, more assimilated. Gays seemed privatised in Thatcher's Brighton, apolitical, invisible – and even more so, unsurprisingly, after the less discreet elements of their community were savagely turned over by the police in a murder investigation. But there was another side as well: pioneering

HIV centres, educational work. And in the nineties, gay Brighton was gayer than ever with Gay Pride celebrations and a huge yearly carnival in Preston Park.

Yet it would not do for Brighton, any more than its gay community, to become too respectable, too mainstream, or too touristic. Too much rebranding of its atmosphere, too much obeisance to the conference market would lead to its destruction. Too many commuters would make it too respectable. On the other hand too much Camden Lock would also be bad news – or may already be if Oliver Bennett's vitriolic 1998 attack on the city is anything to go by. He accused Brighton of having a massive inferiority complex and chip on the shoulder about not being London. It was a scuzzy, dirty town, he said, it was 'basically Luton on sea', the Metroland of the 1990s, a suburb too big for its boots. At the same time it was not so much London by the sea as Camden Lock by the sea, full of ageing punks and ancient hippies, for people who 'will not, shall not, cannot grow up: those steadfastly avoiding the call to maturity' (Bennett, 1998: 3). Even he, however, in the midst of this rant, the motivation of which remained obscure, could not resist the *Brighton Rock* reference, alluding to the seedy underbelly and the riffraff of 'unemployed psychopaths'.

A year later, however, Julie Burchill went to the opposite extreme, celebrating her adopted home town as a thriving machine for living in, a sexy, marvellous place with something for everyone, *toujours gai* (Burchill, 1999: 2). This, too, seems to miss the ambivalence at Brighton's heart (although Burchill does briefly allude to it). When Victorians enquired of a woman, 'Is she gay?' they meant was she a prostitute, and 'gay' meant tragic, not jolly, and not joyful, but fallen, sullied and destroyed. Brighton is 'gay' in both senses of the word, and perhaps that's its charm. You are captivated by its bittersweetness. On the surface so bright, a town of pleasure, the face it turns to the visitor is a painted mask, and at a moment's notice the smiling mask can be whipped away and replaced with a mask of melancholy, while the face behind the masks is never fully visible. Is it the casual beach, the crunching pebbles, or the carousel or the Grand Hotel? Is it *grande dame* Brighton, or the gypsy Sosotris? Is it the joyous gay days in Preston Park or the seedy failure of lives leaking away in the back streets of another time? Is it the paddling pool in the hot, blue July meridian, or the suicide off the chalk-white cliffs of Beachy Head? Brighton has moods, has all its moods together, and all its periods – the Regency, the Edwardian, the thirties – endure. Yet it is also ephemeral, its memories the memories of outings, jaunts and mysteries, of holidays and celebrations, the candy floss of festival rather than the meat of daily life.

Enduring and ephemeral, like the sea. You can stand on the shingle and watch the waves as they gather their watery muscle into a translucent knot, rear up, roll down and fan out extinguished in a foamy hem. It is soothing to listen to the breakers sucking at the stones, with a growl and the sigh of sliding shingle forever rocked to and fro, milled together and ground to sand in another million years. You can often find a piece of broken glass that has been rubbed into a rounded green or milky white pebble by the motion of the waves. I have collected a whole bowl of them over the years.

It is the sea that will always prevent Brighton from being another London. The 'London by the sea' sobriquet, in fact, completely misses the point. There *are* capital cities by the sea – Havana, for example, or Stockholm – but the whole point of Brighton lies in *not* being London. Its melancholy is of aspirations unachieved, of pleasures that fell short, of exclusion amidst the tinsel carnival from some greater excitement elsewhere. But at the same time, it is a city of disappointments redeemed by the presence of the sea, of failures that have become a willing renunciation in the light of some stranger, less obvious purpose.

Marcel Proust wrote that: 'The sea will always fascinate those to whom world-weariness and the lure of mystery have already brought early sadness, like a premonition of the inadequacy of reality to satisfy them' (Tadié, 2000: 90). And this seems a fitting summary of the mournful, hopeful Brighton vistas, where the manic fun of the fair is poised against the calm eternal indifference of the sea.

13

DOGS IN SPACE

In 1996 a fox was sighted in the mews at the back of our house, which fronts on to a large London square. It was later suggested that the fox might actually have been only a cat, since the eyewitness was drunk at the time. By the summer of 1999, however, *everyone* had seen the fox. He was so tame that he came to the back door to beg for food in the early morning, and each evening the neighbours left out a series of little bowls for him, as if for some household god to be appeased. One neighbour even claimed to have seen the fox use a pedestrian crossing to negotiate the adjacent main road.

But even if no-one had actually seen a fox, everyone 'knows' there are foxes in the neighbourhood. There are other woodland species after all: squirrels by the dozen, an owl (though recently deceased), jays, even a hedgehog – and all this in the middle of the capital. Nature penetrates the city, and it appears that the larger the city, the more plants and animals it will shelter. For example Glasgow, with a population of 700,000, has about 1,200 plant species, London with seven million has well over 2,000 types of plant, while 'in the biodiversity stakes, Vienna may have more wild plants than many of its surrounding woods, themselves a pastoral inspiration for past composers and writers' (Smith, 1994).

This rather goes against the way in which, in western thought, nature and the city, rural and urban are positioned as contrasting opposites. The urban seeping into the rural is acknowledged, as a negative force, destructive and polluting, but movement in the opposite direction is rarely discussed.

Lewis Mumford believed that clear boundaries are necessary to our sense of order. The city, he asserted, was, or should be, a container; to be a proper city it had to be a finite, bounded space. This clear-cut entity was threatened by the 'sprawling giantism' of the modern city, which was leading inexorably to 'megalopolis' and thence to 'necropolis', the death of the city. The sharp division between country and city no longer exists, he wrote:

> As the eye stretches towards the hazy periphery one can pick out no definite shapes . . . one beholds rather a continuous shapeless mass . . . the shapelessness of the whole is reflected in the individual part, and the nearer the centre, the less . . . can the smaller parts be distinguished. (Mumford, 1960: 619)

Using an organic metaphor, he described such city growth as cancerous, social chromosomes and cells run riot in 'an overgrowth of formless new tissue':

the city has absorbed villages and little towns, reducing them to place names . . . has . . . enveloped those urban areas in its physical organisation and built up the open land that once served to ensure their identity and integrity. . . . As one moves away from the centre, the urban growth becomes ever more aimless and discontinuous, more diffuse and unfocused. . . . Old neighbourhoods and precincts, the social cells of the city, still maintaining some measure of the village pattern, become vestigial. No human eye can take in this metropolitan mass at a glance. (Mumford, 1960: 619–20)

Mumford's description might apply to cities in many parts of the world, and perhaps particularly the developing world, but nature, in London at least, seems to give its varied districts a shape rather than rendering them shapeless.

The acquisition of a dog has given me a new awareness of the importance of urban nature, although I am not sure whether domestic pets can themselves be seen as a form of nature in the city. Although my partner and I were interviewed and accepted by our local authority as suitable to adopt a child, the first breeder from whom we attempted to buy a dog turned us down. She considered us unfit to be canine carers because we were both working, and therefore not prepared to stay at home with the animal. Also, our house had stairs, which, if he attempted to go up them, would dislocate the back of the overbred dachshund we were trying to acquire. (He was so long that if he'd had more legs he'd have resembled a caterpillar rather than a dog.) Undeterred by this rejection, we later succeeded in becoming the owners of a large and lively poodle, Pip, ownership of which made us realise that whether or not a pet is part of urban nature, it is certainly part of urban politics.

Large, owner-occupied houses surround our local square. There is a small council estate near the top, and the whole district is a typical, mixed inner London neighbourhood, with council and private housing cheek by jowl in all the surrounding streets. The square is planted with beautiful horse chestnut and plane trees, but these block much of the light from its upper end. The lower part is more open and at the very bottom a large – and it must be said unsightly – adventure playground was built in the 1970s.

The main users of the square have always been dog owners; 'It's just a large dogs' toilet,' as one of my neighbours said. Non-dog-owning residents have continually tried to extend its use; indeed a bitterly fought class war of attrition has been waged over this space for some years.

In 1996 antagonisms came to a head when the local municipal authority, Camden Council, appointed a new Director of Public Spaces, whose remit was to improve those 'green amenities', which, like our square, were held to have deteriorated. Fresh from successes in the neighbouring borough of Islington, the new boy on the block was full of enthusiasm for the much greater challenge of Camden, with its sixty-two open spaces, not including Hampstead Heath (which is not managed by the Council).

One of his first initiatives was to call a series of public meetings to ascertain the wishes of local users. At the meeting called specifically to discuss our square the bitter dispute over dogs came fully into the open, as two opposed groups – dog owners, and dog haters determined to get dogs banned from the square – squared up to each other.

A year earlier I should not have cared, and might well have sided with the anti-dog forces, but dog ownership naturally determined my perception of the issue. Besides, my visits to the square with Pip had made me aware that it was much more than a dog's toilet. There was a social culture in the square. This consisted primarily of a group of elderly women who not only exercised their dogs there, but also sat and chatted for hours, even in the winter, except on the very coldest days. Most of them seemed poor, working-class, perhaps lonely. One, referred to only as 'Billy's mum' – Billy being an arthritic, adenoidal pug dog – seemed to be what might have once been described as 'a bit simple'. Emotionally, however, she was very much on the ball, a sweet-natured woman who was always friendly, and interested in everything that was going on. Sometimes, especially in the summer months, the old ladies held court with three or four apparently unemployed men of indeterminate age, usually slightly drunk. The group discussed world politics and the general decline of the West. Voices were sometimes raised – the European Union was an especially contentious issue – but there was never any violence.

At the meeting called by the Director, a vociferous group of the middle-class and middle-aged took the opportunity to object to the presence of dogs in the square and to demand a complete ban. Yet it was immediately obvious that it was the culture of the square – the people rather than the dogs – they wanted to banish. As they hectored and bullied, an elderly Irish woman shouted back that they were anti-working-class. The new director seemed stunned at the violence with which feelings were expressed, but rallied, and made it clear that a compromise had to be reached if possible. A vote, he announced, would be held.

After the meeting, rumours that Camden Council was about to ban dogs from all sixty-two of its green spaces spread to the surrounding streets and a petition was circulated as panic grew. The old women 'regulars' of the square asserted that the London Borough of Westminster had already banned dogs from its parks and squares and were convinced that Camden would soon follow suit. They *knew* that the residents' association wanted a locked-up square on the lines of fashionable West End spaces such as Eaton Square to which only the residents have a key. They became more and more resentful and distressed as the rumours spread and became increasingly wild. The residents' association continued to demand a bye-law to exclude dogs from the square altogether. The paranoia of the regulars reached a stage at which they claimed they were being photographed by 'someone from the council' every time they set foot in the square. 'It's to see if outsiders use it,' they claimed – the residents' association definition of an outsider being anyone who brought their dog to the square in a car.

The Director's plan for a vote, in effect a referendum, at least gave all sides their chance to affect the outcome. It was not really clear who was entitled to vote, and those who did turn up were not asked to prove residency. In the event sixty-three votes were cast. The options given, and the method by which the votes cast were converted into an outcome, were complicated. Nevertheless, a week or so after the vote a notice appeared on the gate announcing that dogs were to be allowed in 40 per cent of the square, and that the dog exercise area was to be separated from the rest by a low railing and shrubs.

Because the railing followed an already existing path, the size of the dog exercise area was less than 40 per cent. It was also located at the sunny south end of the square. In the months after the vote, dog owners used and mainly kept to the exercise area, but few residents appeared in the upper (darker) end of the square to stroll and chat beneath the chestnut trees. For hours at a time this part of the square was deserted. Only in the autumn evenings did children invade it, to hurl bricks up at the trees to bring down the conkers.

The residents' association was still determined to achieve a complete ban. The old women grew even more paranoid. The Council, which is blamed for almost everything that goes wrong in the borough, and sometimes with good reason, made a valiant attempt on this occasion to arbitrate and bring about some permanent satisfactory resolution. The Director of Public Spaces called yet another meeting, and shared with the warring residents his knowledge of the many financial constraints on the Council and the expense of erecting railings, employing gardeners and monitoring the square. Perhaps he hoped that this would assist residents to develop a set of shared meanings and a shared sense of responsibility concerning the square. His vote had also been an attempt at a democratic solution through community participation. Essentially it failed, for the long-running battle was an example of a form of class prejudice as entrenched as racism, but quieter and perhaps more acceptable, since hardly anyone stands up for down and outs, drunks and penniless old women. Eventually a kind of armed truce was reached. Residents' association activists continued to scour the square for signs of abuse by dogs. Billy's mum died. A few more couples and mothers with children used the upper part of the square in the hot days of the following summer.

As a dog owner, I was bound to side with the old ladies, but I have never needed the square in the way they need it. Far more mobile than they, I have always preferred to walk the dog on Hampstead Heath.

There I discovered that to be a dog owner was a social statement, and that with a dog one gained entry to another social world. Dogs, like babies, act as a passport to safe interaction with strangers, and now and again I have found myself in conversation with this or that dubious-looking solitary male dog owner to whom I would in any other circumstances have given a very wide berth indeed. I have become familiar with the 'professional' dog walkers who roam the heath with whole packs of dogs and an armful of leads. I have become adept at the exchange of mutually admiring comments with other owners of the many breeds of dog I had never heard of before I acquired a poodle – Weimaramas, Cuban Bichons, Rhodesian Ridgebacks. I have also discovered that the etiquette of dog chat is that it is *required* to exchange pleasantries and even advice with owners of the same breed as your own, while it is optional to converse with owners of different breeds.

Poodles are so playful and bouncy that passers-by often spontaneously burst out laughing at the joyous energy and unselfconsciousness of these rather absurd animals. Even satiric comments such as 'he looks like my kitchen mop' are delivered with a smile. Yet poodles are also associated with deviant (human) sexualities, part of the social construction of the identity of the effeminate gay man – giving a new meaning to the term 'gay dog'. On one occasion a man on a bicycle circled round us hurling abuse: 'Get lost, you pouffy dog! That's a poufta dog!' The invective continued for at least ten minutes and became quite threatening. On several occasions I have been at the receiving end of – literally – shaggy dog stories that played on the effeteness of poodles. These were delivered by friendly, courteous individuals, with no apparent intention of being deliberately homophobic. I was even once greeted in a paper shop (admittedly this was far from London) by a man who announced in ringing tones: 'Oh, I see you have a homosexual dog!'

By contrast, the owner of a pit bull terrier told me that when he and his boyfriend – 'two fairly obviously gay men' – stroll down the street with their dog, the perceived gendered qualities of the dog completely overwhelm those of its owners. Burly lorry drivers lean out of their cabs and shout: 'Pit bull! Magic! *Yeah*! Mine can hang by his jaws from a tree for fifteen minutes!' Then with a thumbs up and a final '*Great* dog, Squire!' they accelerate away in the certainty that all is well in the macho world of the pit bull in particular, and gender identity in general.

I seldom visited the Heath before I had a dog, and I am grateful to him for raising my awareness of its value and its beauty. To walk over its parkland and through its glades has made me aware of the special significance of nature in the city. As Pip thuds like a racehorse over the dry turf in summer or hurls himself ecstatically through the mud in winter, fulfilling his canine nature, it is better than being in the country, for the Mozart Café and the South Hampstead Tea Rooms are near at hand. On weekdays it is quiet, but never threatening. At weekends the postprandial promenade of North London families turns it into a veritable Coney Island.

Much has changed since the early nineteenth century, of course, yet to stand on the grassy slopes and look down towards London at the silver hulks that hang across the hazy skyline from Canary Wharf to the Telecom Tower is to experience a sense of continuity with the early Victorian landscape, and, as with the sea at Brighton, to feel that the city is both near and far away.

14
NOTES ON THE EROTIC CITY

When I saw the title of Beatriz Colomina's edited collection of essays, *Sexuality and Space*, I imagined that its subject-matter would be sex in public and private places. There would, perhaps, be papers on gay male 'cottaging', on museums as pick-up grounds for intellectual singles, on the rooms and back streets used by sex workers, on brothels, on the public park as a site of sexual congress and on the underground system as promoting 'perversion' ('frotteurism' in the rush hour). Instead, its subject-matter turned out to be *gender* – rather than sex – and space. It explored familiar territory: the exclusion of women from public space and their confinement within the domestic interior. Its purpose was not to look 'at how sexuality acts itself out in space, but rather to ask: How is the question of space already inscribed in the question of sexuality?' The project was 'to identify precisely the kinds of close relationships between sexuality and space hidden within everyday practices, many of which appear to be concerned neither with space [n]or sexuality' (Colomina, 1992: no page number).

My disappointment caused me to reflect on what the contents of a book that *did* take as its main concern the exploration of 'how sexuality acts itself out in space' – especially urban space – might have been. Histories of sexuality in the western world have almost always emphasised the role of the city in facilitating sexual adventure, but to my knowledge there have been few books that have investigated the geography or architecture of sex in the contemporary city.

Nineteenth-century cities grew because people travelled to them, not because they were born in them. The expansion of cities was not due to an increase in the birth rate. Indeed individuals were more likely to die than to be born in the city. The stereotype of the city was not of a more sexual environment than the countryside, but of a differently sexual environment, a more deviant and dangerous place.

Rural and Urban

Life must certainly have been different in the old rural communities. One reconstruction of pre-industrial life in Europe suggests that sexual arrangements were comparatively relaxed. Young couples engaged in various degrees of sexual intimacy and formalised the relationship when pregnancy occurred. (In Britain until the Marriage Act of 1753, the marriage ceremony might be of the simplest kind, consisting sometimes only of an exchange of vows, so that the distinction between marriage and cohabitation was considerably less clear than it had become by the nineteenth century.) This representation of traditional village life suggests a world that was sexually uncomplicated and non-coercive, yet regulated by familiarity and stability. On the other hand, the absence of coercion may have been more apparent than real. Some historians have argued that urbanisation in the industrial period made it possible for men to lose themselves in the cities in order to escape the responsibilities of fatherhood. Therefore the transition from 'going steady' to some form of marriage may not always have been willingly made, but simply unavoidable in pre-industrial times. The 1834 Poor Law Amendment Act further stigmatised unwed mothers. Some hid their shame by taking flight, also to the cities, where they too often became the fallen women of the streets, the 'great social evil'. None of this was peculiar to Britain. Sooner or later similar changes occurred everywhere with the industrialisation of the West.

Whether rural life was a haven and the industrial city the site of new and harsher attitudes towards transgression, or whether the village maintained strict social control through gossip, spying and bullying, by contrast with a city in which misdemeanours went undetected, the idea of the urban erotic depends on its contrast with the rural. One image of rural sexuality is of Breughelesque peasants drinking and fondling in the hay, an image of uncomplicated sensuality; and our image of pre-industrial society must certainly be of a world in which there was a closer connection with nature than in the city, and a world, therefore in which rural eroticism, too, was more 'natural'.

Yet there is a second image of rural sexuality which links it to the violent and oppressive, to incest in enclosed communities, to late marriage and enforced celibacy, to coercion and to the persecution of all who step outside a set of rigid, narrowly enforced conventions. A third image, related to both of the other views, is of the elemental: a *Wuthering Heights* idea of romantic passion, in which wild landscapes engender wild love. Our images of rural eroticism therefore represent it both as freer, more natural and more relaxed than urban sexuality, *and* as enclosed, suppressed and more restrictive.

Michel Foucault described a pre-industrial world in which sexual behaviour was regulated by ecclesiastical systems of thought. Paradoxically, the result was that many aberrant forms of sexual behaviour escaped censure because they were barely even named or noticed, all lumped together under the rubric of 'concupiscence' or 'sin' and linked rather to witchcraft and treason than to minutely specified kinds of perversion (Bray, 1982). Philippe Ariès (1973) described a sixteenth-century world in which, at least at the court, or as Foucault put it: a certain frankness was still common:

> Sexual practices had little need of secrecy; words were said without undue reticence, and things were done without too much concealment. . . . It was a time of direct gestures, shameless discourse, and open transgressions, when anatomies were shown . . . and knowing children hung about amid the laughter of adults. (Foucault, 1976: 3)

Foucault's well-known argument is that, far from 'repressing' sexuality, the Victorian age saw an unprecedented explosion of discourses on sexuality, including, eventually, all the resistances conjured up by the very proliferating definitions and prohibitions that sought to eradicate them. In the case of same-sex eroticism, changing definitions of homosexuality (including the invention of the very word) involved not greater disapproval, but *different forms* of prohibition. These in their turn produced resistances such as Magnus Hirschfeld's belief in the 'third sex', the homophile movements of the 1950s, and Gay Liberation in the 1970s.

Sex in the City

Foucault does not especially explore the link between an urban way of life and the development of this multitude of sexual discourses. His account of the industrial period as one in which attempts were increasingly made to control sexual behaviour through knowledge is not, however, inconsistent with a view of the city as a sexually dangerous place – or at least as simply a more sexual place, a region of sexual opportunity. (To reformers, zealots and rulers the danger lay precisely in the opportunities.) 'Pornography as a regulatory category', suggests Lynn Hunt, 'was invented in response to the perceived menace of the democratisation of culture', itself an urban phenomenon. Here she is speaking of the growing attempts to curb pornography in the nineteenth century. Yet in the early modern period, the development of erotic literature had meant something rather different:

> pornography came into existence, both as a literary and visual practice and as a category of understanding, at the same time as – and concomitantly with – the long-term emergence of Western modernity. It has links with most of the major moments in that emergence: the Renaissance, the Scientific Revolution, the Enlightenment and the French Revolution. Writers and engravers of pornography came out of the demimonde of heretics, freethinkers and libertines who made up the underside of those formative Western developments. (Hunt, 1993: 10–11)

The urbanisation of society, even before the industrial period, was one of the most important of these developments. This was a world whose social life, suggests Margaret Jacob,

> filled a public space that emerged after the mid-seventeenth century in the cities and larger towns of Western Europe. . . . In contrast to the traditional sociability anchored in family, guild, court and church, the new social universe possessed a signal characteristic: men and some women met as individuals, not as members of the traditional corps and corporations where birth, kinship and occupation counted above all else. Freer, more anonymous, they socialised as buyers and sellers, as habitués of coffee houses, cafés, taverns and salons. . . . They met as merchants, shopkeepers, travellers, readers of newspapers, consumers who had some leisure and some extra money; they negotiated, discussed, and, occasionally, even conspired, or spied, or had sex with relative strangers. (Jacob, 1993: 159–60)

The only two female roles mentioned are of actress and prostitute, but Jacob maintains that women did operate as shopkeepers and in other commercial and mercantile roles, although less often than men. Nevertheless, they were and continued to be defined in terms of their sexuality in a way that most men were not.

This picture of a purposeful urban social world is at odds with a whole series of nineteenth- and early twentieth-century images of city life. In these the industrial city is represented as a jungle or labyrinth, a chaotic space of anomie and anarchy where normal social controls and rules of behaviour are suspended. The city is a sexual jungle, a Babylon of licentiousness and unnatural vice in which anything goes. It is disordered and disorderly. Yet there is another, more measured point of view. This perceives sexuality, or rather sexualities, as *more* ordered and *more* organised in cities than in the rural areas.

Marcel Proust's Homosexual City

Marcel Proust illustrates this in an extended section of that part of *À la recherche du temps perdu* devoted to the analysis of homosexual love. He tells the story of a young man living in the country who wordlessly discovers his true nature during the walks he was in the habit of taking with a male friend. At the end of one of these walks, as they reach the cross-roads at which their paths diverge, the friend silently flings his companion to the ground, and a mute, unexplained sexual act occurs, an event thereafter repeated many times, but never discussed. Eventually the friend departs on a mountaineering expedition, leaving the young man heartbroken and alone. He becomes a recluse. After some time, however, the friend returns; but alas he is married, his wife radiantly pregnant. The young man who was cruelly abandoned is so naïve that this makes him even more unhappy; until, that is, one evening when the walks are resumed – the wife in her condition having retired to bed early – and when at the end of the stroll the 'mountaineer soon to be a father' once more flings his friend to the ground for the familiar wordless act; and this pattern is again continued, not until the baby is born and marital relations presumably recommenced, but until the married friend finds a new male companion, from whom he becomes inseparable, leaving the country bumpkin heartbroken once more. This is not the love that dare not speak its name; it is the love that has not even yet got a name, it is almost pre-social.

Proust then compares this rural naïvety with the fate of another young man, a poor but ambitious young bourgeois, who leaves home for the city in order to make his way in some prestigious profession. Such young men, Proust observes, rapidly acquire the social graces and the appearance of successful members of their intended profession; in other words they conform to prevailing conventions in the interests of their career. The homosexuals among them conform as much as the rest, with, however, one exception, which, on certain evenings, 'compels them to miss some meeting advantageous to their career'. While for the most part they mix 'only with brother students, teachers or some fellow provincial who has graduated and can help them on, they have speedily discovered other young men who are drawn to them by the same special inclination'. Proust likens these groups to hobby clubs:

> No-one . . . in the café where they have their table knows what the gathering is, whether it is that of an angling club or an editorial staff meeting, so correct is their attire, so cold and reserved their manner, so careful are they to avoid any but the most covert glances at the young men of fashion . . . who, a few feet away, are making a great to do about their mistresses, and among whom those who now admire them . . . will learn only twenty years later, when some are on the eve of admission to the Academy and others are middle-aged clubmen, that the most attractive among [the young swells] . . . now stout and grizzled . . . was in reality one of themselves, but elsewhere, in a different social world, whose language of signs was indecipherable to them. (Proust, 1981: II, 641)

There is, in other words, not one homosexual grouping, but many and diverse, and at different stages in their development. So,

> just as the 'Union of the Left' differs from the 'Socialist Federation' or some Mendelssohnian music club from the Schola Cantorum, on certain evenings, at another table, there are extremists, who permit a bracelet to slip down from beneath a cuff, or sometimes a necklace to gleam in the gap of a collar, and [who indulge in] persistent stares, cooings . . . and mutual caresses. (Proust, 1981: II, 642)

These elaborate homosexual worlds, described by Proust with ironic detachment, function as a microcosm of the city as a whole. Sometimes intertwined, sometimes almost entirely disconnected, they form part of a vast social formation. This, the metropolis, has been frequently described in terms of metaphors such as formless jungle, wilderness or labyrinth. These terms are used almost interchangeably, although they do not all share exactly similar characteristics, but in any case, the great city, far from being unorganised and chaotic, is highly organised in a series of overlapping and interlocking, almost cellular, structures. Proust recognised that in the city the erotic needs of hundreds of thousands of individuals create a huge net of interlocking relationships and formal and informal structures.

This has especial importance for homosexuality and other minority sexualities. Indeed, gay historians have held the growth of great industrial cities to be key in the very creation of the lesbian/gay identity. It was only in the great city, with its opportunities for meeting individuals far outside the ranks of kin and the narrow networks of rural society, that opportunities arose for sexual minorities to congregate and seek out others of their own kind. Proust's young country dweller didn't even have a name for his desires; but the different groups in Proust's imagined café not only know that they are homosexuals, they know also that there are different kinds of homosexual, different gay identities, that desires can be more and more minutely specified and that someone somewhere will organise and cater for every single one of these desires.

Stephen Spender described this as 'a terrifying mystery of cities' akin to ancient Greek religious rites. While living in Hamburg in the 1920s, he felt that the great city was indeed a labyrinth, for while the adjective 'labyrinthine' is used to suggest the impenetrability of a jungle, a world of confusion without a pattern, a labyrinth is not formless or chaotic, but guards a dangerous secret. And for Spender, exploring the Hamburg and Berlin of the Weimar Republic, the secret was that

> at every moment of the day the most hidden wishes of every human being are performed by people who devote their whole existences to doing this and nothing else. Along a road there walks a man with a desire repressed in his heart. But a few doors away there are people, utterly devoted to accomplishing nothing but this desire. What has been crushed, never spoken of for generations by his family, revolves there night and day like the wheels of a machine. He has only to know a secret word, open a door, and he may enter into this continuity of things which are elsewhere forbidden. (Spender, 1951: 120)

Women in the City

In the Paris of Proust's time, the *Belle Époque*, one of the most important structures organising sex was female prostitution, organised formally by the state, which required brothels to be licensed, as well as informally at many different levels from the great courtesans to the poorest streetwalkers. The relationship of modernist writers and painters to working-class women who were considered sexually available in general, and to prostitutes in particular, has been deeply problematic to contemporary feminists. For Manet, for Baudelaire, for Benjamin, let alone a horde of lesser artists – Francis Carco, say – women in the city and prostitutes were almost interchangeable categories.

In her discussion of Walter Ruttmann's 1927 film, *Berlin: Symphony of a City*, Anke Gleber, for example, has shown that scenes of an unaccompanied woman window shopping, of another young woman waiting on a street corner, and of a third speaking to a man, were interpreted by Siegfried Kracauer in 1947, and by another critic, William Uricchio, in 1982, as scenes about prostitutes; but a woman critic, Sabine Hake, has read them quite differently (Gleber, 1997: 76).

Men – white middle-class men at least, or in particular – own the street without thinking about it. Women must always make a conscious claim, must each time assert anew their right to be 'streetwalkers'. Each time is the first time, even today. As a feminist commentator on Alfred Döblin's *Berlin Alexanderplatz*, expresses it:

> Cities are no longer forbidden spaces [for women]. . . . But in the streets we continue to move strategically, always alerted to having to justify our presence. We learn self-assertion, we practise . . . the aim-oriented walk which is to demonstrate that we are protected and bound: at least bound by an agenda, on

our ways to a secure location, to a job, to a clearly defined aim – and that we are not just loitering around. (Scholvin, 1985: 8)

It has been suggested that urban space favoured the development of special 'perversions'. The crowded Metro or subway, as Le Corbusier noted, was a paradise for *frotteurs*. Cinemas were temples of voyeurism (and, at one time a haven for courting couples), while flashers, gropers and sadists lurked in alleyways, hovered in secluded corners of parks and lay in wait on lonely corners.

Women, harassed by unwanted encounters, had to learn to deal with them, enduring them as simply part and parcel of masculine oppression in public spaces, pretending not to notice, encasing themselves in a kind of invisible burka, a cloud of unknowing to protect them from these importunities. Thus, 'the female *flâneur*'s desire for her own exploration of the world ends where it encounters its limits in male pedestrians and fantasies, assaulting, annoying, disturbing and perpetually evaluating her in the street' (Gleber, 1997: 81).

Yet there were eroticised spaces for women too. The nineteenth-century department store was an incitement to women, an almost erotic experience. In his novel *Au bonheur des dames*, Émile Zola describes how on the opening day of his fictional department store, one bourgeois lady, trying on gloves, appears to be involved in a seduction scene as, almost lying across the counter, she allows a young male assistant to hold her hand, 'taking her fingers one by one, pulling on the glove with a long caress . . . while he looked at her as if waiting to see her swoon with joy', and other female customers, dazzled by a display of textiles arranged like a waterfall tumbling into a lake, 'were thunderstruck with such luxury and seized with an irresistible desire to throw themselves in and be lost in it' (Zola, 1984: 120).

In his study of Berlin and its popular press at the turn of the century, Peter Fritzsche emphasises the fragmentary, fluctuating nature of the modern city. Sharply defined boundaries were blurred, and it was particularly at transitional times of day, above all at dusk, that women transgressed these already shaky boundaries: 'Crossing conventional class and gender demarcations, these women stood as symbols for the disorderly spectacle of the city' (Fritzsche, 1996: 112). Although writers were primarily enthralled by the promise of 'possibility, pleasure and deception' for men in the streets, dance halls and cafés, yet 'female readers found the escapism of the night streets enticing as well' (Fritzsche, 1996: 113). In fact, as he notes, the brightly lit, crowded street in the early evening was actually a rather 'safe location for the erotic imagination'.

Baudelaire and Benjamin cited the lesbian as a new kind of urban woman, and for women as for men, although not to the same extent, urban space presented the opportunity to *be* (in their case) lesbian, to develop an identity. In Paris before 1914 Colette and her circle of upper-class lesbian friends had already developed a lesbian 'look', a specific mode of dress. Like Mammen's appearance, this may have seemed to ape masculinity, but to lesbians themselves it represented a different sexuality, denoting, for some, membership of a 'third sex' that confounded binary genders, blurring sexual conventions, just as the social conventions were blurred in the city.

It seems as if urban space is *inherently* eroticised. One reason perhaps – largely unacknowledged – for migration from country to city is the promise of the bright lights, of excitement, glamour, of night made day and sexual encounters. It is a particular kind of eroticism, an erotic life kindled between strangers, based on chance, unregulated.

Pure Sex

Or perhaps it is simply that, in cities, sex can be separated out from the rest of experience. The gay men's scene in large cities (and its representation in Britain in the television series *Queer as Folk*) might be cited as an example. There are many mixed gay clubs, many inclusive, welcoming scenes and many friendships between gay men and women, heterosexual and lesbians. Yet women may find some aspects of the gay men's city unnerving. The waves of hostility if a woman disrupts the atmosphere of certain gay pubs and bars may not be an expression exactly of misogyny. It may express the psychic disturbance caused by the irruption of something, or rather someone, who interferes with the atmosphere of pure sex. In a space – the gay bar – in which not only is sex defined as men cruising men, but in which identity is fundamentally defined as *gay-male*, the appearance of an alternative is a reminder of ambiguities the habitués would prefer to forget, or rather obliterate, negate. (In one London bar a photograph by Della Grace [who has since become Del LaGrace] decorated the wall: a figure in a leather jacket and tutu, with muscly legs and cropped hair. When the clientele realised that it was a photograph not of a boy but of a lesbian, it was quickly removed.)

A men's gay bar of such a kind provides a sexual or sexualised space freed from ambiguity. It is also a space defined by sex. And this is sex-for-itself, theoretically (although not in practice) separated from social regulation. Yet ambiguity is also of the essence of the erotic city.

Public and Private

This results from the long-developed attempt in western society to mark the division between public and private more and more clearly and strictly. In practice this results in intermediate zones that are not so defined.

The Renaissance architect Alberti wrote at length about the forms of spatial organisation in the city and the home appropriate to a patriarchal society (Alberti, 1969; Wigley, 1992: 327–89). He wished to restrict women to the private, domestic sphere. Within that he recommended a degree of privacy for the marital couple such that no-one else in the household should or need know when the couple had sexual relations, for their separate rooms should have an intercommunicating door so that they could come and go unseen. By the nineteenth century the cult of privacy had fetishised sexual relations to an extreme degree, and those beliefs about privacy and sex still influence us today. We have dispensed with many of the ideas of the lawful and the illicit in relation to sex. The proliferation of representations of sex in contemporary western society testifies to a widespread wish to transgress sexual privacy, to see and watch *everything*. One scandalous, yet banal, terminus of this was the way in which the sexual activities of the President of the United States were broadcast to the whole world.

In spite of this compulsive 'showing' of sex, we have not cast off the idea that consensual or even non-consensual relations *in private* are licit. It is for this reason that rape and child abuse are taken less seriously when they occur in 'the home' than when they take place outside the domestic realm. By contrast sexual activity in any public space moves fairly rapidly outside the parameters of the normal and allowable. The distinction between the private, sexualised space and the public desexualised space is ever-present, yet it is constantly breached.

There are, of course, public spaces that are gendered as well as being sexualised. Women (other than the ones who work in them) seldom see the inside of brothels. Porn shops too are predominantly male preserves (but then so are betting shops). Gay men have cruising grounds, 'cottages' and public baths; lesbians do not.

But there are more ambiguous, eroticised spaces in the city, neither quite public nor really private: secluded corners of parks and commons, offices, cafés, art galleries and department store changing rooms. This is one of the many unsettling paradoxes of urban eroticism. It has escaped from its licensed quarters, whether the bedroom or the brothel, and lies in wait everywhere.

Theorising Sex in the City

In *The Condition of Postmodernity* David Harvey quotes Roland Barthes as having written in *The Pleasure of the Text* that 'the city is a discourse and this discourse is truly a language' (Harvey, 1989: 67). I was unable to find the quotation in Barthes's essay, nevertheless some of the ideas Barthes explored in it seem applicable to the eroticism of cities.

Barthes distinguishes between pleasure and *jouissance*, used to refer to the moment of orgasm. The reader of a text is, he suggests, searching for *jouissance*. This *jouissance* is something striven towards but not predictable, not to be counted upon:

> as a writer, I have to search for my author – I have to dredge him up *without knowing where he is*. A space of *jouissance* is thus created. It is not the reader I need, but the space: the possibility of a dialectic of desire, or an unpredictable *jouissance*: the knowledge that the dice have not been thrown, that there is the possibility of a game. (Barthes, 1994: 1496)

Barthes is writing of literature, but his discussion is transferable to the discussion of the erotic urban space. As he describes it, literary *jouissance* is an unpredictable, fleeting moment. The search for it involves risk, since it is 'like that untenable, impossible, purely romantic moment, experienced by the libertine at the culmination of a daring arrangement whereby he cuts the cord by which he is hanging at the moment of orgasm' (Barthes, 1994: 1497). It is risky, forbidden. It occurs at the point where there is a gap, or a split, where something is inadvertently revealed. 'It is the intermittence that is erotic', as when you catch sight of a glimpse of skin where two garments do not quite meet. As well as being forbidden, therefore, it is also hidden, something that appears where there is a cut, where there is a wound on the surface of the text of the city.

'It's a drifting [*dérive*],' writes Barthes, 'something that is both revolutionary and asocial. . . . [It is] scandalous . . . because it is *atopique*, it has no place' (Barthes, 1994: 1505). The *dérive* had been an important concept for the Situationists in the 1950s. Guy Debord described it as 'the technique of locomotion without a goal' (quoted in Fillon, 1970: 155) – the locomotive equivalent of automatic writing. 'One or more persons during a certain period drop their usual motives for movement and action, their relations, their work and leisure activities, and let themselves be drawn by the attractions of the terrain and the encounters they find there' (Debord, 1981: 50). The Surrealists had engaged in similar activities, indeed the whole of Louis Aragon's *Paris Peasant* consists of *dérives* through mysteriously eroticised, neglected parts of Paris. In turn, the Surrealists were descendants of the nineteenth-century *flâneurs*, for whom the city had also been an eroticised space.

These ideas may go some way towards explaining, or at least exploring, the eroticisation of certain city spaces in a way that psychoanalysis – the obvious theory for the investigation of sexuality – cannot. Psychoanalysis locates sexual experience and erotic fantasy within the individual. However suggestive, this may not be the most illuminating, or at least may not be the only, way of understanding the erotic city.

Freud himself wrote one of the most atmospheric accounts of a kind of sexual encounter in the city:

> As I was walking, one hot summer afternoon, through the deserted streets of a provincial town in Italy, which was unknown to me, I found myself in a quarter of whose character I could not long remain in doubt. Nothing but painted women were to be seen at the windows of the small houses, and I hastened to leave the narrow street at the next turning. But after having wandered about for a time without enquiring my way I suddenly found myself back in the same street, where my presence was now beginning to excite attention. I hurried away once more, only to arrive by another detour at the same place yet a third time. Now, however, a feeling overcame me which I can only describe as uncanny. (Freud, 1985: 359)

This Kafkaesque passage is surely an instance of Barthes's 'gap'. Yet in Freud's anecdote, the possibility becomes threatening – another facet of the ambiguity of the (seemingly) unanchored erotic in urban space although it was of course Freud, not the prostitutes, who was unanchored in this case.

Walter Benjamin made an even more uncanny suggestion. In *Berlin Chronicle* he suggested that the child – of any class or either gender – is at first confined to the district in which his family, along with other members of that class, live. For Benjamin, the crossing of the invisible barrier that separated this district (in his case a wealthy bourgeois *quartier*) from the rest of the city was associated initially with journeys out of the city altogether, beginning with the drive to the railway station. Later, it was associated with sex. 'There is no doubt', he comments, speaking very much from his specific class and gender position, 'that a feeling of crossing the threshold of one's class for the first time had a part in the almost unequalled fascination of publicly accosting a whore in the street . . . whole networks of streets were opened up under the auspices of prostitution' (Benjamin, 1979: 301).

Yet more profound than the irruption of sexuality was another gap, another a-topos which Benjamin, always the prophet of doubt, uncertainty and disappointment, discovered beyond the promise of the erotic encounter. Was this crossing of boundaries, he wondered, really a crossing, was it not, rather,

> an obstinate and voluptuous hovering on the brink, a hesitation that has its most cogent motive in the circumstances that beyond this frontier lies nothingness? The places are countless in the great cities where one stands on the edge of the void, and [both] the whores in the doorways of tenements and the . . . sonorous asphalt of railway stations' platforms are like the household goddesses of this cult of nothingness. (Benjamin, 1979: 301)

– a thought consistent with his view, explored in Chapter 7 of this volume, that the urban labyrinth encourages impotence rather than *jouissance*.

More positively, the ambiguity explored in such different ways by these writers, and, apart from Benjamin, only marginally in connection with urban spaces, moves us beyond the stark dichotomies of pleasure/danger and public/private. In these cities, the erotic is a formless, haunting suggestion. For Freud, the ambiguity lay not in the street in which he found himself, but in his own motivation in finding himself continually returning to it; but for all those who explore great cities, their erotic charm may reside in the hope of encounters that remain forever unspoken, unrealised, permanently in the realm of utopian possibility, unspoilt by being realised, 'love at last sight'.

15

AGAINST UTOPIA

The Romance of Indeterminate Spaces

In her first published novel, *Under the Net* (1954), Iris Murdoch wrote that 'some parts of London were necessary and some were contingent'. This was a philosophical in-joke of the period, but seemed to me when I first read the novel to represent a profound truth not only about London but about all great cities. The 'necessary' parts of London – the old, central districts of Soho and the Law Courts, the sophisticated shopping streets in Knightsbridge, and the gracious parks and romantic residential districts such as Hampstead and Maida Vale – represented its essence. The contingent parts – suburbs, industrial estates, rubbish tips, railway sidings, dead ends and wasteland – were not the 'real' London. When travelling abroad, the parts of cities a tourist had to traverse before reaching the centre were even more contingent and unnecessary and had to be mentally bracketed off in order for the impact of the 'essential' city to be enjoyed to the full. The planless modern mess that surrounds most contemporary cities was merely an unfortunate accident on the way to the transcendental experience that was the truth of these cities.

The search for the 'necessary' city is part of the operation of what John Urry has termed the 'tourist gaze'. As he points out, 'the gaze is constructed through signs . . . "the tourist is interested in everything as a sign of itself. . . . All over the world the unsung armies of semioticians, the tourists, are fanning out"' (Urry, 1995: 133) in search of the 'necessary' experience, the experience, that is, that is adequate to its imaginary anticipation.

Few cities are free of this double arrival – the contingent arrival through the detritus of the outskirts, and the necessary arrival in front of Notre Dame or the Prinsengracht canal. Venice is a partial exception because arrival is across a railway causeway, or, from the airport, by boat, a lengthy journey along mysterious canals. Los Angeles is an exception for the opposite reason, that it is *all* contingent and therefore *all* necessary. So where Venice can without too much effort be envisaged as distinct from the modern world, embalmed on its slowly sinking piles and, as Proust saw it, transformed into a natural, organic piece of matter, a crystalline formation, Los Angeles is a fibre-optic installation, a microchip motherboard; although it is also, like London, a conglomeration of villages and cities within the city, separated by chasms of difference in ethnicity or wealth.

It would seem likely that the more the visitor's expectations are formed by a superfluity of images of the city she or he is about to encounter, the greater is the likelihood of disappointment. No city can live up to its media image. Proust had already discovered that before the First World War. As a child he lived to a large extent through books and art, and as a result his aesthetic sensitivity was developed to a point at which, as he himself recognised, an over-stimulated imagination outstripped the possibilities of experience. As an adolescent he became intoxicated with the names of the cities he longed to visit – Venice, Florence, the Normandy seaside resort of Balbec – so that each of these names triggered a whole dream world. The single word 'Florence', for example, unfurled a picture of 'the meadows of Fiesole with lilies and anemones, and gave Florence a dazzling golden background like those in Fra Angelico's pictures'. Proust knew that these cities of his imagination were more beautiful 'but at the same time more different from anything that the towns of Normandy or Tuscany could in reality be, and, by increasing the arbitrary delights of my imagination, aggravated the disenchantment that was in store for me when I set out upon my travels' (Proust, 1981: II, 419).

Since Proust's time the mass media have increased the circulation of images to the extent that we may feel as if we have been to many cities we have not, in fact, visited in the flesh. Yet these cities may be hyperreal, their contingent bits sliced away in order to perfect images of 'Paris-ness' or 'London-ness', over and above the use of well-known landmarks to signify a particular city. In the late 1960s movie *The Killing of Sister George*, for example, the eponymous heroine was filmed on a journey from work to home made up of picturesque bits of Chelsea and Hampstead knocked together into an impossible route, presumably for the American audience. Heritage films have reinforced a representation of historic cities before the Fall of motorised traffic and mass tourism. It would take more than one film of the violent Paris *banlieus* (*La Haine*) to undo decades of cobbled streets and accordian accompaniment.

Urry suggests that 'it is not the pedestrian *flâneur* who is emblematic of modernity but rather the train-passenger, car driver and jet plane passenger' (Urry, 1995: 134). In fact, though, the majority of journeys *to* tourist destinations are produced as non-events, while wandering around the cathedral on foot is 'the real thing'. This is particularly true of journeys by air, since both in airway terminals and during the flight itself, everything conceivable is done to give the impression that nothing is happening at all. On the plane, although the passenger is *en route* from departure point to destination, there is *nothing* in between, the journey itself is a kind of limbo. The whole journey is 'contingent'; it is the 'historic quarter', the 'old city', that is the 'necessary' object of desire.

Only many years after I first read *Under the Net* did I come to understand that this selective tourist gaze represented a very restricted view of what a city is. Iris Murdoch's 'necessary' parts of cities have increasingly become the parts cleansed, sanitised and rearranged for the delectation of the tourist gaze.

François Maspero (1994), for example, suggests that since the centre of Paris has been wholly 'Disneyfied' the 'real', living Paris is now to be found in precisely the despised and even dangerous peripheral estates, suburbs and shanty towns surrounding the core. His *Roissy Express* is the account of a journey through those Paris suburbs. The idea for such a book came to him after a brief meeting at Roissy (Charles de Gaulle) Airport with an old friend and former lover. Later, alone in the empty train back into Paris, Maspero formed the idea for a journey of exploration through the unknown Paris of the *banlieus*. He had, he tells us, made a documentary about China – but had he ever truly explored his own city?

Maspero suggests that the growth of tourism, the globalisation of travel, and the way in which television gives audiences of millions a possibly specious familiarity with distant places gives rise to a sense of the loss of the immediate and local. At the same time tourism has transformed the immediate and the local. Since the 'necessary' Paris of the centre was now a tourist location, he embarked with a photographer friend, Anaïk Frantz, on a journey in search of the 'real' Paris and the real Parisians in the despised and neglected suburbs, rather as the *flâneurs* of the nineteenth century had done, but now in the benighted municipal housing estates beyond the *Périphérique* motorway rather than off the rue St Antoine or in the slums of the south-east *arrondissements*.

As well as being an exploration of a forgotten present, their journey constituted a return to the past. The travellers planned to excavate a forgotten history of the suburbs. In order to do this they decided to travel in a manner characteristic of an earlier period. Instead of flashing past the suburbs along the motorway or circling over them in an aeroplane, they took short, slow journeys, one stop a day on the train.

The journey began at Roissy Airport. Maspero launches into his mixture of travel diary, documentary, autobiography and historico-geographical exploration with a vivid description of the way in which the Airport has devastated the area for miles around. The old village of Roissy, some way away from the terminal, was once a prosperous farming community with an ancient eighth-century church. As recently as 1954 'Pauline Réage' chose Roissy as the setting for her scandalous sado-masochistic work of pornography, *The Story of O*. This was because her novel needed a location that was near Paris, yet which seemed remote from it. By the 1980s it was no longer remote, and had become a 'restored rural habitat', that is to say, a monument to – rather than a survival of – a lost way of life. It was now marooned in an enormous no-man's land of indeterminate spaces; islands of scrub between motorways, deserted, ruined landscapes where no-one either lived or walked. Maspero noted that one of these had been designated as the site for a park: 'Parc du Sausset is, they say, one of the big operations of "Suburbs 89", a great idea from Roland Castro. In his distant youth, Roland was a great Maoist leader. He used to say that imagination should be empowered' (Maspero, 1994: 31). Now, Castro had become President Mitterrand's urban planner, and, aware of the ambiguous irony of the destiny of the revolutionary turned bureaucrat, had thought up 'Suburbs 89' as a grand municipal plan to regenerate and civilise the Parisian periphery.

Soon Maspero and his companion arrived at the first of the huge housing estates for which outer Paris is notorious, but, unlike most commentators, they refused simply to throw up their hands in horror at a stereotype of life in these grim locations, the usual litany of drugs, crime and delinquency. Instead, the reader is made aware of the rural past; of a more recent past of post-war shanty towns and of immigrants provided with work but nowhere to live; of a yet more recent, largely Communist past in which local politicians built well-intentioned, if grandiose, housing projects to improve the lives of the newcomers; and of the situation by the end of the eighties, when the residents had somewhere to live, but the jobs had disappeared – layers and layers of superimposed, sedimented history.

This new situation was exemplified in the huge estate at Aulnay known as the '3000'. Built in the early 1970s to house workers for the nearby Citroën factory, 'the Communist town council . . . must certainly have dreamed of a radiantly happy proletariat living on a happy estate' (Maspero, 1994: 37). Unfortunately, no sooner was the place built than Citroën started to lay off its workers. Maspero disposes of the argument that the monolithic 'Stalinist' architecture was to blame for its subsequent alienation, drugs problems and crime, by comparing it to another, later suburb, Beaudottes. There, changing fashions in architecture led to the creation of a more 'user-friendly' estate, built to look like a 'real town'. There were 'terraces, varying levels, columns, pedestrian streets opening on to large courtyards where children can play . . . balconies at unexpected angles and even . . . a row of vaguely Moorish concrete arches, fine and slender. Façades are pink, ochre or white earthenware' (Maspero, 1994: 67). Yet despite the planners' attempt to avoid the monotony of the 1970s monoliths, the new town, sprung from nowhere, without a history, quickly became as crime-ridden and godforsaken as the others. Architecture, implies Maspero, cannot solve the social problems of unemployment and displacement.

As well as creating a kind of palimpsest of histories, Maspero peels off the superimposed layers of experience, lifting away the seeming chaos of the contemporary to reveal a pattern and a meaning, or many meanings. He refers to the way in which the suburbs provide what he calls 'geological stratifications', a stratified history of a hundred years of ideas about housing. His skilful method of literary impressionism, whereby he creates a patchwork experience, is also, however, mindful that this journey is not just the discovery of the 'geology' of the past. This is not a search for fossils, although 'fossils' – for example the Air Museum at the former aerodrome of Le Bourget – do appear from time to time. There is a more important political agenda in that Maspero is concerned to demonstrate that these suburbs are inhabited by hundreds of thousands of lively and resourceful individuals surviving in often unfriendly and difficult circumstances.

He and his friend found that urban alienation could coexist with pockets of the old rural life that survived until very recently at the threshold of

Paris. By the Canal de l'Ourcq 'it feels faintly like a weekend at the time of
the Popular Front' (Maspero, 1994: 107). This leads Maspero back into a
yet more distant past when the countryside surrounding the capital was
studded along its waterways with *guingettes* and cafés at which the
Parisians enjoyed themselves on their days off – scenes painted by Pissarro,
Manet and Seurat and reproduced by Jean Renoir and others in the heyday
of French film in the 1940s. A double nostalgia is at work here: for a lost
and more gracious Paris, and for a lost political vision, the vision of the
Left, symbolised in part by the ambivalent character of Roland Castro the
(ex-?)Maoist, but also by the grand schemes of the triumphal Communist
municipalities who ruled the *banlieus* throughout the post-war period until
ousted (although not everywhere, even in the 1990s) by Le Pen's *Front
National*.

Nostalgia occasionally slips towards a romantic, even sentimental, recall.
Maspero cannot really be certain, for example, that a Sunday afternoon at
the Canal de l'Ourcq retains the lost innocence and working-class authenticity of the late 1930s. He may simply be remembering the past seen at
second or even third hand, mediated by scenes from charming Renoir films
or *Hôtel du Nord* (at one point Maspero and his companion actually spent
the night in a hotel with that name). The plangent note of political indig-
nation – with its unspoken suggestion of massive betrayals by the Left –
can also sound a little too easily. Yet his account of Drancy – once a
housing estate, then a Fascist concentration camp, then, incredibly, not
razed to the ground, but simply reorganised into a block of seedy flats once
more – expresses much more sharply than overt moralising could do the
horror of the Nazi period and the implied failure of the French to come to
terms with the collaboration and betrayals of the Occupation.

So in all sorts of ways *Roissy Express*, which is full of nuggets of
seemingly disjointed, inconsequential and arbitrary information, a crazy
quilt of bits of knowledge, combines these to create a rich representation
of the texture of a city, or part of a city. However, the book becomes
increasingly disorganised towards the end, and Maspero acknowledges the
impossibility of ending it. His journey seems proof of something intermin-
able about the progress of the *flâneur*. The huge metropolis always offers
the tantalising prospect of something *more*. The explorer never does reach
either the centre or the end.

The idea of 'contingent' aspects of the urban as a legitimate topic to
explore first came to me on a train from Brighton to London. During the
latter part of the journey the train snakes round the back parts of
Southwark, Bermondsey, the City of London and Blackfriars on its way to
King's Cross: a journey through some very old parts of the metropolis,
which have been destroyed and rebuilt many times. The viaduct passes over
these areas and as it does so the traveller catches sight of the backs of many
different buildings, both important and obscure. There are glimpses of
alleys, decayed pubs and offices, new apartment blocks, old warehouses and
even a few remaining bombsites left from the Second World War. The

bird's-eye view from the railway line above the urban maze reveals the way in which these buildings have accumulated like geological strata (much as Maspero noted), sedimented one on the other, so that the sight provides an awareness of a city almost organically developing over time. The Blitz is still visible over the Edwardian world of pubs and dockers and tenements. This in turn covers a still faintly discernible Dickensian world – the opening pages of *Our Mutual Friend* describe the eerie scene of a scavenger dredging the Thames for dead bodies near the Bermondsey shore. Beneath all this, traces even of the medieval world still survive. Then the train suddenly breaks free from all this agglomeration of buildings to cross the Thames with a panoramic view of St Paul's cathedral and the new skyscrapers of the financial mile. At one point I planned to make a video of the journey, to be called 'The Backs of Buildings' – until I realised that Patrick Keiller's *London* was such a film on a much larger and more imaginative scale than I could ever have achieved.

Soon afterwards my interest in the topic was enhanced when I found a flyer for an exhibition which announced itself as a project about 'non-places'. The flyer invited its readers to send in their accounts of 'non-places' in which they had had some significant experience.

An interest in obscure, forgotten, hidden parts of the great cities of modernity is not new. These lost corners had an enormous romantic charm for the *flâneurs* of the nineteenth century. Writers such as Dickens, Baudelaire and his friend Alexandre Privat d'Anglemont provided a counter-chorus to the reformers and planners who wished to reshape the city and thereby to banish dirt, disease and crime. Indeed Dickens and to some extent Privat d'Anglemont spoke at different times with both voices.

An interest in these spaces, which have been termed interstitial spaces, may represent a rejection or at least a suspicion of urban space as utopia. The majority of literary utopias, from Thomas More onwards, have tended towards the authoritarian in their prescriptions for every detail of life, so that the cities they envisaged became merely part of a much grander plan for human economic, social and cultural life. No part of human experience was to be left unregulated in the majority of these plans. Above all, *nothing was hidden* in utopia. Utopia was to be barren of secrets and of anything resembling an alternative world. Françoise Choay in her book *The Rule and the Model* (1997) demonstrated that historical architectural treatises closely resembled utopian literature, and this was certainly true of Le Corbusier in *The Radiant City* and other works, in which life was to become perfectly regulated along eugenic and rational lines.

Utopia is therefore problematic, yet to reject utopia outright can easily become, or be equated with, a rejection of planning *per se*. It is important therefore to disassociate the exploration of indeterminate spaces both from some postmodern celebration of the fragmentary and from a post-Marxist rejection of planning. Planning is simply the search for urban solutions. Plans that are put into practice often represent a compromise between conflicting views or needs, and democratic planning, which takes into account the views and wishes of local communities, is a laborious and long-drawn-out process, but a very necessary one. Planning is unavoidable and indeed desirable. The question that remains is how the need for an ordered and liveable environment is to be reconciled with the need for the spontaneous, and unexpected: in other words the *unplanned*.

There is a second use of the term 'utopian', in which it appears not as prescriptive rigidity, but rather as a gesture towards intimations of alternative redemptive possibilities in our chaotic contemporary world and contemporary cities. In this use it has a visionary aspect; it is about aspiration rather than perfectibility. It is still not quite the right term for the interstitial places of *unspecified possibility* to which I refer, however.

What are non-places, or interstitial or indeterminate spaces? The panorama of the backs of buildings from Blackfriars to King's Cross is the wrong side of the fabric of the city, a hidden and secret aspect of urban life where traces of former worlds and lives may be found. It is in these spaces that, in Michel de Certeau's words, the dominated weave a language as they make a path through the city, or their fragment of the city. It is the place in which they 'poach' on the preserves of the powerful and manufacture a silent or surreptitious resistance, and although Certeau's influential article 'Walking in the City' (Certeau, 1984) is over-romanticised, it does identify a way in which individuals make their parts of cities their own.

Whereas most theorists distinguish place from space by describing the former as a specific historical and geographic location, as opposed to a space, which is abstract and in a sense empty, for Certeau space is a 'frequented place', 'an intersection of moving bodies'. It is the pedestrians who transform a street into a space. For Certeau, that is, space implies movement and interaction.

Marc Augé (1995) has identified a third kind of location: non-place, or non-places. He writes not of postmodernity but of a 'supermodernity' in which non-places become not only increasingly common but also increasingly characteristic. Non-places are spaces such as airports, 'that space outside real time and space' (Maspero, 1994: 7), and supermarkets. They are also the relationships such spaces enjoin. They have the peculiarity that they are 'defined partly by the words and texts they offer us: their instructions for use, so to speak' (Augé, 1995: 83). Persons in these non-places are meant to interact only with texts; so, for example, the motorway networks of France (or Britain for that matter) no longer pass through towns, but lists of their notable features – indeed whole commentaries – appear on big signboards nearby. 'Motorway travel is thus doubly remarkable: it avoids, for functional reasons, all the principal places to which it takes us; and it makes comments upon them' ('You are now passing historic Poitiers', etc.) (Augé, 1995: 97). The same is true of supermarkets, where shoppers wander around reading texts (apricots contain calcium; cereals are full of vitamin C; there are even instructions on how to cook exotic ingredients) which may have relatively little to do with what they actually purchase and later eat.

Augé's non-places are the absolute opposite of the interstitial spaces referred to by the organisers of the exhibition whose flyer I picked up. Augé's non-places are utopian in a wholly negative sense, in that they are over-determined, totally prescriptive and usually provide an impoverished experience. Interstitial spaces, by contrast, are indeterminate places or spaces, which precisely because their purpose is ambiguous or because they are places in between, leading from one more clearly defined place to another, can facilitate imaginative uses by individuals.

The message that appeared on the flyer, or rather postcard, for the non-place exhibition read as follows:

> We are ever increasingly in transit through 'non-places'. Corners that lurk at the edge of activity. Passageways where activity occurs but the relationship between use and place remains unnamed. Places where names are incidental, meaningless because the need for communication – or the passage of time spent – is already deemed to be transient, insignificant, minimal, empty. Street corners, bus stops, shopping malls, motorways, airport lounges . . .

Thus the anonymous writers or film makers of the project merge the two sorts of space that I have just suggested are polar opposites. They seem to be looking for a new way in which to articulate another narrative of urban space, something that is hidden, pre-conscious almost, inarticulate, the secret experience of the underside of cities. These non-places do not yet have a language. Marc Augé, by contrast, sees the anti-utopia of the non-place as founded on rhetoric. He writes:

> the use of 'basic English' by communications and marketing technologies [and in travel] is revealing [because] it is less a question of the triumph of one language over the others than of the invasion of all languages by a universal vocabulary [of words such as transit, freeway, cashpoint, and so on]. What is significant is the need for this generalised vocabulary, not the fact that it uses English words. Linguistic enfeeblement . . . is attributable more to this generalisation than to subversion of one language by another. (Augé, 1995: 110)

Writers such as Maspero reject the pessimism of this vision of contemporary life. Zurbrugg (1993: 5) suggests that such pessimism falls into an 'apocalyptic fallacy', leading to a denunciation of all aspects of postmodern culture.

The novelist Iain Sinclair manages to combine an apocalyptic vision of London with a relish for the details of the urban landscape, and in *Lights Out for the Territory: Nine Excursions into the Secret History of London* he sought to excavate some of the meanings of the hidden places or non-places of the capital. The book begins with a meditation on graffiti writing, which he sees as a hidden language, 'playful collages of argument and invective, not the publicly displayed, and quietly absorbed papers of the Chinese, but editorials of madness'. Graffiti, in Sinclair's imagination, constitute an alternative language bubbling up from the postmodern chaos of the inner city. Everything in the area he is describing, Hackney, is a fragment: torn bits of posters or newspaper; amateur advertisement cards in the windows of newsagents; flotsam cast up on the urban shore, corresponding to the transient lives of immigrants, fugitive East End criminals, shabby stall holders, Punks, Turkish revolutionaries, pentacostalists. And, as he embarks on his walk through the obscurity of the borough, Sinclair invokes the Situationists and their concept of the *dérive* or drift. 'The notion,' he writes, 'was to cut a crude V into the sprawl of the city, to vandalise dormant energies by an act of ambulant signmaking. . . . I would transcribe all the pictographs of venom that decorated our near-arbitrary route' (Sinclair, 1997: 1). He would get under the skin of East London in Hackney by cataloguing all the graffiti, every corner shop small-ad and all the sheets of newspaper drifting along the gutters. He would orchestrate them into 'editorials of madness', the unceasing murmur of the dispossessed, the implication being that to notice and record *everything* would be eventually to get at the heart of the hidden city.

Sinclair's journeys are as untidy as those of his French fellow urban explorer, though he takes less care than Maspero to interrogate the stereotype of the city's underbelly as unliveable. His take on London was especially apocalyptic in his novel *Down River*, where it bordered on the self-indulgent – there must be some scepticism about a protagonist who lives in such squalor, surrounded by such infernal urban blight, himself in such a bad way, yet who nevertheless always manages to have great sex.

In his search for the hidden London Sinclair (1997) rejects the rehabilitation of Abney Park Cemetery and Victoria Park. These redemptions banish eccentricity and rage, as do his non-places, 'interzones' such as Broadgate, the revamped Liverpool Street train terminal or the Barbican concert hall complex, 'an honorary airport without the stress of departure'. His anger flails about making hits and misses, with moments of blinding insight and over-coruscating prose.

In the end, London defeats him, not only geographically endless, but also bottomless. The attempt to record every inch, every event, every character, is a hopeless one and we end with a Dickensian vision of London as the golden dustman's mound, still a nineteenth-century city:

> That mysterious paper currency which circulates in London when the wind blows, gyrated here and there and everywhere . . . it hangs on every bush, flutters in every tree, is caught flying by the electric wires, haunts every enclosure, drinks at every pump, cowers at every grating, shudders upon every plot of grass, seeks rest in vain behind the legions of iron rails. In Paris, where nothing is wasted, costly and luxurious city though it be, but where wonderful human ants creep out of holes and pick up every scrap, there is no such thing. There it blows nothing but dust. . . .
> The wind sawed, and the sawdust whirled. . . . When the spring evenings are too long and light to shut out and such weather is rife . . . London is at its worst. Such a black shrill city . . . such a gritty city, such a hopeless city, with no rent in the leaden canopy of its sky; such a beleaguered city. (Dickens, 1983: 191)

In the 1940s Claude Lévi-Strauss described his surprise on finding that New York was not the modern metropolis he had expected. Instead it was 'an immense horizontal and vertical disorder . . . [and] despite the loftiness of the tallest buildings and the way they were piled up and squeezed together on the cramped surface of an island . . . on the edges of these labyrinths the web of the urban tissue was astonishingly slack' (Lévi-Strauss, 1987: 261).

It is at these slack edges that Barthes's gap in the fabric of the city may be found. Sinclair's search is for a language – the opposite of the transit lounge language of Augé's non-places – that is adequate to the mystery and uncertainty that is their ever-unfulfilled, romantic promise.

REFERENCES

Acton, W. (1968) *Prostitution*, (ed.) Peter Fryer, London: MacGibbon and Kee, 1968. Orig. publ. 1857.

Adams, T. (1995) 'Elegy to the Bull Ring', *Observer*, 'Life' section, 5 March.

Adorno, T. (1967) *Prisms*, Cambridge, MA: MIT Press.

Alberti, L.B. (1969) *The Family in Renaissance Florence*, Columbia, SC: University of South Carolina Press. Orig. Publ. 1434.

Anderson, P. (1984) 'Modernity and Revolution', *New Left Review*, 144 (March/April): 96–113.

Anderson, P. (1998) *The Origins of Postmodernity*, London: Verso.

Ang, I. (1983) *Watching Dallas: Soap Opera and the Melodramatic Imagination*, London: Methuen.

Ang, I. (1996) *Living Room Wars: Rethinking Media Audiences for a Postmodern World*, London: Routledge.

Ankum, K. von (ed.) (1997) *Women in the Metropolis: Gender and Modernity in Weimar Culture*, Berkeley: University of California Press.

Anon. (n.d. [1806]) *Le Flâneur au Salon, ou M. Bonhomme, examen joyeux des tableaux, mêlé de vaudevilles*, Paris: Aubry.

Anon. (1862) *Brighton: The Road, The Place, The People*, London: J.H. Thomson.

Appignanesi, L.(ed.) (1989) *Postmodernism: ICA Documents*, London: Free Association Books.

Ariès, P. (1973) *Centuries of Childhood*, Harmondsworth: Penguin. Orig. publ. 1960.

Attfield, J. (1989) 'Inside Pram Town: A Case Study of Harlow House Interiors, 1951–1961', in J. Attfield and P. Kirkham (eds), *A View from the Interior: Feminism Women and Design*, London: The Women's Press.

Augé, M (1995) *Non-Places: Introduction to an Anthropology of Supermodernity*, London: Verso.

Baldwin, F.E. (1926) *Sumptuary Legislation and Personal Regulation in England*, Baltimore: Johns Hopkins University Press.

Barret-Ducroq, F. (1991) *Love in the Time of Victoria*, London: Verso. Trans. John Howe.

Barthes, R. (1957) *Mythologies*, New York: Hill and Wang.

Barthes, R. (1994) *Le Plaisir du Texte*, in *Oeuvres Complètes*, vol. 2, 1966–1973, Paris: Éditions du Seuil.

Batifol, I. (1930) *The Great Literary Salons*, Paris: Musée Carnavalet.

Baudelaire, C. (1971) 'Le Dandy', *Écrits sur L'Art*, 2, Paris: Gallimard.

Baudelaire, C. (1992) 'The Salon of 1846', in C. Baudelaire, *Selected Writings on Art and Around Literature*, Harmondsworth, Penguin.

Baudrillard, J. (1981) *For a Critique of the Political Economy of the Sign*, St Louis, MO: Telos Press. Orig. publ. 1972.

Baudrillard, J. (1988) *America*, London: Verso.

Baudrillard, J. (1990) *Seduction*, London: Macmillan. Orig. publ. 1979.

Bauman, Z. (1988) 'Is There a Postmodern Sociology?', *Theory Culture and Society*, 5 (2–3): 217–38.

Bauman, Z. (1994) 'Desert Spectacular', in K. Tester (ed.), *The Flâneur*, London: Routledge.

Beaton, C. (1954) *The Glass of Fashion*, London: Weidenfeld and Nicolson.

Bell, Q. (1947) *On Human Finery*, London: Hogarth Press.

Benjamin, W. (1973) *Charles Baudelaire: A Lyric Poet in the Era of High Capitalism*, London: Verso.

Benjamin, W. (1979) *One Way Street*, London: Verso.

Benjamin, W. (1985) 'Central Park', *New German Critique*, no. 34, Winter.

Bennett, O. (1998) 'I don't want to go to Brighton', *Independent on Sunday*, 'Real Life' section, 7 June.

Berard, T.J. (1999) 'Dada between Nietzsche's *Birth of Tragedy* and Bourdieu's *Distinction: Existenz* and Conflict in Cultural Analysis', *Theory Culture and Society*, 16 (1): 141-66.

Berman, M. (1983) *All That Is Solid Melts Into Air*, London: Verso.

Betjeman, J. and Gray, J.S. (1972) *Victorian and Edwardian Brighton from Old Photographs*, London: Batsford.

Bourdieu, P. (1980) *Distinction*, London: Routledge.

Bradbury, M. (1959) *Eating People is Wrong*, Harmondsworth: Penguin.

Bray, A. (1982) *Homosexuality in Renaissance England*, London: Gay Men's Press.

Breward, C. (1999) *The Hidden Consumer: Masculinities, Fashion and City Life 1860–1914*, Manchester: Manchester University Press.

Brighton Ourstory Project, (1992) Brighton, Queen's Park Books.

Buci-Glucksmann, C. (1986) 'Catastrophic Utopia: The Feminine as Allegory of the Modern', *Representations*, no. 124.

Buck-Morss, S. (1986) 'The *Flâneur*, The Sandwichman and the Whore: The Politics of Loitering', *New German Critique*, 39 (Fall): 99–140.

Burchill, J. (1999) 'Brighton Rocks', *The Guardian*, 28 August.

Bürger, P. (1984) *The Theory of the Avant Garde*, Manchester: Manchester University Press.

Butler, J. (1990) *Gender Trouble*, London: Routledge.

Cagle, Van M. (1995) *Reconstructing Pop/Subculture: Art, Rock and Andy Warhol*, London: Sage.

Callinicos, A. (1990a) 'Reactionary Postmodernism?', in R. Boyne and A. Rattansi (eds), *Postmodernism and Society*, London: Macmillan.

Callinicos, A. (1990b) *Against Postmodernism: A Marxist Critique*, New York: St Martins Press.

Carey, J. (1994) *The Intellectuals and the Masses*, London: Faber and Faber.

Carver, T. (1998) *Postmodern Marx*, London: Macmillan.

Castells, M. (1978) *City Class and Power*, London: Macmillan.

Certeau, M. de (1984) 'Walking in the City', in M. de Certeau, *The Practice of Everyday Life*, Berkeley, CA: University of California Press.

Chaney, D. (1997) 'Authenticity and Suburbia', in S. Westwood and J. Williams (eds), *Imagining Cities: Scripts, Signs, Memory*, London: Routledge.

Chapman, B. (1996) *Brighton in the Fifties*, Lewes: The Book Guild.

Choay, F. (1997) *The Rule and the Model: On the Theory of Architecture and Urbanism*, Cambridge, MA: MIT Press. Orig. publ. 1980.

Cixous, H. (1980) 'The Laugh of the Medusa', in E. Marks and De Courtivron (eds) *New French Feminisms*, Brighton: Harvester Wheatsheaf.

Clarke, A. (1997) 'Tupperware: Suburbia, Sociality and Mass Consumption', in R. Silverstone (ed.) *Visions of Suburbia*, London: Routledge.

Clark, T.J. (1999) *Farewell to an Idea: Episodes from a History of Modernism*, New Haven: Yale University Press.

Colomina, B. (1992) (ed.) *Sexuality and Space*, New York: Princeton Architectural Press.

Corbin, A. (1986) 'Commercial Sexuality in Nineteenth-Century France: A System of Images and Regulations', *Representations*, Special Issue on the Body, (ed.), Catherine Gallagher and Thomas Lacquer, no. 14, Spring.

Coward, R. (1993) *Our Treacherous Hearts: Why Women Let Men Get Their Way*, London: Faber and Faber.

Coward, R. (1999) *Sacred Cows: Is Feminism Relevant to the New Millennium?* London: HarperCollins.

Craik, J. (1994) *The Face of Fashion: Cultural Studies in Fashion*, London: Routledge.

Cross, G. (1997) 'The Suburban Weekend: Perspectives on a Vanishing Twentieth Century Dream', in R. Silverstone (ed.), *Visions of Suburbia*, London: Routledge.

Curran, J. (1996) 'Rethinking Mass Communications', in J. Curran, D. Morley and V. Walkerdine (eds), in *Cultural Studies and Communications*, London: Arnold.

Dale, A. (1967) *Fashionable Brighton, 1820–1860*, London: Oriel Press. Orig. publ. 1947.

Davidoff, L. (1973) *The Best Circles: Society Etiquette and the Season*, London: Croom Helm.

Davies, J. and McCann, G. (1985) 'All Bingo Barbie and Barthes?', *Times Higher Education Supplement*, 10 March.

Davis, M. (1985) 'Urban Renaissance and the Spirit of Postmodernism', *New Left Review*, 151 (May/June).

Debord, G. (1981) 'Theory of the Dérive', in K. Knabb (ed.), *Situationist International Anthology*, Berkeley: Bureau of Public Secrets.

Denzin, N. (1991) *Images of Postmodern Society: Social Theory and Contemporary Cinema*, London: Sage.

Dickens, C. (1983) *Our Mutual Friend*, Harmondsworth: Penguin. Orig. publ. 1864.

Dior, C. (1957) *Dior by Dior*, London: Weidenfeld and Nicolson.

Duplessis, R.B. and Snitow, A. (eds) (1998) *The Feminist Memoir Project: Voices from Women's Liberation*, New York: Three Rivers Press.

Dworkin, A. (1980) *Pornography: Men Possessing Women*, London: The Women's Press.

Eagleton, T. (1996) *The Illusions of Postmodernism*, Oxford: Polity Press.

Eco, U. (1986) *Travels in Hyperreality*, London: Picador.

Engels, F. (1962) *The Condition of the Working Class in England*, Moscow: Progress Publishers. Orig. publ. 1844.

Etzioni, A. (1995) *New Communitarian Thinking: Persons, Virtues, Institutions and Communities*, Charlottesville, VA: University of Virginia Press.

Featherstone, M. (1988) 'In pursuit of the postmodern: introduction', *Theory, Culture & Society*, 5 (2–3): 195–216.

Feminists Against Censorship (1991) *Pornography and Feminism: The Case Against Censorship*, London: Lawrence and Wishart.

Ferguson, P.P. (1994) 'The *flâneur* on and off the streets of Paris', in K. Tester, *The Flâneur*, London: Routledge.

Fillon, J. (1970) 'New Games', in C. Ulrichs (ed.), *Programmes and Manifestoes on Twentieth Century Architecture*, London: Lund Humphries.

Fiske, J. (1986) *Understanding Popular Culture*, London: Routledge.

Flugel, J.C. (1930) *The Psychology of Clothes*, London: Hogarth Press.

Foster, A. (1999) 'Dressing for Art's Sake: Gwen John, the *Bon Marché* and the Spectacle of the Woman Artist in Paris', in A. de la Haye and E. Wilson (eds), *Defining Dress*, Manchester: Manchester University Press. pp. 114–27.

Foster, H. (ed.) (1983) *The Anti-Aesthetic: Essays on Postmodern Culture*, Port Townsend, Washington: Bay Press.

Foster, H. (1985), *Recodings: Art, Spectacle, Cultural Politics*, Port Townsend, Washington: Bay Press.

Foucault, M. (1976) *The History of Sexuality: An Introduction*, Harmondsworth: Penguin.

Fraser, K. (1985) *The Fashionable Mind: Reflections on Fashion, 1970–1982*, Boston: Godine.

Franks, S. (1999) *Having None of It: Women, Men and the Future of Work*, London: Granta.

Freely, M. (1999) 'Nice Work If You Can Get It', *Observer* 'Review' section, 4 July, p. 1.

Freud, S. (1949) *Civilisation and Its Discontents*, London: Hogarth Press. Orig. publ. 1930.

Freud, S. (1985) 'The Uncanny', in *The Pelican Freud Library*, vol. 14, *Art and Literature*, Harmondsworth: Penguin. Orig. publ. 1919.

Fritzsche, P. (1996) *Reading Berlin 1900*, Cambridge, MA: Harvard University Press.

Garb, T. (1994) *Sisters of the Brush: Women's Artistic Culture in Late Nineteenth-Century Paris*, New Haven, CT: Yale University Press.

Gautier, T. (1874) *Histoire du Romantisme*, Paris: Charpentier.

Gilbert, E.W. (1954) *Brighton: Old Ocean's Bauble*, London: Methuen.

Gillet, L. (1930) 'Introduction', in I. Batifol (ed.), *The Great Literary Salons*, Paris: Musée Carnavalet.

Gilloch, G. (1996) *Myth and Metropolis: Walter Benjamin and the City*, Oxford: Oxford University Press.

Gleber, A. (1997) 'Female Flanerie and the *Symphony of the City*', in K. von Ankum, *Women in the Metropolis: Gender and Modernity in Weimar Culture*, Berkeley: University of California Press. pp. 67–88.

Guibaut, S. (1983) *How New York Stole the Idea of Modern Art: Abstract Expressionism, Freedom and the Cold War*, Chicago: Chicago University Press.

Hall, S., Critcher, C., Jefferson, T., Clarke, J. and Robert, B. (1978) *Policing the Crisis: Mugging, the State and Law'n'Order*, London: Macmillan.

Hall, S. (1980a) 'Reformism and the Legalisation of Consent', in National Deviancy Conference (ed.) *Permissiveness and Control: The Fate of the Sixites Legislation*, London: Macmillan.

Hall, S. (1980b) 'Popular Democratic versus Authoritarian Populism', in A. Hunt (ed.) *Marxism and Democracy*, London: Lawrence and Wishart.

Hall, S. (1981) 'Notes on Deconstructing the Popular', in R. Samuel (ed.) *People's History and Socialist Theory*, London: Routledge, 1981, pp. 227–41.

Hall, S. and Jacques, M. (eds) (1983) *The Politics of Thatcherism*, London: Lawrence and Wishart.

Harrison, J.F.C. (1995) *Scholarship Boy: A Personal History of the Mid-Twentieth Century*, London: Rivers Oram Press.

Hartley, J. (1999) 'Editorial', *International Journal of Cultural Studies*, 1 (1).

Harvey, D. (1973) *Social Justice and the City*, Oxford: Blackwell.

Harvey, D. (1989) *The Condition of Postmodernity*, Oxford: Blackwell.

Haye, A. de la and Wilson, E. (eds) (1999) *Defining Dress*, Manchester: Manchester University Press.

Healey, P. et al. (eds) (1995) *Managing Cities: The New Urban Context*, Chichester: John Wiley.

Hertz, N. (1983) 'Medusa's Head: Male Hysteria under Political Pressure', *Representations*, 1 (4).

Hoggart, R. (1999) 'Interview with Richard Hoggart', *International Journal of Cultural Studies*, 1 (1).

Hollander, A. (1994) *Sex and Suits: The Evolution of Modern Dress*, New York: Knopf.

Holt, L. (1998) 'Diana and the Backlash', in M. Merck (ed.), *After Diana: Irreverent Elegies*, London: Verso.

Holtby, W. (1978) *Women and a Changing Civilisation*, Chicago: Academy. Orig. publ. 1935.

Hoy, D.C. (ed.) (1986) *Foucault: A Critical Reader*, Oxford: Blackwell.

Hunt, L. (1993) 'Introduction: Obscenity and the Origins of Modernity, 1500–1800', in L. Hunt (ed.), *The Invention of Pornography: Obscenity and the Origins of Modernity, 1500–1800*, New York: Zone Books.

Huyssen, A. (1986) *After the Great Divide: Modernism Mass Culture and Postmodernism*, London: Macmillan.

Irigaray, L. (1985) *Speculum of the Other Wman*, Paris: Éditions de Minuit.

Jacob, M. (1993) 'The Materialist World of Pornography', in L. Hunt (ed.), *The Invention of Pornography: Obscenity and the Origins of Modernity, 1500–1800*, New York: Zone Books.

Jacobs, J. (1961) *The Death and Life of American Cities*, Harmondsworth: Penguin.

James, O. (1997) 'The Happiness Gap', *The Guardian*, G2, 15 September, p. 2.

Jameson, F. (1984) 'Postmodernism; or the Cultural Logic of Late Capitalism', *New Left Review*, no. 146, July/August.

Jameson, F. (1991) *Postmodernism; or the Cultural Logic of Late Capitalism*, London: Verso.

Jay, M. (1986) 'In the Empire of the Gaze: Foucault and the Denigration of Vision in

Twentieth Century French Thought', in D.C. Hoy (ed.), *Foucault: A Critical Reader*, Oxford: Blackwell.

Kaplan, E.A. (1984) 'Is the Gaze Male?', in A. Snitow, C. Stansell and S. Thompson (eds), *Desire: The Politics of Sexuality*, London: Virago.

Knabb, K. (ed.) (1981) *Situationist International Anthology*, Berkeley: Bureau of Public Secrets.

Kracauer, S. (1937) *Jacques Offenbach and the Paris of His Time*, London: Constable.

Laver, J. (1969) *A Concise History of Costume*, London: Thames and Hudson.

Lebas, E. (1996) 'Les Nouveaux Flâneurs', in B. Catterell (ed.), *City*, vol. 1, no. 2.

Lees, A. (1985) *Cities Perceived: Urban Society in European and American Thought, 1820–1940*, Manchester: Manchester University Press.

Leopold, E. (1992) 'The Manufacture of the Fashion System', in J. Ash and E. Wilson (eds), *Chic Thrills: A Fashion Reader*, Berkeley, CA: University of California Press.

Leroy-Beaulieu, P. (1873) *Le Travail des Femmes au XIXe Siècle*, Paris: Charpentier.

Lévi-Strauss, C. (1987) *The View From Afar*, Harmondsworth: Penguin

Lütgens, A. (1997) 'The Conspiracy of Women: Images of City Life in the Work of Jeanne Mammen', in K. von Ankum (ed.), *Women in the Metropolis: Gender and Modernity in Weimar Culture*, Berkeley, CA: University of California Press.

Lyotard, J.-F. (1984) *The Postmodern Condition: A Report on Knowledge*, Manchester: Manchester University Press.

MacKinnon, C. (1994) *Only Words*, London: HarperCollins.

McGuigan, J. (1992) *Cultural Populisum*, London: Routledge.

McGuigan, J. (1994) *Modernity and Postmodern Culture*, Buckingham: Open University Press.

McGuigan, J. (1999) *Modernity and Postmodern Culture*, Buckingham: Open University Press.

McRobbie, A. (1989a) 'Postmodernism and Popular Culture', in L. Appignanesi (ed.), *Postmodernism: ICA Documents*, London: Free Association Press.

McRobbie, A. (1989b) 'Second-Hand Dresses and the Role of the Ragmarket', in A. McRobbie (ed.), *Zoot Suits and Second-Hand Dresses: An Anthology of Fashion and Music*, London: Macmillan.

Maffesoli, M. (1996) *The Time of the Tribes*, London: Sage.

Marin, L. (1977) 'Disneyland: A Degenerate Utopia', in *Glyph: Johns Hopkins Textual Studies*, vol. 1, no. 1.

Marks, E. and Courtivron, I. de (eds) (1980) *New French Feminisms*, Brighton: Harvester Wheatsheaf.

Marsh, J. (1985) *The Pre-Raphaelite Sisterhood*, New York: St Martin's Press.

Marsh, J. and Nunn, P.G. (1989) *Women Artists and the Pre-Raphaelite Movement*, London.

Massey, D. (1991) 'Flexible Sexism', in *Environment and Planning D: Society and Space*, vol. 9.

Maspero, F. (1994) *Roissy Express*, London: Verso.

Merck, M. (ed.) (1998) *After Diana: Irreverent Elegies*, London: Verso.

Modleski, T. (ed.) (1999) *Studies in Entertainment: Critical Approaches to Mass Culture*, Bloomington, IN: Indiana University Press.

Moretti, F. (1983) *Signs Taken for Wonders*, London: Verso.

Morris, M. (1988) 'Politics Now (Anxieties of a Petty Bourgeois Intellectual)', in M. Morris *The Pirate's Fiancée: Feminism: Reading: Postmodernism*, London: Verso.

Morris, W. (1986) *News From Nowhere and Selected Writings and Designs*, Harmondsworth: Penguin. Orig. publ. 1890.

Motion, A. (1993) *Philip Larkin: A Writer's Life*, London: Faber and Faber.

Mukerji, C. (1983) *From Graven Images: Patterns of Modern Materialism*, New York: Columbia University Press.

Mulvagh, J. (1999) *Vivienne Westwood: An Unfashionable Life*, London: HarperCollins.

Mulvey, L. (1975) 'Visual Pleasure and Narrative Cinema', *Screen*, 16 (3): 6–18.

Mumford, L. (1960) *The City in History*, Harmondsworth: Penguin.

National Deviancy Conference (ed.) (1980) *Permissiveness and Control: The Fate of the Sixties' Legislation*, London: Macmillan.

Nead, L. (1993) 'The Female Nude: Pornography Art and Sexuality', in L. Segal and M.

McIntosh (eds), *Sex Exposed: Sexuality and the Pornography Debate*, New Brunswick, NJ: Rutgers University Press.

Negrin, L. (1999) 'The Self as Image: A Critical Appraisal of Postmodern Theories', *Theory Culture and Society*, 16 (3): 99–118.

Oakley, A. and Mitchell, J. (eds) (1997) *Who's Afraid of Feminism? Seeing Through the Backlash*, London: Hamish Hamilton.

Oliver, P., Davis, I. and Bentley, R. (1981) *Dunroamin: The Suburban Semi and Its Enemies*, London: Barrie and Jenkins.

Osborne, P. (1995) *The Politics of Time: Modernity and the Avant Garde*, London: Verso.

Owens, C. (1983) 'Discourse of Others: Feminism and Postmodernism', in H. Foster (ed.), *The Anti-Aesthetic: Essays on Postmodern Culture*, Port Townsend, WA: Bay Press.

Parent-Duchâtelet, A. (1836) *De La Prostitution dans la Ville de Paris*, Paris: H. Baillière.

Perry, G. (1995) *Women Artists and the Parisian Avant Garde*, Manchester: Manchester University Press.

Phillips, R. (1980) *Family Breakdown in Late Eighteenth-Century France: Divorces in Rouen, 1792–1803*, Oxford: Oxford University Press.

Pollock, G. (1988) *Vision and Difference: Femininity, Feminism and the Histories of Art*, London: Routledge.

Poovey, M. (1989) *Uneven Developments: The Ideological Work of Gender in Mid-Victorian England*, London: Virago.

Priestley, J.B. (1977) *English Journey*, Harmondsworth: Penguin. Orig. publ. 1934.

Proust, M. (1981) *Remembrance of Things Past*, Vols I, II and III, London: Chatto and Windus, 1981. Orig. publ. 1908–1925.

Queen's Park Rates Book Group (n.d. [1983?]) *Brighton On the Rocks: Monetarism and the Local State*, Brighton: Queen's Park Books.

Radway, J. (1991) *Reading the Romance: Women, Patriarchy and Popular Literature*, Chapel Hill, NC: University of North Carolina Press.

Richards, J.M. (1946) *The Castles on the Ground: The Anatomy of Suburbia*, London: John Murray.

Robins, K. (1995) 'Collective Emotion and Urban Culture', in P. Healey et al. (eds), *Managing Cities: The New Urban Context*, Chichester: John Wiley.

Sala, G.A. (1859) *Twice Around the Clock*, London: Houlston & Wright.

Samuel, R. (ed.) (1981) *People's History and Socialist Theory*, London: Routledge.

Samuel, R. (1994) *Theatres of Memory*, London: Verso.

Saunders, F.S. (1999) *Who Paid the Piper? The CIA and the Cultural Cold War*, London: Granta.

Savage, J. (1991) *England's Dreaming: Sex Pistols and Punk Rock*, London: Faber and Faber.

Scholvin, U. (1985) *Döblin's Metropolen: über reale und imaginäre Städte und die Travestie der Wünsche*, Weinhemi and Basel: Beltz Verlag.

Segal, L. (1999) *Why Feminism?*, Oxford: Polity Press.

Segal, L. and McIntosh, M. (eds) (1993) *Sex Exposed: Sexuality and the Pornography Debate*, New Brunswick, NJ: Rutgers University Press.

Sennett, R. (1970) *The Uses of Disorder*, Harmondsworth: Penguin.

Sennett, R. (1974) *The Fall of Public Man*, Cambridge: Cambridge University Press.

Sennett, R. (1993) *The Conscience of the Eye*, London: Faber and Faber.

Sharp, T. (1940) *Town Planning*, Harmondsworth: Penguin.

Silverman, K. (1986) 'Fragments of a Fashionable Discourse', in T. Modleski (ed.), *Studies in Entertainment: Critical Approaches to Mass Culture*, Bloomington, IN: Indiana University Press.

Silverstone, R. (1997) 'Introduction', in R. Silverstone (ed.), *Visions of Suburbia*, London: Routledge.

Sinclair, I. (1997) *Lights Out for the Territory: Nine Excursions into the Secret History of London*, London: Granta.

Sinfield, A. (1989) *Literature, Politics and Culture in Postwar Britain*, Oxford: Blackwell.

Smart, C. (1993) 'Unquestionably a Moral Issue: Rhetorical Devices and Regulatory

Imperatives', in L. Segal and M. McIntosh (eds), *Sex Exposed: Sexuality and the Pornography Debate*, New Brunswick, NJ: Rutgers University Press.

Smith, M. (1994) 'Growing Wild in the City', *The Guardian*, 20 October.

Smith, N. (1992) 'New City, New Frontier: The Lower East Side as Wild, Wild West', in M. Sorkin (ed.), *Variations on a Theme Park: The New American City and the End of Public Space*, New York: Noonday Press.

Snitow, A., Stansell, C. and Thompson, S. (eds) (1984) *Desire: The Politics of Sexuality*, London: Virago.

Soja, E. (1989) *Postmodern Geographies*, London: Verso.

Sorkin, M. (ed.) (1992) *Variations on a Theme Park: The New American City and the End of Public Space*, New York: Noonday Press.

Spender, S. (1951) *World Within World*, London: Hamish Hamilton.

Sprengel, P. (ed.) (1998) *Berlin-Flaneure: Stadt-Lektüren in Roman und Feuilleton, 1910–1930*, Berlin: Weidler.

Tadié, J.-Y. (2000) *Marcel Proust*, London: Viking. Trans. E. Cameron.

Taylor, I. and Jamieson, R. (1997) 'Proper Little Mesters: Nostalgia and Protest: Masculinity in De-Industrialised Sheffield', in S. Westwood and J. Williams (eds), *Imagining Cities: Scripts, Signs, Memory*, London: Routledge.

Tester, K. (1994) 'Introduction', in K. Tester (ed.) *The Flâneur*, London: Routledge.

Thompson, T. (2000) 'Unsolved Murder of Teenage Mother Exposes Brighton's Sleazy Secrets', *Observer*, 28 May, p. 12.

Thorne, R. (1980) 'Places of Refreshment in the Nineteenth-Century City', in A. King (ed.), *Buildings and Society: Essays on the Social Development of the Built Environment*, London: Routledge and Kegan Paul.

Travis, A. (1999) 'Sex in the 90s: The Young Take a Moral Stand', *The Guardian*, 29 December, p. 3.

Tytell, J. (1997) *The Living Theatre: Art, Exile and Outrage*, London: Methuen.

Urry, J. (1995) *Consuming Places*, London: Routledge.

Vaughan, R. (1843) *The Age of Great Cities or Modern Society Viewed in its Relation to Intelligence, Morals and Religion*, London: Jackson & Walford.

Veblen, T. (1957) *Theory of the Leisure Class*, London: Allen and Unwin. Orig. publ. 1899.

Walkowitz, J. (1980) *Prositution and Victorian Society: Women Class and the State*, New York: Cambridge University Press.

Walkowitz, J. (1982) 'Male Vice and Feminist Virtue: Feminism and the Politics of Prostitution in Nineteenth-Century Britain', *History Workshop Journal*, 13, Spring.

Walter, N. (1997) 'Six Months' Hard Labour', *Observer*, Review section, 30 November, p. 7.

Walter, N. (1998) *The New Feminism*, London: Little Brown.

Walters, M. (1997) 'American Gothic: Feminism, Melodrama and the Backlash', in A. Oakley and J. Mitchell (eds), *Who's Afraid of Feminism? Seeing Through the Backlash*, London: Hamish Hamilton.

Weeks, J. (1981) *Sex Politics and Society: the Regulation of Sexuality Since 1800*, London: Longman.

Westwood, S. and Williams, J. (eds) (1997) *Imagining Cities: Scripts, Signs, Memory*, London: Routledge.

Wharton, E. (1952) *The House of Mirth*, London: Oxford University Press. Orig. publ. 1905.

White, J. (1986) *The Worst Street in North London: Campbell Bunk*, London: Routledge.

Wigley, M. (1992) 'Untitled: The Housing of Gender', in B. Colomina (ed.) *Sexuality and Space*, New York: Princeton Architectural Press.

Wilkinson, H. and Howard, M. (1997) *Tomorrow's Women*, London: Demos.

Williams, R. (1975) *The Country and the City*, London: Paladin.

Wilson, E. (1985) *Adorned in Dreams: Fashion and Modernity*, Berkeley, CA: University of California Press.

Wilson, E. (1993) *The Sphinx in the City*, Berkeley, CA: University of California Press.

Wilson, E. (2000) *Bohemians: the Glamorous Outcasts*, London: I.B. Tauris.

Wolff, J. (1985) 'The Invisible *Flâneuse*: Women and the Literature of Modernity', *Theory Culture and Society*, 2 (3): 37–48.

Wolff, J. (1990) 'Feminism and Modernism', in J. Wolff, *Feminine Sentences: Essays on Women and Culture*, Oxford: Polity Press.

Wolff, J. (1994) 'The Artist and the *Flâneur*: Rodin, Rilke and Gwen John in Paris', in K. Tester (ed.), *The Flâneur*, London: Routledge.

Wollen, P. (1993) 'Out of the Past: Fashion/Orientation/The Body', in P. Wollen, *Raiding the Ice Box*, Bloomington, IN: Indiana University Press.

Woolf, V. (1938) *Three Guineas*, Harmondsworth: Penguin.

Wright, P. (1985) *On Living in an Old Country*, London: Verso.

Wright, P. (1995) 'Resist Me, Make me Strong', *Guardian Weekend*, pp. 38–46, 11 November.

Zola, E. (1984) *Au Bonheur des Dames*, Paris: Bernard Grasset. Orig. publ. 1883. (English edn, 1993, *The Ladies' Paradise*, Berkeley, CA: University of California Press.

Zurbrugg, N. (1993) *The Parameters of Postmodernism*, London: Routledge.

Index

Callinicos, A., 1
capitalism *see* consumer culture; late/post capitalism; Marxism
censorship *see* pornography
charity, 34–5
cities
  aesthetic experience of, 66–7
  celebration of dangers, 69–70
  diversity of, 70, 71
  dogs in, 129–33
  growth of, 129–30, 134
  media image, 146
  necessary and contingent parts, 145, 146, 149–50
  'non-places', 150, 151–3, 154
  sex in, 134–7
    homosexual, 126–7, 137–9, 141
    theorising, 142–4
  as space of consumption, 65, 66, 90–1
  strangers in, 70, 86, 132–3
  women in, 72, 79–81, 82, 83–5, 139–41
  writing on, 64, 65–7, 68, 69, 70–1, 91
  see also specific cities
Clark, K., 44
Clarke, A., 111
class
  academics, 68
  divides, 125, 131
    crossing, 74–5, 79, 82, 144
  and fashion, 56, 80
  Paris, 75–7, 78
  rise of bourgeousie, 72
  in suburbs, 74, 104, 108
  see also Marxism; working-class
Cobbett, W., 121
Colomina, B., 134
commercialisation
  nineteenth century, 81–2, 140
  of sexuality, 78, 82, 85
  of writing, 77–8
consumer culture, 6, 24, 48
  of cities, 65, 66, 90–1
  fashion, 50–1, 55, 57, 58
Contagious Diseases Acts, 74
counter-cultures, 6–8, 60, 61
Courbin, A., 80
Craik, J., 50–1, 53
crime, 121, 122–3
  and architecure, 148
cultural populism, 110–11

cultural/media studies, 5, 7–10, 12–13, 110
Curran, J., 110

dandies, 53
  see also flâneur
de Certeau, M., 151
dérives, 143, 153
Diana
  myth of, 26–7
  politics of death of, 33–7
  responses to death of, 31–3
  romantic tragedy of, 28–9
  soap opera of, 30–1
Dickens, C., 120–1, 150, 153
dogs in cities, 129–33
domestic sphere, 20–1, 79, 141–2
drifting (*dérives*), 143, 153
DuPlessis, R.B. and Snitow, A., 18
Dworkin, A., 23–4, 40–1

Eagleton, T., 1–2, 10, 11–13
elitism, 8, 10–11, 32, 123
  city life, 68
  haute couture, 56
  suburban life, 109, 110
emotion, 32–4, 36
Engels, F., 72
Evington, Leicestershire, 108

fashion, 5
  and class, 56, 80
  and 'dress', 50–1
  haute couture, 52, 54–5, 56, 58
  mass production, 52, 54–5, 56
  nostalgia, 58–60, 62, 99
  and postmodernism, 56–8, 60–3
  of sixties, 6, 56, 99
  and urban life, 64–5
Featherstone, M., 2
'feminine values', 20
'feminisation' of British society, 26, 31, 32, 34
feminism, 17–20
  anti-pornography campaign, 23–4, 39–41, 43–4, 46–8
  attitudes to fashion, 60, 61–2
  'backlash' against, 22, 23
  cultural populism, 110–11
  debates within, 15–16, 38–41
  decline in, 16, 38–9, 47–8
  and Marxism, 4
  postmodern perspective, 24–5
  views of the *flâneur*, 78–9, 82–4, 92–3
  see also gender; women
feminist icons, 18
  Diana, 29, 31

housing estates, 105, 147–8, 149
nostalgia, 97–8, 111
utopian quality of, 106, 107, 108
'supermodernity', 151

Thatcherism, 32, 34, 42, 43
Tomorrow's Women see Wilkinson, H. and
Howard, M.
tourism, 147
tourist gaze, 145, 146

urban life
ambiguity of, 86–7, 142
vs rural life, 67–8, 134–6
urban planning, 69–70, 98–9, 105, 147–8,
150–1
urban space
Marxist analysis, 65–6
postmodern, 66, 67
urbanisation, 134, 135, 136–7
hostility to, 72–3
Urry, J., 145, 146
utopian ideal
arguments against, 150–1, 152
suburban, 106, 107, 108
urban, 86–7, 99, 101–2

Walter, N., 14, 21–2, 23
Walters, M., 23–4
Warhol, Andy, 6, 56, 113
wealth/poverty gap, 119
women, 16–17, 20–1, 92–3
Wharton, Edith, 28, 29
Wilkinson, H. and Howard, M. (*Tomorrow's
Women*), 19–20, 21–2

Wol, J., 79, 80, 81, 84, 93
women
ambiguity of lives, 17–25, 28–9
artists, 4–5, 93–4
bourgeois, 74, 80, 81, 140
in cities, 72, 79–81, 82, 83–5, 139–41
diversity of, 19–20, 24
as dolls, 116
domestic sphere, 20–1, 79, 141–2
equality at work, 19
fallen, 135
Diana as, 28, 29
fashions, 54–5, 59, 62
as *flâneuses*, 84, 85, 91, 92–4, 140
Labour MPs, 14, 21, 48
lesbians, 140–1
Pre-Raphaelite, 83–4
wealth/poverty gap, 16–17, 20–1, 92–3
working-class, 79, 82, 84
see also feminism; gender; prostitution
Woolf, Virginia, 53
working-class
areas, 95–6
nostalgia, 7, 149
women, 79, 82, 84
see also class, divides
writing/writers
Brighton, 119–20, 122–3, 124
on cities, 64, 65–7, 68, 69, 70–1, 91
journalists, 77–8
on women in cities, 139–41
see also British fiction; *specific writers*

youth cultures, 9